Enemies of the State

Enemies of
the State

The Cato Street Conspiracy

M J Trow

Pen & Sword
MILITARY

First published in Great Britain in 2010 by
Pen & Sword Military
an imprint of
Pen & Sword Books Ltd
47 Church Street
Barnsley
South Yorkshire
S70 2AS
Copyright (c) M J Trow 2010
ISBN 978-1-84415-964-2

The right of M J Trow to be identified as Author of this Work has been asserted by him in accordance with the Copyright, Designs and Patents Act 1988.

A CIP catalogue record for this book is available from the British Library

Typeset in 11pt Ehrhardt MT by
Pen & Sword Books Ltd., Barnsley, South Yorkshire

Printed and bound in England by the MPG Books Group

Pen & Sword Books Ltd incorporates the Imprints of Pen & Sword Aviation, Pen & Sword Maritime, Pen & Sword Military, Wharncliffe Local History, Pen and Sword Select, Pen and Sword Military Classics, Leo Cooper, Remember When, Seaforth Publishing and Frontline Publishing.

For a complete list of Pen & Sword titles please contact
PEN & SWORD BOOKS LIMITED
47 Church Street, Barnsley, South Yorkshire, S70 2AS, England
E-mail: enquiries@pen-and-sword.co.uk
Website: www.pen-and-sword.co.uk

Contents

List of Illustrations vi

1.   Dinner at Lord Harrowby's 1

2.   The Winter of Discontent 11

3.   The Shadow of the Guillotine 25

4.   Desperate Men and Desperate Measures 39

5.   'A Plot, a Plot! How they Sigh for a Plot!' 57

6.   Pig's Meat 75

7.   Oliver the Spy 87

8.   Bloody Fields 99

9.   Men of Colour 113

10. 'Dreadful Riot and Murder' 127

11. 'On a Charge of High Treason' 141

12. The Hand of Death 156

13. 'This is But the Beginning . . .' 170

Notes 179

Bibliography 187

Index 188

List of Illustrations

Arthur Thistlewood, 'on the day sentence of death was passed'

James Ings, the Portsmouth butcher

Richard Tidd, radical and conman

William Davidson, the 'man of colour'

John Thomas Brunt, conspirator

Robert Adams, who turned king's evidence

Thomas Hyden, the cow-keeper

John Monument

Lord Harrowby's house

Robert Stewart, Lord Castlereagh, hated Cabinet minister

Henry Addington, Lord Sidmouth, Home Secretary

John Scott, Lord Eldon, Chancellor of England

The Cato St stable as it looked in May 1820

The stable today

Plan of the hay-loft, marking the spot where Smithers died

Newgate Gaol

The Central Criminal Court on the site of the Session House and Newgate

Excavations outside the Central Criminal Court

Execution day, 1 May 1820

This book is dedicated to my wife, Carol –
Susan Thistlewood and Catherine Despard rolled into one.

'Assassination is political murder, where the motives, no matter how mixed, are all about power; those who do not have power assassinate to get it and those who have power assassinate to keep it.'

(Richard Belfield, *The Secret History of Assassination*, 2005)

Chapter 1

Dinner at Lord Harrowby's

The first carriage arrived a little after seven. The hour had been called, on that chill, cheerless night, by the square's Charlie, Thomas Smart, as he hobbled by with his lantern and his staff – 'seven o'clock and all's well.' All was well – for now.

Arthur Thistlewood recognized the Londonderry arms painted on the carriage door and he knew the occupant, too, his boots grating on the pavement as the footman held the steps steady. He was over six feet tall, strikingly handsome, even in the eerie half-light of the new gas-lamps. There was a rumour that the Marquess of Londonderry, Lord Castlereagh, went armed these days; that despite the sang-froid he always showed in public, he went in fear of his life. There were two pistols concealed in the lining of his frock coat.

The carriage jerked away at the crack of the driver's whip, dark lackeys atop the coach, swathed in layers, their breath snaking out on the night air. Castlereagh was silhouetted for a moment in the lighted doorway, a perfect target for Thistlewood's gun. But Thistlewood waited. He had no intention of deviating from the plan. Castlereagh would go, but he would go with the others – catch one, catch them all.

The flunkey at Lord Harrowby's door was ancient, silver-haired and stooped; he'd prove no problem. And Thistlewood was determined he'd give the man a choice – give all the servants a choice. Join the Government of the People or follow your masters into eternity. It was what lay beyond the bobbing flunkey that grabbed Thistlewood's attention. The New Times *had carried news of this dinner only two days ago. There had been no time to reconnoitre, to plan in detail. The shock of what was to happen would be enough. The blazing lights of the vestibule led into a carpeted corridor that reached a staircase. That was the way Castlereagh went, his greatcoat and hat removed, just before the door closed.*

Thistlewood eased himself back into the shadows. It was a minute, perhaps two, before the target appeared in an upstairs window, overlooking the square. He had a glass in his hand and was smiling and shaking hands with his host.

William Davidson was in the shadows too and recognized at once the man with whom Castlereagh was hob-nobbing. It was Lord Harrowby, Lord President of the Privy Council, a kindly old boy with a twinkle in his eye. Davidson had worked for the man in days gone by, as a master carpenter working on some grand design the old man had. But it was not this house. It was Harrowby's country estate near Birmingham and that was a pity. If Davidson had known the layout of the town house, how much simpler the whole thing would have been. For a moment, he caught the laughter of two girls on the far side of the square. What were they? Eighteen, perhaps? Unfortunates? Probably. But Davidson shook himself. Now was not the time. On any other night, when Thistlewood or Edwards had no need of him, he would have crossed the square, tipped his hat to them, waited for their reaction. William Davidson was a free man of colour, as the whites called people like him. But he was tall, good-looking, quick-witted. His father had intended him for the Bar, but fate had driven him to another kind of bar altogether, at the Horse and Groom, the White Lion or anywhere where the disgruntled went. But all that would come later, when William Davidson was a member of Thistlewood's government. Tonight, he stayed in the shadows, checking his carbine lock for the umpteenth time.

John Brunt could see Davidson's carbine quite clearly – too clearly, bearing in mind the desperate enterprise now under way. He had seen carbines like that before when he'd worked for the army at Cambrai. He could see Thistlewood too, from his vantage point in the south-east corner of the square, but he had an oblique, awkward view of the house, merely a series of grand columns and chandelier-lit windows. Mechanically, he checked the brace of pistols under his shabby topcoat. Then the second carriage rattled past him, causing him to duck into the darkness.

He didn't see the gilded crest on the paintwork, but he knew the coach's occupant well enough. Even before he turned to enter the house, nodding to the flunkeys, he recognized the set of the shoulders, the great stride. Wellington. He'd seen the man, all nose and iron, in his days working with the Blues, when the saviour of Europe had inspected the Horse Guards. He was the hero of Assaye,

Talavera, Salamanca and Waterloo; he would not go quietly. All Brunt knew of the general's reputation told him that Wellington would not be armed, but he knew, too, that there would be weapons enough in that dining room for a man like him – knives, forks, candelabra, chair legs. No, Wellington would not go quietly.

James Ings carried no watch. He'd pawned that years ago to keep the wolf from his family's door. So he had little idea of the time as the third carriage squealed to a halt, hard on the wheels of Wellington's. But he recognized the occupant, helped down by a footman – the smirking, furtive features of the Home Secretary, Lord Sidmouth. His was the throat he would cut in a few minutes' time. He had rehearsed this moment a thousand times in his dreams. The tune of that damned song drummed through his brain – 'Give me liberty or give me death'. Liberty was an alien concept to Sidmouth, a lost cause. This was the man who had suspended habeas corpus, denying freeborn Englishmen their basic rights. He had passed the Six Acts in that cesspool of corruption, Parliament, increasing the government's arbitrary powers. This was the man who had smirked still wider when he read the news from Manchester, of the massacre there, when the Hussars had trampled the unarmed crowd and the Yeomanry butchers had hacked down the people who had only gone to listen to Mr Hunt. He spat onto the cobbles as Sidmouth reached the safety of Harrowby's front door. Under his greatcoat, Ings was proud to wear his butcher's apron and under his left arm bulged the cleaver that was the tool of his profession.

Richard Tidd was not a happy man. He'd kissed his daughter Mary as he left Hole-in-the-Wall. And yes, he'd stopped off for some grog at the White Lion. It had been nearly empty then as dusk had settled on the West End. It seemed a long way from there to the Horse and Groom and his nerves were frayed. He'd looked across from the pub's candle-lit windows to that ill-lit stable in Cato Street which was their rendezvous. He'd seen that idiot Davidson, strutting backwards and forwards with his carbine on his shoulder and his white cross-belt bright even under the waxing moon, like some London version of the slave-leader l'Overture. Tidd had downed his rum and gone to join him. That must have been two, nearly three hours ago. Now, his head ached from the grog and his clogs slipped now and then on the frosty cobbles as he moved between the plane trees. But he was still in command, he told himself, still ready to do his duty.

'Eldon', a voice hissed in the darkness. George Edwards had been there for

longer than any of them, chatting with the Charlies, Bissex and Smart, with some cock-and-bull story that he was waiting for his master and he hoped the watchmen would ignore him so that no one would notice his pockets were bulging with large amounts of mail for the master who was arriving that very day from the Indies. As Edwards had hoped, Charlie Bissex and Tom Smart weren't the brightest apples in the barrel and they'd waved their staves at him as he fingered the hand-grenades that lay waiting in his deep pockets.

Tidd jumped as Edwards passed. It was a toss-up really between the two of them, Edwards or Thistlewood, who was the more focused, the more determined. Which of them, Tidd wondered again, would run the People's Government when the time came? Thistlewood was the gentleman certainly and from Tidd's own county but Edwards, the impoverished doll-maker, was dressed very flash these days.

Eldon's coach was already rattling away and the Lord Chancellor of England looked decidedly small without his huge wig, his gold chain and his glittering robes of office. But he had sat heavy on mankind for too long. He did not invent the Bloody Code, but he approved it and day after day he had presided over the law courts which hanged little boys for stealing a shilling and saw women whipped at the cart's tail. Neither Tidd nor Edwards knew that, in his cups, Eldon had said that if he had his life to live over again, he would be an agitator, damn his eyes. They would not have believed it had they known, but they would damn his eyes all right – forever.

Now, all the carriages had come and gone. True to form, Lord Westmoreland had been the last to arrive. He'd only had to cross the square, from the north side and he came alone, with no servant at his elbow. He nodded to the Charlies who saluted him and tipped his hat to the decently dressed man who would kill him four minutes later.

Arthur Thistlewood was making his rounds for one last time, the fake letter from Carlton House in his pocket. It must have been about a quarter to eight and all the guests had now assembled. His Majesty's Secretaries of State, the King's Ministers, the whole nest of noodles in one, helpless trap. Thistlewood had fifteen men around the square and there were fifteen members of the Cabinet inside. How many servants Harrowby had was anybody's guess, but Davidson's carbine would overawe the lot until Edwards could lob his grenades into the kitchen passages.

The carpenter Richard Bradburn straightened as he passed. James Gilchrist was checking his shoemaker's knives. John Monument looked pale, but something in his eyes told Thistlewood he was ready. John Shaw was leaning against the portico of a house in the south-west corner, whittling silently as the night deepened. Cooper the bootmaker, Ings the butcher, Wilson the tailor, Tidd the bootmaker, Davidson the cabinet-maker and Edwards the man recently come into money; money he'd spent on the arsenal for tonight. They were all ready, ready to end tyranny and to make history their own.

It was time. Thistlewood crossed the square boldly, from left to right, his boots crunching on the hoar frost. He saw Charlie Bissex wandering in the pool of the gas light. He'd call the hour shortly − 'eight o'clock and all's far from well'.

He rapped on Harrowby's door, the brass knocker barking his arrival. The flunkey opened it, rather bemused. Everyone was here. What late arrival was this?

'My apologies,' said Thistlewood. 'I have an urgent letter for the Prime Minister, from his Majesty.'

He thrust the envelope into the flunkey's hand. The old man frowned. There was no royal crest. Nothing at all. Only a badly scrawled name 'Lord Liverpool'. He looked up, as if to ask for an explanation and found himself staring down the barrel of a horse pistol pointing at the bridge of his nose. Thistlewood held his left index finger to his lips and motioned to the flunkey to step back.

George Edwards was at his elbow and he ducked inside, to his left, to the stairs that must lead down to the kitchens. Gilchrist was with him and Cooper and even before he disappeared around the corner of the stairway, Thistlewood saw Edwards handing out the grenades.

The others were with him now, blinking in the unaccustomed brightness of Harrrowby's hall. Strange was the last and he clicked the door closed. Thistlewood could wait no longer. He had been planning this or something like it for over two years. He brought the pistol barrel down hard across the old flunkey's temple and hopped over the fallen man, who lay slumped and bleeding on the lower stairs. Then they rushed upwards, three abreast, to reach that room and begin their work. The West End job was under way at last.

The double doors along the upstairs landing were closed. Davidson at least knew that there were likely to be two attendants flanking the other side of it. He would cover one with his carbine if Ings took the other. That would leave Thistlewood to go about his business, confront the smug, murdering bastards around the table.

'Ready, T,' he nodded to his captain.

Thistlewood kicked open the doors and stood there, the horse-pistols cocked in both hands. Ings grabbed the nearest flunkey and threw him against the wall, scattering silver tureens off the sideboard. Davidson jabbed the servant on his side in the waistcoat and he fell back with the others.

For the briefest of moments, the only noise in the room was the rolling of the last tureen around the floor. All fifteen men at the table sat frozen, their appalled faces lit by the flickering candles reflected off the silverware – the silverware that would keep Ings's family fed for years.

A burly butler broke the silence, striding towards Thistlewood and his cocked pistols. 'What the devil do you mean, sir?' he asked him.

'It's all right, Joseph,' a kindly voice rang from behind him. Lord Harrowby was sitting, as host, at the head of the oblong table. He dipped his spoon into his soup and turned to his Prime Minister, Lord Liverpool, to his left. 'Farley's White Soup,' he said, as though someone had just dropped a napkin. 'Cook tells me you put a knuckle of veal into six quarts of water, with a large fowl and a pound of lean bacon. Add half a pound of rice, two anchovies, a few pepper corns . . .'

'My Lord!' Thistlewood's broad Lincolnshire accent stopped Harrowby's flow. 'We are representatives of the People's Government. As I speak the Committee of Two Hundred is raising London. You, gentlemen, have one chance. Refuse and you will die now.'

'Here's men as good as the Manchester Yeomanry!' Ings bellowed. It was a line he had been rehearsing for some time.

Another silence. There had been no explosions from downstairs. Edwards had not used the hand-grenades; had not fired a shot. That was to the good. If the servants and lackeys of the West End had come over, everyone would follow and by dawn, the whole of London would be reformist. Manchester would be avenged. There would be a new world.

'The most important thing', Harrowby continued in his calm, collected voice, 'is the celery heads and the sweet herbs, because . . .'

But the President of the Privy Council never finished his sentence because Thistlewood's pistol crashed with a spark and a roar and Harrowby was thrown sideways, a neat dark hole in his right temple. Liverpool tried to catch him as he went down, his hands instantly soaked in blood and brains.

Now everyone was on their feet. On the far side, Castlereagh had a pistol in his hand. Davidson saw it first and fired the carbine with one hand from his hip. The handsome Foreign Secretary jack-knifed as the lead tore a path through his stomach. He staggered backwards, kicking over his chair as he went down, the pistol gone from his grasp.

What happened next was a frenzy of killing. There was no time to reload and Davidson hacked about him with the carbine butt, clubbing anyone who stood in his way, flunkey or lord, it made no difference. This was a new world and he was removing the old order to make way for it. The guns of the killers crashed again and again and the dining room was full of screams and curses. Wellington, true to form, downed Harrison with a candelabra and was ready to tackle the next man, if Thistlewood hadn't shattered that famous nose with his third pistol.

No one knew how long the slaughter lasted. No one knew how many windows were broken or how the sounds of the killings had travelled through the West End night. They stood there, the men who had come from Cato Street, breathing hard, flushed, covered in blood and soup. There was a sob from a corner – a servant still alive, whimpering. The last thing he saw was Brunt's solid frame, shutting out the candle-light. The last thing he felt was Brunt's boot, one he had made himself, in his face.

Now was Ings's moment, the one he'd planned, the one he'd rehearsed. He tore off his greatcoat and stood there in his butcher's apron, drawing the long, steel cleaver from its sheath. Out of his pocket he pulled two canvas bags and laid them on the sideboard. Then he squatted on the other side of the table. No one else moved, sharing in that weird stillness, the moment of triumph. There was a ripping sound and the twisting of muscle and sinew and bone. Then Ings stood upright, the cleaver still dripping in his right hand. In his left were the no longer handsome features of the head of the Foreign Secretary. His eyes were half closed and the hair gripped in the butcher's hand was matted with blood. His throat had been slashed at an angle and a piece of vertebra gleamed white in the bloody mess.

'Behold,' gasped Ings, eyes shining in the slaughter. 'The head of a traitor.'

And he stuffed it into one of the sacks.

Thistlewood didn't wait to see more. He spun on his heel and left the killing room, almost colliding with Edwards on the landing.

'All well, T?' the man asked.

'Well,' said Thistlewood. 'You?'

'I think we can say the servants are with us. They're all but singing Ça Ira down there.'

Thistlewood clapped the man on the shoulder. 'Ings has taken Castlereagh's head. Now he's after Sidmouth's. Keep them close. I want them on poles on the bridge come morning.'

And he made for the stairs.

Out on the leads of Lord Harrowby's, high over Grosvenor Square, Arthur Thistlewood looked across London. He could hear the shouts and the singing as the new world began. There was no gunfire, so the Committee must have got their cannon from the Artillery Ground without a fight. He could see the fires already flaring where John Palin and his men had fired the barracks – to his left in Portman Street, to his right in Knightsbridge and beyond that to Birdcage Walk. He could imagine the horror and the disbelief on the faces of the well-to-do as the ragged masses smashed in their doors and windows, helping themselves to food and valuables. But, above all, to food.

There would be chaos for a while, perhaps for days, perhaps for weeks. But then, a calm would descend and order would be restored. Thistlewood would have the king brought to him at the Mansion House and the Archbishop of Canterbury. As he stood there, unaware of the biting cold and watching the magic of the fires, he knew the new world was at hand.

The Government of the People of Great Britain had begun.

*

The account you have just read never happened. But it, or something like it, was supposed to. We do not know how Thistlewood's conspirators would actually have coped at Lord Harrowby's dinner because they never got there. Instead, they were arrested in the early evening of 23 February 1820, in a dilapidated hay-loft of a stable in Cato Street, ten minutes walk away, arming themselves for what would have been the most devastating assassination in

British history.

This is the story of that conspiracy, of what might have been and what was not. It is a story of hopes and dreams, of cruelty and kindness, of high drama and of farce. It is a tale of one injustice heaped on another. The men who should have dined – and died – with Lord Harrowby that winter's night long ago have all found honourable graves and have won their places in the pantheon of history. The men who tried to kill them have vanished, their bodies indistinguishable from the clay under what today is the Central Criminal Court of the Old Bailey.

This is their story.

Chapter 2

The Winter of Discontent

'Merde!'[1]

The famous shout of defiance from General Cambronne as he stood with the shattered remnants of the Old Guard near Hougoumont as dusk fell on 18 June symbolized in so many ways the days of 'la gloire', the extraordinary military adventure on which France had embarked after 1791.

The battle of Waterloo has passed into legend, destroying forever the French domination of Europe that had lasted for one and a half centuries. From now on, the language of diplomacy, the currency of power, was English and Britain was on her way to becoming the mightiest power the world has known.

But there were casualties along the way and never more so than in the months and years following that famous victory in the fields on the road to Charleroi. At first, of course, all was well. Britain celebrated the end of a gruelling twenty-two years of war, first against Revolutionary France, then Napoleon. The bells rang out, there were services of thanksgiving. And gentlemen in England, then-abed, read over and over, to their families and servants, the words of Wellington's despatch to *The Times*.[2]

Wellington's army would stay in France for a further three years, just to make sure that the restoration of the Bourbons was not a last flicker of monarchy and that Bonapartism would not raise its head again. The Emperor of the French – known to most Englishmen as Boney – was sent on board the *Northumberland*, bound for the grim, black rock that was St Helena. He would leave it as a partially mummified corpse twenty-five years later.

John Thomas Brunt, the Cato Street conspirator, supplied boots to the cavalry regiment the Blues, soon after Waterloo, and would have heard grumblings about the regiment's quota sailing home. These men had served their country and in the months to come, at the insistence of the Duke of

Wellington, they would receive their Waterloo medal, the first of its kind ever awarded to ordinary soldiers. Brunt's co-conspirator James Ings might have attended street parties in his town of Portsmouth, jostling the crowded alleyways of the harbour with the sailors who had won their battle honours at Cape St Vincent, Copenhagen, the Nile and Trafalgar. He would have been stood rounds of drinks in the port's taverns, hearing over and over again, 'with advantages', the deeds the Tars carried out on those days.

But by the late summer of 1815, James Ings was already in London, and would have read the signs in the London parks – 'No dogs – and no soldiers in uniform'.

The euphoria of victory soon gave way to reality and to despair. What kind of England did men of the Blues come home to that summer? For all the nineteenth century was 'the age of the cities', we would be struck by how rural everything was. Britain was not yet the workshop of the world and if the 'dark Satanic mills' were increasing in number and London was the largest city in the world, England still had 'mountains green' and the metropolis was ringed with fields. The hay-loft in Cato Street, from which the conspirators planned to launch their revolution, was on the edge of civilization. Beyond the Edgware Road were pastures (the Cato Street building was a cow shed) and Hyde Park much more countrified than it is today. In the 1830s, Princess Victoria, writing her diary from the perspective of a 13 year old, talked of Kensington where she was born as 'our dear village'. And from exactly the same vantage point, but many years older and of a more bitter disposition, the radical pamphleteer William Cobbett watched with revulsion the 'great Wen' that was London creeping inexorably across the fields towards him.

Most men and women worked on the land and were slaves of the seasons. In the summer, they toiled at the back-breaking work of the harvest, with sickle and scythe – it would be half a century before steam-driven threshing machines did some of the work for them. They rose with the sun and crawled home in the darkness, ready to sing lustily in church on Sunday of the harvest home. 'Come, ye thankful people, come.' In the winter, before the spring sowing, they huddled around peat fires in the tied cottages and prayed the squire for whom they worked would not evict them before the next harvest.

The fields themselves were still new in some places. The enclosure movement, which cleared woodland and drained marsh, was two generations old, but the trend had been speeded up in recent years by desperation. Britain had been a fortress on the edge of French-dominated Europe and had had to become self-sufficient or surrender. In 1801 parliament had passed the General Enclosure Act which cut through much of the red-tape surrounding the lengthy mechanics of enclosure. So now, in the south, hedges and fences surrounded the old common land. In the north, dry-stone walls criss-crossed the moors. There was still the need to prove land ownership. Without an actual written deed, a man whose great-grandfather had owned the land was forced to see it bought up by the local squire.

> The law arrests the man or woman,
> Who steals the goose from off the Common,
> But lets the greater thief go loose,
> Who steals the Common from the goose.

His choice then was to leave, to find work elsewhere or to stay put as a 'landless labourer'. Most took the latter road and carried on as before. But not quite as before. In the long, dark nights of winter such men huddled around their fires and puffed on their pipes. The firewood that crackled in their hearths was no longer free. The tobacco they smoked had a duty on it. Even the rabbit stewing in the pot belonged to somebody else and they risked gaol by trapping it. Most men muttered, shrugged, stirred the fire in the grate. But some men 'knew no harm of Bonaparte and plenty of the squire' and perhaps, as the fire died and their children cried with hunger, they plotted murder and revolution.

Fifty years ago, social historians believed that the effects of change on the land – the combination of enclosures and the patenting of labour-saving devices like the horse-hoe and the seed-drill – drove thousands to the towns in a mass exodus. We now know that this was not the case. There was movement, certainly, but it was localized and piecemeal. Landless labourers moved to the next parish or the one beyond that and they continued to work the land. Even when the second generation[3] did reach the towns, they tried to find work with animals or delivering foodstuffs. Thomas Hyden, one of the key witnesses in the trials of the Cato Street conspirators, was a cow-keeper. Edward Hucklestone, who gave evidence at Thistlewood's trial, had become a shoemaker, but was 'now articled to a cow-doctor in Newman Mews'.[4] It was not until the 1770s that we see the first appearance of industrial mills and not until the decade of Cato Street that machinery began to be steam-driven.

In the long term of course, the complex series of interlocking events we call by shorthand convenience the Industrial Revolution was beneficial to everyone. The kind of poverty which the Cato Street conspirators believed, naively, could be laid at the door of Lord Liverpool's Cabinet, has long vanished and it takes an extraordinary leap of imagination for us to see the world as Arthur Thistlewood saw it. The massive changes in British society from a rural way of life in which men lived in villages, were born and died in the same parish, to an urban existence, where the flotsam of society moved to the thud and grind of the machines, had no precedent. There was no blueprint and when mistakes were made – and they were, in large measure – it was because no nation in the world had experienced such changes before.

The new men of the Industrial Revolution – Josiah Wedgwood, Jedediah Strutt, James Watt, Jethro Tull and countless others – were men of vision driven by a thirst for knowledge or a thirst for profit or both. Improving landlords like Tull, 'Turnip' Townshend and Coke of Holkham, had the money, the time and the leisure to try out revolutionary new techniques on sections of their estates. Tull's seed-drill, for example, made nonsense of the New Testament parable of the sower. No longer would seeds fall on stony ground or among weeds; neither could the wind blow them away, because the machine dug a hole for each seed and buried it. The result would be a massive increase in productivity and in food to fill hungry mouths in the long winters ahead. In the short term, however, it saw the laying off of labour and angry farm workers tried to smash the drill and beat Tull to a pulp.

Josiah Wedgwood built his Etruria factory along the banks of the Trent so that the water could power his machinery. He saw that the rising middle classes wanted to emulate their betters. The aristocracy and the gentry might eat off porcelain imported from China; Wedgwood could make the stuff in Staffordshire at a fraction of the cost. It was probably not his intention, but in creating a quality product at a cheap price, Wedgwood was obeying every rule in the capitalist book (some would say he wrote the book) and he was, incidentally, helping to narrow the vast poverty gap that existed in his day.

Other manufacturers and industrialists got the point and followed suit.

Since machinery was made largely of timber and ran on water, whole forests disappeared and mills, with their distinctive rows of windows, sprang up along river banks, especially in the Midlands and the North. Obtaining money in the increasingly prosperous eighteenth century was not difficult. Until the wartime-engendered collapse of finance houses in 1797 there were over 300 banks in Britain, all of them operating under the shadow of a powerful financial system that was already over a century old. Interest rates for most of the century ran between 3 and 4 per cent. Without the need for planning permission, an entrepreneur could build on a fast-flowing river bank (for his power) as close as possible to an existing town (for his raw materials and a ready market) and he would advertise his goods in the increasingly widespread newspaper and printing businesses springing up everywhere.[5] By the 1790s, Britain was indeed the nation of shopkeepers described as such nearly twenty years before by Adam Smith.[6] But we were above all a nation of manufacturers. If we look at the nine men arrested by the Bow Street Runners on the night of 23 February 1820: James Ings and James Wilson were butchers; Richard Bradburn and John Shaw were carpenters; James Gilchrist and John Monument were shoemakers; Charles Cooper and Richard Tidd were bootmakers; William Davidson, always a little apart, had the highest status of them all – he was a cabinet-maker.

But the entrepreneurs of the eighteenth century had fixed costs which they could not avoid. They had to buy land and build suitable premises. They had to pay for their raw materials and their machinery. They had to pay the going rate for transport costs, both for raw materials and finished goods. They had to pay to advertise and if they were sensible, they would insure all they had. Where they could save money – and virtually all of them did – was in the paying of wages to their workforce. Here, there were no fixed costs, no going rate. Each hiring was a private transaction between the employer – always, and until the 1870s legally, known as the Master – and the employee – the Servant. The terminology spoke volumes for the great poverty divide of the time. It was not until twenty-five years after Cato Street that Benjamin Disraeli used as the subtitle of his novel *Sybil*, the Two Nations, by which he meant the rich and the poor in England. It would be another three years after that, that Karl Marx and Frederick Engels wrote the Communist Manifesto, a blueprint for doing something about that monstrous inequality.

So the entrepreneurs of the first phase of the Industrial Revolution built cheap houses for their workers as close as possible to the factory. That way, time would not be lost in travelling to and from work. They built them quickly so that profits would grow from the first day and they built them in terraces to save space. These 'back-to-back' tenements formed the nucleus of cities in the last decade of the eighteenth century, built haphazardly by individual industrialists with no recourse to civic planning, so that street upon street and alley upon alley became warrens of overcrowding and despair.

In the 1830s when the Whig government commissioned Edwin Chadwick and his team of civil servants to investigate the problem, a house built for a single family was home to sixty individuals, of both sexes and all ages. Typically, the attic, with no fireplace, a single window and a sloping ceiling, housed eight. The only means to the ground was via the floors below. The upper storey, intended of course as a bedroom, had perhaps two windows and a fireplace, but it routinely housed up to twenty people. The ground floor was identical, with two extra people crammed in here somehow. Below ground, steps led down to the cellars, often inches deep in water, where ten miserable souls had no view but other people's shoes clattering at street level. The walls of every storey were wringing wet and every house was awash with vermin. People slept eight to a bed, children tucked into every conceivable angle and corner.

Water for these first- and second-generation industrial families came from stand-pipes that were owned by private water companies and these taps were usually turned on for two hours a day. Children queued to fill buckets and the water collected had to last for twenty-four hours, to be used for drinking, cooking, washing bodies and clothes. The toilet was a privy, a single shed on the ground next to the terrace. Its door was often hanging off and there would be no flush mechanism until the 1850s.[7] The human waste was carried away into a neighbouring sewer (in effect an open drain) or merely collected in a pit until it was removed – and dumped nearby – by the euphemistically named night soil men.

Landlords were under no obligation to repair or maintain these premises and no tenant had the time or money to turn to law for redress. The overcrowding was appalling because tenants continually sublet in an effort to be able to pay their rent. And of course the bitterest pill of all was that the landlord was very often the factory master too. If a man lost his job, he would lose the roof over his head. There was no such thing as a fair rents tribunal and, like the wages he paid, the rent was fixed by the Master/landlord without any external control whatever. If a labourer would not work for the money offered, if he would not pay the rent demanded, there were plenty who would.

To too many men of Arthur Thistlewood's generation, home was a rat-infested hovel where cholera and typhoid would become endemic killers by the 1830s. Work was a suffocating mill, where stringent rules led to swingeing fines or dismissal. In the stifling cotton mills of Manchester, the most technologically advanced of their day, small children as young as 5 crawled under the eighty-spindled 'jennies', tying snapped fibres. Asthmatics died in their hundreds. The 'healthy' ones, with their long hair, ragged clothes and bare feet were walking disaster zones among the unguarded, moving machinery. Whole families went to work in the dark and came home in the dark, with bread and cheese for their only meals, taken alongside their machines. Some of them worked up to eighteen hours a day, the women earning half of their menfolk's wages, the children half of that.

It is easy to wax too lyrical on the plight of the factory workers, as Marx and Frederik Engels would in the 1840s. We have to see their lives in the context of what they had known in their early lives and what their fathers knew. And we have to acknowledge that, in terms of child labour at least, the first tentative steps of reform and government improvement, had been taken as early as 1802.[8]

Whichever way we look at the social/industrial problem, what we are witnessing is the effects of an unprecedented series of upheavals onto an expanding generation in a brave, but terrifying, new world. But that was only the background – the long-term work and living patterns that had been developing by 1815 for a generation. Bolted onto all that was the peculiar set of circumstances that followed the end of the war.

In terms of pure economics, the months following Waterloo were positive. So much of the investment, manifest today in the world's hysterical stock markets, is about confidence. And in the summer of 1815 Britain was confident indeed. The Treaty of Paris, signed in May 1815 by the allies who had overthrown Napoleon, promised 'perpetual peace and friendship'. To this end, various dignitaries – Talleyrand from France, Nesselrode from

Prussia, Tsar Alexander of Russia and Lord Castlereagh from Britain –
reconvened with their entourages (and in the case of Castlereagh, his wife)
in Vienna under the genial auspices of Prince Metternich to establish thirty
years of European cooperation. By this arrangement, Britain added to her
territories and British businesses could congratulate themselves as being the
richest, best organized and most technologically advanced in the world.
Their nearest rivals, the French, were humiliated and beaten. They would
never rise again.

But the short-lived boom of 1815 hid a hornets' nest of problems. The
long years of war had created an economy that was inevitably geared to the
war effort. In the 1790s, William Pitt as the Prime Minister launched a black
crusade against the viciousness of the French Revolution, manufacturing
turned to making weapons of war. In textiles, the most mechanized of all
British industries, there was a huge demand for uniforms. Every soldier was
issued with a new jacket or coatee every Christmas Day. It would be over a
century before conscription was introduced by a British government, but at
the height of the war against Napoleon, there were perhaps half a million
men serving with the army and navy; they all had to be clothed. Sails were
needed for ships of the line. The 104-gun *Victory*, Nelson's flagship at
Trafalgar, carried 6,500 square yards of canvas. Likewise the army needed
tents, in all the theatres of war where they fought. Even in relatively non-
confrontational areas like the West Indies or the virtually pointless
campaigning of the Duke of York in 1794, the demand for textiles was
voracious. And of course, the industry rose to the challenge. These were the
great days of the handloom weavers, earning up to 22 shillings a week.[9]
There are accounts of these men swaggering through Manchester with gold-
topped canes and pound notes stuffed into their hatbands.

The huge demand for woollen and cotton textiles carried the seeds of
destruction, at least from the point of view of employment. James
Hargreaves's 'Spinning Jenny', patented in 1769 but not in widespread use
until the 1790s, could do the work of eighty individual spinning wheels
which had been the centre of the domestic industry. Increasingly, the
independent spinners and weavers were going to the wall by 1810. They had
a stark choice: work in the new, all-pervasive mills or starve. Out of this
dilemma, from 1811, were born the Luddites, weavers, spinners and
stocking-frame knitters from Lancashire, Derbyshire and Nottinghamshire,

who in desperation and naivety saw the hated machines as their enemy and used their huge, two-handed lump hammers, made by the firm of Enoch & Co. to shatter their rivals. 'Great Enoch still shall lead the van; Stop him who dare, stop him who can'. Matters were made worse by the year of Cato Street when the Revd Edmund Cartwright's power-loom was in widespread use, cutting the ground from under thousands of weavers in the Midlands and the North. Many of the 60,000 who attended the fateful meeting at St Peter's Fields, Manchester, in August 1819[10] were weavers. They had gone to hear speeches about universal suffrage but only because they believed the vote would safeguard their livelihoods.

As with textiles, so with the iron industry. Swords for the cavalry, bayonets for the infantry, guns for everybody – the demand was huge. John Wilkinson remained the longest-serving supplier of swords for the army,[11] but he was matched in the 1790s by Gill, Osborn and nearly 200 makers and cutlers. Thomas Gill's sabres for the Light Cavalry had the boast 'Guaranteed to cut iron' stamped on their blades. A small firm, that of Underwood, became involved in Cato Street because Hector Morrison, one of the cutlers, was engaged by James Ings to sharpen two sword blades in February 1820.

'They were made extremely sharp from heel to point', Morrison told the jury at Ings' trial. 'The prisoner directed that they should be made as sharp as a needle at the point and that they should be made to cut both at the back and front.'[12]

Cannon and wheel rims for the Artillery, shot of all proportions, buckles and hooks and buttons – all of it came under the aegis of iron. The new Hussar jackets for certain regiments of cavalry after 1805 had no less than 97 buttons – only 19 of them actually fastened anything! Much was made at the Cato Street trials of the appalling weapons of mass destruction made by the conspirators in the days and weeks before 23 February. When Samuel Taunton, a Bow Street Runner, searched Richard Tidd's house in the Hole-in-the-Wall Passage, he found 965 cartridges, 10 grenades and 'a great quantity of gunpowder'. There were 434 balls (bullets) along with 69 ball cartridges and 11 bags of gunpowder, each weighing one pound. Sergeant Edward Hanson of the Royal Artillery shocked the jury at Thistlewood's trial by describing the devastating effect of a hand-grenade:

The [tin] case contains three ounces and a half of gunpowder. The priming in the tube is a composition of salt-petre, powder and brimstone. The tin was pitched and wrapped round with rope-yarn which was cemented with rosin and tar. Round the tin, and in the rope-yarn, twelve pieces of iron were planted. From the lighting of the fusee to the explosion might be about half a minute. If one of them were to be exploded in a room where there were a number of persons, it would produce great destruction. The pieces of iron would fly about like bullets.[13]

Chain-shot, bar-shot, canister shot and grape shot, as well as cannon balls weighing between 9 and 64 pounds, were being produced in their thousands for use against the French, giving the iron masters huge profits and creating work for the new industrial classes lured into the workshops by the promise of high wages. It was dangerous, hot and dirty, but the money was good.

And demand for iron and textiles did not end there. Britain was rich enough by the 1790s to become the effective paymaster of Europe, supplying cash, cloth, iron and much else to keep the armies of Austria, Prussia and Russia in the field against the French. Four such coalitions were smashed by the combination of luck and zeal that characterized the Revolutionary armies. Under Napoleon, the coalitions collapsed even quicker. So the Austrians, for example, adopted a pattern of British cavalry sword they still used, in essence, up to 1914 and, in one memorable exchange of goods which flew in the face of all logic, Napoleon sent shiploads of corn to Britain in exchange for Nottingham-made boots so that his troops could go on killing ours!

We have already seen the impact of the wars on agriculture. Enclosure was the watchword. After 1806 Napoleon's Continental System, though never fully functional, was designed to seal Britain off from the rest of Europe. We had never been self-sufficient in terms of foodstuffs and now the situation was worse. Reliance on the harvest and good weather became absolutely crucial and rural distress remained a burning issue for years to come.

In terms of paying for the war, the poor had what, with hindsight, was something of a lucky break. To keep the coalitions sweet, Pitt arbitrarily withdrew gold from the banks and issued paper 'promissory notes' instead. In 1797, the same year as the naval mutinies at the Nore and Spithead, the banks collapsed in a spectacular crisis of confidence. Bank employees were beaten up and their windows smashed as investors were told their gold had gone. A recurring theme of the pugnacious William Cobbett's pamphlets from 1802 was hatred of 'Mr Pitt's paper money'. In 1799, Pitt hit upon the obvious and introduced a tax on incomes, graduated so that the rich paid most, on incomes of over £60 a year. Since no working man earned anything like that (farm labourers, for instance, subsisted on anything between £5 and £8), the poor found their financial burden lighter in these years. Direct taxation, which they did not pay, had largely replaced indirect taxation, which they did.

And then, suddenly, from 1814, all that changed. Napoleon's escape from his first imprisonment on Elba and the subsequent hundred days campaign that culminated in Waterloo proved to be a mere last gasp of 'la gloire'. And after that long June day certainly, the demand for wartime industries collapsed overnight and the world had changed.

No one needed swords, guns, bayonets, sail, tents, buckles, ammunition and warships. The Elizabethan statesman Lord Burghley had famously said, 'Soldiers in peacetime are like chimneys in summer' and in the summer of 1815, an estimated 300,000 of them came home.

There were, no doubt, parties and handshakes and heart-warming reunions of families and friends. But reality must have kicked in quickly. An infantryman who had been lucky might have served under Arthur Wellesley, later Duke of Wellington, since 1808 in Portugal and Spain. That meant he had been out of the workforce for seven years and the workforce had learnt to do without him. If he been a spinner or a weaver, he would find no chance of setting up again independently. If he went, cap in hand, to a Master, he would be asked what experience he had. None, except killing Frenchmen. The door would be slammed in his face. One of the five men who died at Newgate after the Cato Street conspiracy was ex-military; so was one of the principal witnesses against them. It would be fascinating to know how many ex-soldiers joined the Luddites to smash the hated machines, marched with the radicals at Spa Fields in 1816,[14] faced the yeomanry at St Peter's Fields two years later and were in that crowd outside Newgate when the men of Cato Street met their maker. For the world had turned. Any cold analysis of revolution, any attempt to explain why one works and the other does not, must hinge on the role of the army. In France in 1789, in Russia in 1917, the army was divided, shaky, disloyal. In Britain in 1815–22, the army was rock solid. But those who had left the army were a different matter. In some cases, whole regiments, like the 23rd Light Dragoons, were disbanded. In others, their strength was halved. The government of Lord Liverpool was desperate to save money and this was one obvious way of doing it. In the navy, the story ran the same as ships' companies were axed. It was, perhaps a slow and painful death, personified by the painter J M W Turner in his haunting *The Fighting Temeraire*, as a graceful ship-of-the-line gilded by a dying sun, is towed along by a black, ugly steam tug to be broken up. Soldiers and sailors had seen death up close and personal. Life, to them, was cheap. Murder was always a solution. Such men were dangerous.

William Pitt died, worn out by his exertions, in January 1806, but true to the promise he had made seven years earlier, as soon as was expedient after the war, the hated income tax was dropped. This of course meant that indirect taxation – duties on goods – had to increase. And this time all consumers were hit, including and most especially the poor. In 1815, Liverpool's government spearheaded by the men who were due to dine with Lord Harrowby in February 1820, introduced the Corn Laws, one of the most divisive and class-conscious pieces of legislation ever put forward. Napoleon's Continental System had totally collapsed by 1814 as Prussia, Russia and Britain conspired to drive his armies back into France. This meant that European ports were open and cheap, foreign corn was available and bread – the staple diet of most Englishmen – was affordable. 1813, 1814 and 1815 were also years of good harvests at home, so for a very brief period as war came to an end, rural distress was lessened and there seemed a light at the end of the tunnel of economic gloom.

The Corn Laws changed all that. Faced with a loss of profits because of foreign competition, parliament (by definition and to a man, all landowners) placed a price on corn which affected the opening and closing of ports. Economically, this was slow and cumbersome, but to the people it seemed (and it is difficult to argue against this) that the real aim of government was to keep the cost of bread artificially high. If bread was dear, everything was dear – rent, clothes, other foodstuffs. The euphoria at the end of the war quickly changed to a dark mood of defiance and the scene was set for a class war bordering on revolution.

Over all this was the enigmatic figure of William Cobbett. From 1802, the pamphleteer had written a series of polemical, from-the-shoulder articles in his *Weekly Political Register*. As the essayist Charles Hazlitt wrote of Cobbett, he would take on everyone and anyone. As a writer, he is enormous fun to read, if only because he is so inconsistent. In one passage, he extols the courage and honesty of Sir Francis Burdett, the radical MP. In another, he fairly burns paper:

> he is a sore to Westminster; a set-fast on its back; a cholic in its belly; a cramp in its limbs; a gag in its mouth; he is a nuisance, a monstrous nuisance in Westminster and he must be abated.

He attacked: Pitt and his paper money; Robert Peel, the War Secretary; Thomas Malthus, the population parson,[15] William Wilberforce, hero of the anti-slavers; Scotsmen; Americans; tea; corruption; Methodists; Quakers; Unitarians; and the landlord of the George Inn, Andover.

In fact, he was by no means so bold face-to-face with his opponents and, although he served time in prison for his views, was just as likely to run to the safety of America (whose towns he said at one stage should be burnt down) as to stay. Ironically, the thing that Cobbett hated most was hypocrisy and in this, he was as guilty as the next man.

Why is Cobbett so important in this story? Because the *Political Register*, especially in its cheaper form of the *Twopenny Trash*, reached thousands of the working class and was more of a Bible to them than any other radical tract.[16] Those who read it believed it. Those who could not read it had it read to them, and still believed. Oddly, Samuel Bamford, the radical weaver from Middleton who witnessed 'Peterloo',[17] believed that Cobbett's works calmed the working class. This is difficult to accept; every line of Cobbett's is contentious – it was in his nature.

And the recurring dripfeed of the *Register* was how glorious it was in the good old days and how appalling things were now. This nostalgia is nonsense, but it is an all-pervading part of the human condition. For men, women and children, squatting in damp, freezing cellars, moving to the jar and grind of inhuman machines, to be told that their fathers and grandfathers had lived an idyllic, rural existence with roses twining around the door was hardly likely to instil a sense of contentment.

The loss of jobs, the change in taxation, the arrival of the Corn Laws, the overcrowding of an increasingly desperate people into foul-smelling tenements and dangerous workshops and mills – this was the reality in a nation that had just emerged victorious from a quarter of a century of war.

That there was economic distress and a discontented workforce in Lord Liverpool's England cannot be doubted. But was it this alone that led James Ings to get his swords sharpened and George Edwards to put the fuses in the grenades?

For that, there had to be something more.

Chapter 3

The Shadow of the Guillotine

The future Cato Street conspirator, William Davidson, was 3 when a ragged 'army' of *sans-culottes*, carrying scythes and pitchforks, swarmed through the alleyways and avenues of Paris on its way to the Bastille, long the symbol of governmental tyranny. It was 14 July 1789 – a day to be remembered.

For three days Paris had effectively been in the hands of the mob – the terrifying peasantry whom the Whig politician Edmund Burke described as 'the swinish multitude'. The rigid political structure in France – the three estates of Church, Aristocracy and Everybody Else – gave an unhappy country nowhere to go. Superficially, the list of complaints by the Third Estate (representing 96 per cent of the French population) against the first two were very much what the Cato Street conspirators would level at the Cabinet in 1820. The crucial difference was social mobility. The Prime Minister, William Pitt, was the son of an Earl (of Chatham) but the grandson of an official of the East India Company. In other words, in two generations the Pitt family had risen from the 'middling sort' to the aristocracy and to holding the most important political position in the land. Such meteoric rises were impossible in France, or indeed anywhere else in Europe and liberals there looked with longing and envy at the relative egalitarianism of the British constitution.

Suffering prolonged economic difficulties, both in agriculture and industry, plagued by a series of failed foreign wars (mostly against the victorious British) and politically stagnant, the beleaguered Louis XVI called a meeting of the Estates General for the first time since 1614. The distinctions with which the three estates were supposed to greet the king underlined everything that was wrong with France. The Clergy were to show him homage, the Aristocracy respect and the Third Estate 'humble supplications'.

But the Third Estate had changed since 1614. Fed by the liberal writings of men like the Frenchman Jean-Jacques Rousseau, the American Thomas Jefferson and the Englishman Tom Paine, the literate, pushy middle-class elements demanded a constitution along British lines in which the privileges and tax-exemption of the Church and Aristocracy should be swept away and the king drop the archaic notion of Divine Right. Calling itself the National Assembly, the Third Estate stood its ground against reactionary opposition and more and more of the Clergy and Aristocracy went over to its side. Noblemen like the Duke of Orleans and the hero of the American Revolution, Lafayette, joined the braying Deputies of the Assembly, as did the Abbé (Bishop) Sieyes, quickly assuming the role of oracle.

In the first two weeks of June, the 'grande peur' took place. Hostile mobs encouraged by the extraordinary events in Paris, vented their spleen over local grievances and burnt down the chateaux that had dominated their lives and the lives of their grandfathers. Rumours flew everywhere and by 11 July Paris was in open revolt. On the 14th, the aim was not only to release the handful of political prisoners in the Bastille, but to steal the arsenal of weapons stored there. The Cato Street conspirators tried a watered-down version of the same thing thirty-one years later. The stubborn, but at the same time indecisive Louis XVI ordered the army back to the Champ de Mars and left the 110-strong Bastille garrison to its fate. When the mob trained stolen cannon on the prison's walls, the governor, Bernard de Launay, was forced to surrender. The chanting, hysterical mob hacked off his head and carried it in triumph on a pole through the streets. It was quickly followed by that of the Intendant of Paris. Then, the Bastille was demolished.

The storming of the Bastille was the outward symbol of a revolution that would shatter the peace of Europe for a quarter of a century. The most cultured and sophisticated nation in the world appeared to have gone mad, destroying forever the ancien regime and introducing a bizarre version of democracy which has never gone away. No matter that the greed and envy which characterizes human nature ruined the whole idealistic crusade, the original notions of 'liberté, égalité, fraternité' struck a chord with liberal philosophers and starving peasants alike.

The French Revolution was a defining event. In part it was a reaction to the 'shot heard round the world' which signalled events at Concorde and Lexington when American Minutemen exchanged musket fire with British infantry. The French lent their support to the American colonists, largely as a chance to win *one* military engagement against the British, but somehow the ideology too rubbed off. What was actually a self-centred and chauvinist squabble about trade was turned by the Americans into a just war in which the prize was freedom from tyranny.

But the Revolution created armed camps. For some, tub-thumpers like Camille Desmoulins, military opportunists like Napoleon Bonaparte and plain psychopaths like Maximilien Robespierre, it was heaven-sent. For others, essentially the governments, landowners, churches and entrenched establishments of Europe, it was the end of civilization. In Britain, the aristocracy, the gentry and the church rallied around George III. Briefly, the 'king who had lost America' experienced a popularity he had never known before in his life and coming, as it did, on the heels of one of George's inexplicable bouts of dementia,[1] the Tory establishment saw all this as some sort of test.

The Revolution became a party issue. Pitt hinted darkly that grim days lay ahead and he was echoed from an unlikely quarter. Edmund Burke, very much the philosopher and diarist of the Whigs, was known as the 'dinner gong' because his speeches were so dull that most of the Commons would file out to eat rather than listen to him. In 1790 however his *Reflections on the Revolution in France* was a runaway bestseller, perhaps because it was a 'doom and gloom' book of the type which still has huge readerships today. We like to be frightened by prognostications of disaster, especially if it is going to happen to somebody else. Burke also struck a nostalgic chord: 'But the age of chivalry is gone. That of sophisters, economists and calculators has succeeded and the glory of Europe is extinguished for ever.'[2] In taking this stand, which delighted Pitt and the king, Burke helped to split his own Whig party. His leader, the mercurial Charles James Fox, wholeheartedly supported the revolution, largely because he misunderstood it. He saw 1789 as a rather belated action replay of British events in 1688 when the wannabe despot James II was overthrown by his parliament and the timely defection of much of the army under John Churchill. On hearing of the fall of the Bastille Fox wrote: 'How much the greatest event it is that ever happened in the world! And how much the best!'[3]

The Cambridge undergraduate and future Lakeland poet William Wordsworth found himself on a walking tour of France in 1790 and wrote:

> Bliss was it in that dawn to be alive,
> But to be young was very heaven![4]

But no one captured the spirit of the Revolution like Tom Paine – his 'damnable works' were quoted in the Cato Street trials as being the cause of the madness that led men there. Paine, the son of a Quaker from Thetford, Norfolk, was a born agitator. Variously a corset-maker, sailor and teacher, he was dismissed from his post as an exciseman[5] for fighting for an increase in his men's wages. Having met Benjamin Franklin in London in 1774, Paine settled in Philadelphia as a radical journalist and published *Common Sense* in the year that the colonies declared their independence. In 1781 he was in France helping to secure continued backing for the American cause and even served in the continental (i.e. American) army of George Washington. It was either the height of courage or folly then that he returned to England in 1787. Unable to stomach Burke's lily-livered conservatism, Paine wrote the *Rights of Man* between 1791 and 1792, which both outsold Burke and, because Paine had advocated the overthrow of the British monarchy, brought charges of high treason against him. With a price on his head, Paine skipped to Paris where he was made not only a citizen, but a member of the National Convention.

'[Burke] is not affected by the reality of distress,' wrote Paine,

> touching his heart, but by the showy resemblance of it striking his imagination. He pities the plumage but forgets the dying bird . . . His hero or heroine must be a tragedy victim, expiring in show and not the real prisoner of misery, sliding into death in the silence of a dungeon.[6]

He answered Burke almost line for line: 'Man has no property in man. There is a dawn of reasoning in the world.'[7] And he attacked privilege, courtiers, placemen, pensioners, borough-holders and party leaders which, presumably, included Fox.[8]

In many ways of course, Paine heralded the democratic conventions and even the welfare state of the twentieth century. He advocated old age pensions, family allowances, free education and benefits for immigrants and the unemployed. No wonder Pitt's government hated him and he became a hero to the downtrodden and the dispossessed.

And the downtrodden and the dispossessed were now making waves. Before the war against Revolutionary France helped to define attitudes and opinions, there was a rising sense of alarm. By the time the second (and more radical) part of Paine's *Rights of Man* was published, there was a general and growing discontent, as reported by magistrates and MPs throughout the country. In Sheffield, which was quickly becoming the most radical town in the kingdom, 2,500 men – 'the lowest mechanicals' – had formed a Constitutional Society, corresponding with villages in their own area and other towns and cities further afield. The reformer Christopher Wyvill described graffiti daubed on the market cross in Barnard Castle, Durham. It read 'No King', 'Liberty' and 'Equality'. In North Shields, pitmen, keelmen, waggoners and sailors joined forces and were running opponents out of towns naked. William Wilberforce, the anti-slaver, heard that in Leeds Paine's book was being given away free, having been précis-ed down to a sixpenny pamphlet. In Sheffield in November 1792, there were demonstrations to celebrate the victory of the infant French Republic's army over the ancien regime powers at Valmy. The mob carried an effigy of Burke riding a pig and Henry Dundas, the Home Secretary, with the bottom of a donkey.

Nor were these riotous demonstrations one-sided. A pro-establishment 'church and king' mob went on the rampage for two days in Birmingham, and hit the Dissenting support for the Revolution by burning down a Baptist church and two Unitarian meeting houses before ransacking the house of the Dissenter and scientist Dr Joseph Priestley, burning his extensive library and dumping him in a pond. As with the Bastille, the town prison was thrown open and a great deal of looting occurred. In May, Mary Wollstonecraft rattled establishment cages still further with her publication *A Vindication of the Rights of Women*, based on the ideals being floated across the Channel – 'Woman is born free,' wrote Olympe de Gouges, 'and remains equal to man in rights.'[9]

In Scotland, by December, things were now more serious. The Friends of the People Society, meeting in Edinburgh, had 160 delegates. Not only were they jumping on the Revolutionary bandwagon by complaining about London's failure to recognize their local grievances, they were composed of middle-class men, lawyers and merchants, even landowners, lending the considerable weight of education and money to the cause.

While some British liberals played at revolution, wearing the scarlet 'caps of liberty' of the Parisian *sans-culottes* and addressing each other ostentatiously as 'citizen', war broke out in February 1793 and this forced a polarization. A man could sit on the fence no longer. If he supported the Revolution, he was, in effect, a traitor. To many, France had now gone beyond the pale because in January the Republican government publicly executed Louis XVI and his wife, the 'Austrian woman', Marie Antoinette. There was general horror, even among liberal reformers at this move and everyone conveniently forgot that we had done this to our king a century and a half earlier when a masked, anonymous executioner lopped off the head of Charles I.

As British troops were despatched to India and the West Indies in the opening moves of the Revolutionary War, Pitt infuriated Fox and the extremist Whigs by extending the numbers of militiamen and introducing a new force – the yeomanry. These part-time cavalrymen would play a central and appalling role in the Manchester 'massacre' in 1819. Their job was to provide a second line of defence – the motto of many units was 'Pro Aris et Focis', for hearths and homes – in the event of French invasion. Fox and many others saw them as a private army, a return to the dark days of the Protectorate when Oliver Cromwell and the army effectively ran England.

By the spring, there were disquieting voices from some at least of the Celtic fringe. The Catholic Relief Act, which gave Catholics *some* rights after two centuries in the wilderness was a hollow victory. Since voting was based on a rigid property qualification and the majority of Ireland's Catholics were too poor to qualify, their 'victory' was useless. In June, Pitt's Militia Act, attempting to raise 16,000 men for home defence, was causing widespread rioting throughout Ireland, with attacks being made on priests and gentry who tried to interfere.

In September, Thomas Muir, leader of the Scottish Radicals, faced trial on charges of sedition. For over a year, new panicky legislation had outlawed various polemical writings, which is precisely why Tom Paine was an outlaw and William Cobbett spent time in prison. Muir's background as a lawyer enabled him to make a good case, but he was found guilty anyway and sentenced to fourteen years' transportation to Botany Bay.[10]

Burke was proved uncannily prescient when Robespierre's terror struck between 1792 and 1794. The guillotine (probably, before lethal injection, the most humane method of execution[11]) was set up in the Place de Grèves in Paris and its victims were not merely aristocrats, but *anyone* who fell foul of the Revolutionary tribunals across France. Aristocrats had been flying out of the country for months, bringing tales of persecution and horror. Any English landowner, from George III downwards, turned pale at the stories of chateau burning, of previously loyal servants turning on their masters.

On the other hand, the ideologies of Paine stood firm. The man himself might be outlawed and his book illegal – from time to time booksellers' premises were raided, especially in London, by overzealous magistrates – but the ideas lived on. Radicals of every hue were now branded Jacobins after the more extreme French party. These were the warmongers whose proclamation in November 1792 had terrified all Europe, offering 'fraternity and assistance' to anyone who wanted to overthrow their own governments.[12] Briefly, 'Ça Ira', the revolutionary song whose words were actually written by Benjamin Franklin, became the theme tune of English revolution.

This was the heyday of the corresponding societies, the most famous of which was set up in London by men like the shoemaker Thomas Hardy, meeting in the Bell Tavern in Exeter Street. Letters and handbills flew backwards and forwards to similar groups in Sheffield and Norwich and to the Jacobin Club in Paris itself.

To counter these pseudo-revolutionary groups, James Reeves formed the Association of Property Against Republicans and Levellers. This was clearly how the forces of reaction saw Jacobins and tarred them all with the same brush, whether they wanted bloody revolution or cheap bread. Interestingly, there was nothing actually republican in the Cato Street conspiracy – the new king, George IV, in residence at Carlton House, was not among their targets. The Leveller charge is fascinating too. The name comes from the extraordinary time of the English Civil War, a time when men believed the world was 'turned upside down' and all sorts of political and religious lunacy prevailed among the Puritan sects and elsewhere. The Levellers could be regarded as crypto-socialists because they wanted the hedgerows – symbols of private property – to be levelled and equality to reign. They were the forerunners of the Spenceans and in their nostalgic longing for the old, forgotten but somehow better world, they had a belated champion in William Cobbett.

Some of the aims of the corresponding societies and Jacobins in general are hopelessly naive. Ex-naval captain Richard Brothers wrote *Revealed Knowledge of the Prophecies and Times* in 1794. The book was full of millennialist dreams and naïveté, the Thames red with human blood and 'then shall there be no more war, no more want, no more wickedness; but all shall be peace, plenty and virtue'. Brothers was arrested by the Privy Council the following year and confined in a lunatic asylum.

Throughout the 1790s, the corresponding societies came and went in terms of action and membership. Some members never returned as they saw the French Revolution collapse in blood and ultimately, by 1799, a military dictatorship. Others fell apart because of internal bickering and constant squabbles over exactly what the English revolution should be about and how it should be obtained. Their greatest problem was that they had no obvious national leader around which to rally. Parliamentarians like Fox, Wyvill and later Francis Burdett were, when all was said and done, still gentlemen with large fortunes[13] and had nothing in common with an agricultural labourer struggling to keep his family alive. At the lower end in terms of class hierarchy, men like Thomas Hardy in London, Francis Place the radical tailor of Charing Cross and, later, Samuel Bamford the Middleton weaver, did not command the respect of thousands, nor could they sway a mob. Somewhere in the middle came Joseph Gerrald and John Thelwall. Gerrald in particular tried to promote a National Convention along French lines, which would not only have had the effect of welding together the differing strands of Jacobinism in England, but would have included the reformers north of Hadrian's Wall and across the Irish Sea. That concept must have given Prime Minister Pitt and the entire Establishment many a sleepless night.

Like Muir, Gerrald was put on trial in Scotland in March 1794. As a lawyer, he conducted his own defence admirably and the judge, Lord Braxfield, was technically misdirecting the jury when he said to them

> When you see Mr Gerrald . . . making speeches such as you have heard today, I look upon him as a very dangerous member of society, for I daresay, he has eloquence enough to persuade the people to rise

in arms.[14]

Gerrald got fourteen years.

In May 1794, Pitt hit the corresponding societies. Leaders were arrested, habeas corpus (the law by which a man had to be charged with an offence to be held in prison) was suspended. Thomas Hardy's house was attacked by a loyalist mob celebrating Admiral Howe's victory of the 'glorious first of June' and his wife, already on the brink of a nervous breakdown, died. Hardy himself was put on trial at the Sessions House of the Old Bailey (where the Cato Street trials would be held) in October on a charge of high treason. The lawyer John Horne Tooke stood in the dock with him and when asked the usual question as to whether he would be tried by 'God and his country', shook his head and launched into a tirade against the latter. There was an ugly mood in the mob around the Bailey and Hardy's acquittal was met with undisguised joy.

In Tooke's trial, the Prime Minister himself was forced to attend and to admit that, before 1789, he too had been a reformer. Tooke was acquitted. John Thelwall, who increasingly had taken over from Hardy as the main thrust of the London Corresponding Society, was the last to be set free by an increasingly sympathetic jury. It was precisely this problem that led Robert Peel, as Home Secretary in the 1820s, to reform the penal system. Juries were increasingly failing to convict when the cause or circumstances of the case permitted, because of the ferocity of the sentence. Had Hardy, Tooke or Thelwall been convicted, they would, according to the law, have been dragged through London's streets on hurdles, hanged, their heads hacked off and their bodies quartered. Such an ass was the law on high treason that it had not been changed since 1605 and the Gunpowder Plot.

By 1794, Edmund Burke replaced James Reeves as the arch-champion of reaction. He believed that about one-fifth of men with the vote (i.e. men of property) and almost all those without were 'pure Jacobins, utterly incapable of amendment; objects of eternal vigilance'.[15] Hardy, Tooke and Thelwall were little better than assassins.

The success of these three not only encouraged the societies but created new leaders. Irishman John Binns, now a London plumber, became a leading light in the LCS and wrote that many of the members wanted the establishment of a republic. Three of them may have tried to put the theory into practice, although like Cato Street there was an air of farce about it.

Higgins, Smith and Lemaitre were held in the early months of 1795 on a charge of trying to kill George III with a poisoned dart fired from an air gun. Since the evidence against them relied solely on the word of an informer,[16] the case was dropped.

At around the same time, tracts were disseminated from the British Tree of Liberty at 98 Berwick Street, Soho, with such titles as *King Killing* and *The Happy Reign of George the Last*. At the end of October, three days after a huge mass rally, perhaps numbering 100,000, took place at Copenhagen Fields, Islington, parliament opened and the king's carriage was attacked. The satirists had a field day, with cartoons showing wild-looking ruffians armed with cudgels, blasting the windows of George's carriage. In fact there was no such assault, the window being broken by a stone, but the reality of 200,000 Londoners chanting 'No war! No king! No Pitt!' was enough to cause the wildest rumours. As a precaution when the king went to the theatre the next day, he had 100 infantrymen, 200 cavalry and 500 constables in attendance.

In January 1793, to the tune of 'God Save the King', the American Joel Barlow, who had witnessed the execution of Louis XVI, wrote:

> And when great George's poll
> Shall in the basket roll,
> Let mercy then control
> The guillotine.

John Binns toured the country extensively, talking to sailors in Portsmouth where the future Cato Street conspirator James Ings was probably already an apprentice butcher.[17] Francis Place, who had a rather well-developed sense of his own importance, said of the LCS:

> It induced men to read books instead of spending their time at public
> houses. It taught them to think, to respect themselves and to desire
> to educate their children.[18]

Place was anxious to distance himself from the lunatic fringe of the society and the mob, but he seems to have missed the point. A *thinking* working class that had respect for its own ideas was the last thing that Pitt's Establishment wanted. And their numbers were growing. Norwich, a town made rich by the worsted woollen trade, was one centre of Jacobinism. Sheffield, with its cutlery and plate, was another. Spitalfields, long the weaving heart of London, was a third. Jacobinism was not yet to be found in the satanic mills; nor had it focused on Manchester and Birmingham. But there was a hint of revolution in the wind.

At the end of December 1796, international politics appeared to come to the aid of those determined to see reform. Capitalizing on the centuries-old hatred of England by the Irish, a half-baked alliance was concluded between the United Irishmen of Theobald Wolfe Tone and the French government of Paul Barras. Plans for invasion had existed since at least 1789 (*before* the Revolution), but Ireland would have provided an excellent springboard for invasion from the west and would effectively create a war on two fronts for Pitt. But the French navy had mistimed things and General Hoche's 14,000 strong army did not leave Brest until 15 December, by which time storms scattered the 43 ships and not one could land at Bantry Bay. One vessel, limping back home, landed by mistake in Fishguard in Pembrokeshire and its crew were 'routed' by the arrival of a handful of shrieking fishwives and a troop of the Pembrokeshire Yeomanry. In that same month, Horatio Nelson won a spectacular victory over a Spanish convoy off Cape St Vincent, but elsewhere the news was not so good.

While virtual civil war was breaking out in Ireland with a Catholic population bitterly hostile to its puppet Protestant parliament, an alien church and serious economic problems, the cost of four years of war was laid bare. The country had run up a staggering £19 million of debt. The cartoonist Gilray showed Pitt desperately wooing the Old Lady of Threadneedle Street (the Bank of England) in an attempt to squeeze yet more money out of her. In the Commons Henry Addington, the future Lord Sidmouth, suggested voluntary contributions and pledged £2,000 from his own pocket. While the banks wobbled and crashed and Pitt began to formulate his income tax, at Spithead near Portsmouth, the navy mutinied, to be followed by a similar act of defiance at the Nore, in the Thames estuary in May.

Conditions on board warships were appalling. Captain Thomas Hardy's[19] *Victory* for example, which became the most famous of the first-rater ships of the line, had a crew (including marines) of nearly 800, all of them crammed into five decks with very little space. Wages had not risen for a century and the semi-legal use of the press gangs to find likely lads in the ports' taverns had created a class of literate, educated sailors who were prepared to make a stand. What is difficult to say is how important John Binns's meetings were in Portsmouth in this context. Did he rouse the jolly tars of Old England to query something they had accepted meekly for 200 years?

The ending of the naval mutinies speaks volumes for the Establishment and how it dealt with rebellion. Nominally, the fleet's behaviour was treason – refusal to fight in time of war. At Spithead, the delegates from the mutinous ships met around a table with kindly old Admiral Howe, drank large quantities of rum and were promised better pay and conditions. At the Nore, delegates were hanged, perhaps because here violence had been offered to ships' officers. In both cases, the fleets sailed and the country could breathe a sigh of relief.

No sooner was the naval crisis averted however than trouble broke out in Scotland. The Militia Act, by which Pitt hoped to create a serious home defence force, was deeply unpopular, especially in the Celtic fringe. What it meant was that all able-bodied men between 18 and 23 were to be conscripted by ballot. These men could also be raised in the colonies, which led to racial issues and a rather irrational fear of outbreaks of yellow fever and other West Indian diseases. Teachers, whose unenviable job it was to compile ballot lists, had their houses burnt. Tranent in Lothian became the focal point for this unrest, where magistrates looked very closely at the colliers and weavers in the town. Rioting and looting in August was met by the yeomanry cavalry who charged the crowd, killing a 13-year-old boy in the process and leaving the dead in the cornfields 'like partridges'.

The naval mutinies, ominous rumblings in Scotland and the rebellion of Wolfe Tone's United Irishmen the following year – 'they're hanging men and women there for wearing o' the green'[20] – show how precarious was the hold of authority on a country struggling under the double burden of uncontrolled industrialization and war. Secret societies – possibly the United Englishmen, itself a spinoff of Wolfe Tone's group – met after dark in places like Furnival's Inn in Holborn and Richard Fuller was sentenced to death for making inflammatory speeches to soldiers of the Coldstream Guards.

And Richard Parker, the Nore mutiny leader facing the rope, wrote: 'Remember, never to make yourself the busy body of the lower classes, for they are cowardly, selfish and ungrateful'.[21] Parker was talking about the essential divide which existed among the Jacobins. At the heart of their movement, especially as the French Revolution itself led to disappointment and betrayal and the new France of Napoleon Bonaparte looked suspiciously like the old,[22] was the need to keep their children fed. Increasingly, men turned to trade unions and friendly societies, advocating change by peaceful means, brought about by the extension of the vote.

Only a few held out for violence – 'One saying Liberty, the other saying Death'.

Chapter 4

Desperate Men and Desperate Measures

The mood of the nation was ugly as the century turned. The Dissenting millennialists, who had expected some great sign from God, were to be disappointed. The popular general predicted by Robespierre shortly before his execution was Napoleon Bonaparte and he had indeed brought the Revolution to an end, as Robespierre had prophesied, but he had done it with bayonets at his back and few people were in doubt that the Consulate was no more than a trio of military dictators who eventually became one. The unstoppable Corsican was winning battle after battle, smashing yet another alliance against him at Marengo in 1800.

The Act of Union with Ireland was designed by Pitt's government to pacify the provinces, but it failed and determined Irishmen spent the next century trying to repeal it. The Dublin parliament ceased to exist and Ireland became liable for its share of the national debt, cripplingly high as it was of course by now. No Irishman had forgotten the vicious putting down of Wolfe Tone's rising of 1798 and the ex-pats who drifted to London and other cities in search of work brought their sense of grievance with them. At home, famine claimed their families and friends. All over the country there were protests against the malt tax and the window tax. Men denied the right to form trade unions by the Anti-Combinations Acts of 1799 and 1800 met after dark behind closed doors. They were probably still discussing hours, working conditions and wages, but since they were secret, Pitt's government now had no accurate idea what they were talking about. By driving these groups underground, the Establishment had created a potential monster it would be difficult to control.

And there was always an uneasy tension, a sense that some bizarre, brutal act was about to happen. It did, on the night of 15 May 1800, when the king was attending a performance of *The Marriage of Figaro* at Drury Lane Theatre. James Hadfield stepped out to the orchestra pit and fired a pistol at

George, the ball crunching into a pillar to one side of the royal box. Perhaps gambling on the fact that the assassin did not have a second gun and would be grabbed before he could reload, George calmly stood up and inspected the bullet hole. The show's star, Michael Kelly, was impressed – 'Never shall I forget his majesty's coolness' – while the rest of the audience was, of course, hysterical.

Ever one to capitalize on a situation, the poet, playwright and Whig MP Richard Sheridan, who happened to be in that audience, rattled off a new verse of 'God Save the King' –

> From every latent foe,
> From the assassin's blow
> God save the king!
> O'er him thine arm extend,
> For Britain's sake defend,
> Our father, prince and friend,
> God save the king!

Kelly ended the evening with a rousing version of this which brought the house down.

Hadfield's behaviour was decidedly odd. Having missed with his pistol, he said to the king, 'God bless your royal highness; I like you very well. You are a good fellow.' He stood trial on the inevitable charge of high treason and was defended by the brilliant lawyer Thomas Erskine, himself a supporter of the French Revolution and a member of the Friends of the People, set up in 1792. Erskine's acceptance of a retainer from Tom Paine cost him the friendship of the Prince of Wales and a possible appointment as Attorney-General. As MP for Portsmouth, he made speeches on behalf of both Thomas Hardy and Horne Tooke and was a natural to defend Hadfield.

It was clear from Hadfield's demeanour – and indeed, appearance – that Erskine's best bet would be to plead insanity. Hadfield had been a serving soldier until the battle of Tourcoing in 1794, when he took eight sabre cuts to the head. Although nothing is known of his early life, this battle was fought between Austria and France, so presumably he was serving as a mercenary with the Austrians. Released after capture by the French, he came home and joined a millennialist movement in London. He told Erskine that he believed he (Hadfield) would be instrumental in the second coming of Christ by being executed by the government. Conspiring with fellow millennialist Bannister Truelock, Hadfield hit upon the one crime for which he was *certain* to be executed – the killing of the king.

Unfortunately for Hadfield, Erskine had other ideas. It would not be until the 1840s that the British judicial system came to a consensus on how to handle criminal insanity.[1] The standard definition at the time was that a defendant 'must be lost to all sense . . . incapable of forming a judgement upon the consequences of the act which he is about to do'. Going head to head with the judge, Lord Kenyon, Erskine argued that delusion 'unaccompanied by frenzy or raving madness was the true test of insanity' and produced three doctors to prove that Hadfield's mania was caused by his head injuries. Kenyon was convinced before the jury had a chance to deliberate and ended the trial with Hadfield acquitted.

There was an immediate outcry as a would-be king-killer walked free and parliament rushed through the Criminal Lunatics Act, which enabled Hadfield to be detained indefinitely because he was regarded as a danger to himself and society at large. He was sent to Bedlam – the Royal Bethlehem Hospital – where he died from gaol fever, probably tuberculosis.

Altogether more dangerous than the clearly deranged James Hadfield was Edward Marcus Despard, an Irish adventurer with a chip on his shoulder. In many ways, Despard's attempted coup of 1802 was a blueprint for Cato Street. Indeed during the trials of the 1820 conspirators, the name Despard was used disparagingly, as how *not* to carry out an assassination and revolution.

Despard was born in Queen's County, Ireland, in 1751. He entered the navy as a midshipman at the age of 15 and was promoted lieutenant in 1772. For the next eighteen years he served in the West Indies, making a name for himself as an administrator with considerable engineering ability. He was stationed in Jamaica at the same time that the father of the future Cato Street conspirator William Davidson was Attorney-General there. He was promoted captain after the San Juan expedition of 1780 and led a successful attack on Spanish-held territory on the Black River two years later. By 1786, Despard was Superintendent of the Crown Colony of Honduras (today's Belize) on the Mosquito Coast south of Yucatan.

The West Indies were notoriously difficult to police. They had a long history of piracy and running battles between settlers from just about every European state were commonplace. The elder Pitt, adopting a 'blue-water policy' in the Seven Years' War had mounted several campaigns against the French and on the outbreak of the Revolutionary War, his son tried the same thing. By that time, however, Despard had been recalled to London to answer charges of incompetence.

As Superintendent, Despard's brief was to settle the new territory, which he did without considering race and background. So alongside the exclusively British plantation owners were ex-slaves, smugglers, military volunteers and labourers, *anyone* in effect who agreed to purchase land and farm it. He did this, he said, because according to English law, there was no distinction in land tenure. A free man with enough money had no bar to ownership of property at home, but the Baymen did not see it that way and petitioned the Home Secretary, Lord Grenville, for redress. Cleverly, Despard stood for election as a magistrate and won a landslide victory. The racist Baymen would have none of it, complaining that the Superintendent had only won because he had the backing of 'ignorant turtlers and people of colour'.

The people of colour arrived with Despard in London on his return in 1790. One was his wife, Catherine; the other his son, James. A great deal of research has been carried out in recent years on the black history of Britain and Catherine Despard deserves her place in it. Unlike the wives of the Cato Street conspirators, when her husband was accused of high treason, Catherine fought on his behalf. It is highly likely that the Despards were a unique example of a mixed marriage in England at that time. The slave trade would not be abolished for another seventeen years; the ownership of slaves not for another twenty after that. Relatively speaking there was a large number of blacks in the country, especially in London and Bristol, but they were not free (unless they had been enfranchised by liberal owners) and usually appeared in the roles of servants, boxers, prostitutes and menials.

The arrival of the Despards probably filled most whites with horror. It was one thing for British soldiers and administrators of empire to take black mistresses in the colonies and even produce mulatto or half-breed children (William Davidson belongs to this category) but actual marriage was something else. The extraordinary ex-slave Olaudah Equiano had already produced the first edition of his autobiographical *The Interesting Narrative* the previous year and in it he wrote:

> Why not establish intermarriage at home and in our colonies? And
> encourage open, free and generous love, upon Nature's own wide and
> extensive plan, subservient only to moral rectitude, without
> distinction of the colour of a skin?

Two years later, Equiano himself married a white girl from Cambridgeshire.

Race did indeed lie at the heart of Despard's problems. The government
refused to back him, anxious to keep the plantation owners sweet in any
colonial sphere and he found himself dragged through any number of claims
courts by the Baymen who wanted recompense for what they imagined was
criminal mishandling of their affairs. The colonel found himself in the
King's Bench prison for debt in 1792.

The prison itself was new, the old one having been burnt by the mob in
the anti-Catholic Gordon Riots twelve years earlier. Long before the attack
on the Bastille, the English had a reputation for gaol-wrecking. The King's
Bench had been destroyed three times by the time Despard found himself
there. Like most London prisons, it was all things to all men. It had its own
'Rules' by which better off prisoners (who would have included Despard)
lived relatively comfortably, whereas the poor wallowed in the filth they had
known on the outside in the reeking rookeries of St Giles, Wapping and St
James. It was here that the disgruntled colonel read the new book by Tom
Paine . . .

On his release two years later, Despard joined the London
Corresponding Society and shortly after that the United Englishmen, the
offshoot of Wolfe Tone's 'terrorist' organization over the Irish Sea. The
most common meeting houses for this group were either Furnival's Inn in
Holborn (much was to be made of this place in the Cato Street trials) or
Soho Square. Large numbers of Irishmen, like those who lived in Gee's
Court off Oxford Street, met there, as did a hard core of disgruntled
soldiers.

What we have here is the lunatic fringe of the Jacobin movement. We
have no idea of their numbers but Despard, like the men of Cato Street,
seems to have genuinely believed that there was an army of the dispossessed
out there, in London, Sheffield, Leeds and elsewhere, ready to rise at the
drop of a cap of liberty. By 1801, the mutinous rumblings had formulated
into a plan which has some of the elements of urban guerrilla warfare and a

Utopian vision of a rosy future.

Despard's links with the Irish underground are shadowy. He almost certainly met Wolfe Tone in the mid-1790s and probably Robert Emmett, the son of the viceroy's doctor who had joined Tone's United Irishmen in 1789. There is no real evidence in Despard's case that his plan to seize power in London was linked either to a French invasion or Emmett's scheme to capture Dublin castle and imprison the viceroy. In fact between 1797 and 1803, the Franco-Irish plans seem to have been totally disjointed, with timings going wrong and Emmett, in 1803, forced to go it alone, with, for him, fatal consequences.

By the year of Wolfe Tone's rebellion, Catherine Despard was increasingly worried about her husband's political machinations and he took to using a 'safe house' rather than talk sedition with fellow conspirators at their home. Both the LCS and the United Englishmen/Irishmen were hit by the authorities in that year after a traitor was discovered at Margate with plans for an Irish rising he was taking across the Channel to France. Among thirty Jacobins, Despard was arrested and held in Coldbath Fields gaol in Clerkenwell. There was a deep irony here because this prison was known as The Steel (i.e. Bastille) because of its associations with the notorious Parisian gaol. The Jacobin poets Southey and Coleridge wrote of it:

> As he went through Coldbath Fields he saw
> A solitary cell:
> And the Devil was pleased, for it gave him a hint
> For improving his prisons in Hell.[2]

In fact, when Despard was there, the place was only four years old. It had 232 cells and cost a staggering £65,000 to build.

Tone's rebellion broke out while Despard was still inside and, since habeas corpus was now suspended, the colonel could, in theory, be held indefinitely.

Enter the feisty Catherine Despard. She contacted the radical MP Sir Francis Burdett who raised the issue of the Coldbath inmates in the Commons. Burdett was a brilliant choice, the respectable face of English Jacobinism, a rebel by temperament who was the darling of the mob. He read out Catherine's letter to an unruly House, equally divided over their attitudes towards habeas corpus. Colonel Despard, he told them, was being held 'without either fire or candle, table, knife, fork, a glazed window or even a book to read'. He also read out a second letter, an appeal from a Coldbath prisoner written with a splinter of wood dipped in blood. There were cries of 'Burdett and no Bastille' on the one hand, but on the other, the Attorney-General Sir John Scott expressed himself surprised that Catherine Despard wasn't in prison along with her husband.

Once released, Despard returned to his old haunts and his plans were reformulated. In six articles presented to the United Englishmen's Committee, the first attack should be on the Tower. Not only was the place a prison along Bastille lines (several of the Cato Street conspirators would be sent there in 1820) but it contained the Royal Mint, a barracks and a sizeable arsenal of guns and powder. In theory, the massive 80 foot thick walls of the White Tower could withstand the shot and shell of any government-ordered artillery attack. Beyond the outer wall was the hell-hole of Tower Hill, a rookery where would-be insurgents could easily be found to join the rising.

The second article referred to the seizure of the Bank of England in Threadneedle Street. It contained gold bullion as well as Pitt's hated paper money and would provide funds for the revolution. Woolwich was the next target. It was nine miles from London Bridge but the Royal Arsenal there, founded in the seventeenth century, was three and a half miles long and one mile wide. If the rebels could take that, there was nothing that could stand against them. The fourth article, which was rejected, was that parliament should be seized while both houses were sitting. Although attendance was not usually compulsory, at a stroke the political leadership of the country would be in Jacobin hands. The fifth article talked of the pay back for the soldiers who had mounted this revolution. Each man would receive one guinea (£1 1s) per week and to be allowed to retire from the army with 10 acres of land and cash to cultivate it. The final article discussed the idea of winning the many over to the cause. Over London and any other towns that carried out their own coups, flags of liberty were to be flown. 'Conductors' (agitators) were to organize such campaigns in the outlying areas, drill 'soldiers' and obtain weapons for the purpose.

This was a military plan, broadly accepted or perhaps even proposed by Despard. And in essence it was the right thing to do. Had the army and navy gone over to the revolutionaries, there was every chance of success. This had already been proved by the French experience and would be again in Russia in 1917. Where Despard's followers seriously miscalculated was the actual mood of the people of 1802. The Tower garrison would not crack and run up a white flag as de Launay's Bastille men had done. The down-and-outs of Tower Hill could not be relied upon to join the movement and how much use would underfed civilians be against an efficient, well-equipped army?

None of this, of course, was ever put to the test. On 16 November 1802, a large body of Runners from Bow Street descended on the Oakley Arms in Lambeth and arrested nearly forty men, most of them Irish, after a tip-off. The next day they all appeared before a magistrate. Despard, who refused to say a word, was sent to Newgate. This grimmest of London gaols had been totally destroyed by the mob in the Gordon Riots and rebuilt. Only twenty years old when Despard arrived, it was already a slum, with gaol fever claiming large numbers of its shackled inhabitants. Twelve of his followers, six of them soldiers, were sent to the Bridewell at Tothill Fields. Unlike Newgate, this place was well managed by its governor, George Smith, even though it was forced to accommodate extra prisoners after the closure of the Gatehouse Gaol in Westminster in 1777. Twenty others were sent to the New Prison in Clerkenwell, one of the smallest in London after its rebuilding following the Gordon Riots. It was a house of detention with separate male and female wards and specialized in holding people awaiting trial. The remaining ten who had been bundled up in the police raid were found in an adjoining room, had no links with Despard and were released.

The trial opened on Monday 7 February and the Attorney-General went through the motions of his case. In the dock were Edward Marcus Despard, 'a colonel in the army' aged 56; John Francis, a soldier, aged 23; John Wood, another soldier, aged 36; Thomas Broughton, a carpenter, aged 26; James Sedgwick Wratton, a shoemaker, aged 35; John McNamara, another carpenter, aged 50; and Arthur Graham, a slater, aged 53. All of them were married men, many with children. In the course of the trial, other members of the gang were acquitted or pardoned, but these seven were held to be at the heart of the conspiracy.

The problem for any group of men bent on such a desperate enterprise was winning other men to their cause. Revolution could only succeed if sufficient numbers took part, but the more in the know, the greater the chance of someone talking, either maliciously to obtain a reward or carelessly in their cups. In an attempt to gauge the trustworthiness of men, John

Francis had insisted on 'administering unlawful oaths'. Such oaths had only been illegal for five years and the relevant law had been rushed through at the time of the naval mutinies. One of the men approached was Thomas Windsor, who, according to the *Newgate Calendar* which reported the trial, 'soon became dissatisfied' and reported what he knew to a Mr Bonus. It is not clear who this man was, but he was certainly Establishment and shrewd enough to suggest to Windsor that he continued in Despard's company and learn all he could. It was his tip-off that led to the rebels' arrest.

Windsor's evidence was that an integral part of the plan was the assassination of the king on his way to the opening of parliament, which was, of course, an exact action replay of the Gunpowder Plot of 1605, in which James I would have been eviscerated in the parliament house along with his entire government. 'I have weighed the matter well,' Despard had told Windsor, 'and my heart is callous.'

Windsor had several meetings with Despard and the others, first meeting the 'nice man' as Despard was referred to at the Flying Horse in Newington. He also met him at the Tiger on Tower Hill and was supposed to bring four or five intelligent men (he settled for three soldiers) to discuss the best way to take the Tower. It was at this meeting that John Wood hit upon the idea of grabbing 'the great gun in the Park' (St James's) and blasting the king's carriage as it passed by. The prosecution trotted out a number of other witnesses – William Campbell, Charles Reed, Joseph Walker and Thomas Blades among them – who testified to other planning meetings that had been held.

Mr Gurney, who would feature in the Cato Street trials eighteen years later, seconded for the defence under Mr Best. The evidence against Despard was overwhelming; in the twelve years since he had returned from Honduras, he had become a marked man, a known opponent of the government and had been in gaol twice, once as a suspected Jacobin. His habit of walking round London with an umbrella and a black wife merely served to draw yet more attention to himself. So Gurney went for the younger Despard, the virtuous, hard-working officer of his early years. Evan Nepean and Alured Clarke from the Admiralty testified to his zeal. But the star witness was undoubtedly Horatio Nelson, the diminutive Vice Admiral who was by now the nation's hero, with the victories of Cape St Vincent, Aboukir Bay and Copenhagen to his credit.

Nelson testified that he had known Despard well, having met him in Jamaica in 1779. 'He was, at that time, a lieutenant in what were called the Liverpool Blues.' The judge, Lord Ellenborough, was a staunch believer in the Bloody Code and interrupted Nelson to remind him that what was needed was a character reference, not a military CV. He did it politely – after all, Nelson was a lord too and a national treasure Ellenborough was not about to offend. The flat trial transcript gives no hint of the scorn with which the Admiral turned his good eye on the judge:

> We [Despard and Nelson] were on the Spanish Main together. We slept many nights together in our clothes upon the same ground . . . In all that time, no man could have shown more zealous attachment to his sovereign and his country than Colonel Despard did. I formed the highest opinion of him as a man and an officer.[3]

In cross-examination, the Attorney-General got Nelson to admit that it was nearly twenty years since he had seen Despard last. That was before the Irishman had become embittered over the Honduras fiasco and before he had read Tom Paine. It came as a surprise to no one when the jury found Despard guilty, but in view of the man's previous good conduct, recommended mercy. The other conspirators were tried together on Wednesday 9 February where (with the obvious exception of the naval men) the same witnesses gave the same evidence. Nine of the twelve were found guilty, with three more recommendations to mercy.

Ellenborough summed up:

> You have been separately indicted for conspiracy against his majesty's person, his crown and government, for the purposes of subverting the same and changing the government of this realm.

In full flow the judge made sweeping statements which the guilty men, especially Despard, could never have accepted. The constitution, said Ellenborough, had 'established freedoms' and 'just and rational equality of rights' (neither of which was true for the working class). Despard and his traitors offered instead anarchy and bloodshed, 'the subversion of all property and the massacre of its proprietors, the annihilation of all legitimate authority and established order'.

He then passed sentence:

Each of you [shall] be taken from the place whence you came and thence you are to be drawn on hurdles to the place of execution, where you are to be hanged by the neck, but not until you are dead; for while you are still living your bodies are to be taken down, your bowels torn out and burned before your faces, your heads cut off and your bodies divided into four quarters and your heads and quarters to be then at the king's disposal and may Almighty God have mercy on your souls.[4]

Three of the prisoners – Newman, Tyndall and Lander – were respited (held in prison 'until his Majesty's pleasure be known'). The condemned seven were sent to the New Gaol in the Borough at 6 o'clock on Saturday evening and the keeper, Mr Ives, had the unenviable task of serving the execution warrant. Catherine Despard, who had already fought tooth and nail for her husband in 1798, launched herself again. She petitioned Nelson and this and other appeals led to the remission of part of the sentence. Hanged and beheaded the Jacobins would be, but the disembowelling (drawing) and quartering were dropped. It is just as likely that Henry Addington, the Prime Minister now that Pitt had resigned over the issue of Catholic emancipation,[5] was concerned about the crowd's behaviour. When Robert Catesby and his fellow Gunpowder Plotters were executed in this way in January 1606, the mob was hardened to it. Torture was legal in England at the time and the horror of a gunpowder attack on the Lord's anointed made *any* punishment acceptable. Despard's men, like Catesby's, would die publicly in front of a vast crowd. Who knew how many of them might turn on the authorities if the execution were too gruesome?

Despard also wrote to Nelson, to ask him to forward a petition to Addington. The Admiral did, without comment, and uncharacteristically Addington had been deeply affected by it, sitting up with his family after supper, weeping over it. Nelson did intercede however, on the part of Catherine Despard, urging that she be given a pension as a result of her husband's former good service. The *Observer* reported that Catherine

had almost sunk under the anticipated horror of his fate; her feelings, when the dreadful order [for execution] came, can scarcely be conceived – we cannot pretend to describe them.[6]

By the time of their last meeting, however, she was composed and waved her handkerchief out of the window as her carriage rattled away.

Daybreak, Sunday 21 February, seventeen years almost to the day before Arthur Thistlewood's conspirators were arrested in the hay-loft at Cato Street. The entire Bow Street patrol and other constables of the watch had been up all night to guard against any spontaneous and sympathetic uprising. The army ringed London, ready to strike at a moment's notice. The place of execution was the roof of the Surrey County Gaol, commonly called Horsemonger Lane. The prison was really intended for petty criminals and debtors, but the new gatehouse was low and solid enough to provide an excellent platform for the execution,[7] 'drop, scaffold and gallows'.

It was still dark when the drum sounded at the Horse Guards along Whitehall and a squadron of the Life Guards, in black cocked hats and scarlet coatees, moved off at a jingling walk to take up position at the Obelisk in St George's Fields. In twos, the troopers peeled off and patrolled the roads that led to Horsemonger Lane.[8] In the mean time police officers from stations at Queen Square, Marlborough Street, Hatton Garden, Worship Street, Whitechapel and Shadwell formed cordons around the prison itself.

At half past six, still dark at that time of year, the bell was tolled at Horsemonger Lane and the cells were unlocked. The crowd had been gathering for a while, jostling with the law officers and soldiers for a good view. It would be a full two and a half hours before the condemned men stood at the execution site. The solemn bell of St George's church tolled as the County Sheriff, an Anglican vicar and a Catholic priest took their places at the head of the sorry little column.

First was the thick-set Irishman John McNamara, who looked at the sea of faces below him and said loudly, 'Lord Jesus, have mercy on me.' Arthur Graham came next, the oldest of them, looking 'pale and ghastly'. The shoemaker James Wratton climbed the gallows steps 'with much firmness'. Thomas Broughton was next, then the soldiers Wood and Francis. Last came Despard, the man the crowd had really come to see. 'His countenance underwent not the slightest change' as they placed the noose around his neck and the cap (actually a hood) on the top of his head. He helped the executioner fix the rope so that the knot was under his left ear to make the job clean. Despard may or may not have known that the hangman was William Brunskill, notoriously inept at what was still an inexact science. Six years earlier, while he was hanging two murderers outside Newgate, the entire scaffold had collapsed and the men died by accident. Two priests who dropped with them were badly hurt.

John McNamara muttered to Despard, 'I am afraid, Colonel, we have got ourselves into a bad situation.' Despard replied, 'There are many better and some worse', with his usual sangfroid. While Father Griffiths gave McNamara the last rites and five others were similarly interceded for by the prison chaplain, William Winkworth, Despard declined. This atheism appalled Nelson when he read of it, but Despard believed the opinions of Dissenters, Quakers, Methodists, Catholics, savages or even atheists to be equally irrelevant when a man was facing death.

Traditionally men on the scaffold were allowed a last word to the crowd. Indeed, the crowd expected it – it was all part of the Roman holiday of a public execution and Despard was granted permission by the sheriff of Southwark as long as he said nothing 'inflammatory or improper', otherwise Brunskill would operate the drop immediately. The colonel's loud and clear 'Fellow citizens' could have been regarded as inflammatory in itself, but the sheriff let it go. Some stood in stunned silence while Despard spoke, others cheered as he said his goodbyes. The poet Robert Southey, himself a Jacobin who had attempted to set up a pseudo-socialistic society or pantisocracy with fellow poet Samuel Coleridge, was in that crowd and it seemed to him that the rowdy element near the front were not Despard sympathizers but *agents provocateurs* placed there by the authorities to whip the crowd into a frenzy and carry out several arrests. When Despard protested his innocence – 'I am no more guilty of it than any of you . . .' – he may have been referring to the now vanished army of English *sans-culottes* he once hoped would have backed him. He railed against the king's ministers who had

> availed themselves of a legal pretext to destroy a man, because he has
> been a friend to the truth, to liberty and to justice, because he has been
> a friend to the poor and the oppressed.

The sheriff moved in to signal that that was enough and Despard wished the mob 'health, happiness and freedom'. It would be over a century before any of them really had that.

'What an amazing crowd,' John Francis said to Despard when he had finished. ''Tis very cold; I think we shall have some rain.'

At seven minutes to nine, the sheriff gave the signal and Brunskill went to work, beginning with Despard, 'and they were all launched into eternity'.

The colonel made no sound as he fell, his fists clenching twice before he hung, a dead weight at the end of the creaking rope. The crowd was silent now, the men with their hats off, some unable at the last moment to watch.

Brunskill let them all hang for half an hour to make sure that life was extinct, then he and his assistants handed Despard down, stripped off his dark blue coat and cream, gold-laced waistcoat (traditionally a hanged man's clothes became the property of his executioners) and the body was placed on the waiting block, amongst the sawdust strewn there to catch the blood and the head was hacked off 'by persons engaged on purpose to perform that ceremony'. Then, Brunskill lifted the dripping head skyward by the hair. 'This is the head of the traitor, Edward Marcus Despard.' One by one the others followed suit, and the bodies were placed in their shells or coffins and the sawdust swept away.

The police and the cavalry had not been needed. If Despard hoped for a last-minute rising of the people, it did not happen.

Again, the redoubtable Catherine came to the fore. Despard, she claimed, had a right, as an honourable man and one of a family of long-serving soldiers, to burial in St Paul's cathedral. The Lord Mayor of London, responsible after all for the safety of his city, opposed her, but she had her way.

Three black-draped coaches followed the hearse on 1 March as Colonel Despard's body was taken to the cathedral and buried near the north door.[9] Again there was a police and army presence, just in case the mob rallied to their martyr. Again, there was no need.

At some point between the execution and the interment in St Paul's, Madame Tussaud's services were sought. Marie Tussaud, née Grosholtz, was a brilliant artist who had recently arrived in London. Under the auspices of Dr Phillipe Curtius, she had been modelling wax likenesses of famous – and infamous – Frenchmen since before the Revolution. The fall of the Bastille and the Terror that followed gave her a whole range of grisly experiences as scores of severed heads came her way for modelling purposes. Such was the cult of the guillotine that Parisians mobbed Curtius's premises to see the head of their hero Marat, murdered in his bath by ex-mistress Charlotte Corday, the heads of Louis XVI and Marie Antoinette and ultimately that of Maximilien Robespierre, with its shattered jaw.[10]

Taking advantage of the Peace of Amiens which temporarily halted the war against Napoleon, Marie Tussaud (she had married an engineer eight years her junior by this time) arrived in London with her 4-year-old son. She set up a permanent exhibition at the Lyceum Theatre and quickly saw off any opposition, such as Mrs Salmon's waxworks in Fleet Street and Mrs Bullock's 'Beautiful Cabinet of Wax Figures'. Her success was due to the *Caverne des Grands Voleurs* (Cave of the Great Thieves), the Separate Room, to which Edward Despard would now be added. In the years ahead, of course, it became the Chamber of Horrors.

Marie Tussaud took the likeness at the undertaker's premises in Mount Street, Lambeth, working quickly and unobtrusively. Despard was the last celebrity to be modelled by Madame Tussaud herself. The hanged traitor's likeness travelled as a star exhibit to Edinburgh. Wisely, however, when she toured in Ireland in 1804, Despard's head remained in storage. Eight men had been hanged for treason in Dublin the previous September and British troops patrolled the uneasy provinces in the aftermath of the Act of Union. Not until she returned to Scotland in the summer of 1808 did Despard appear again. His name remained in the catalogue until 1818, by which time interest was probably waning.[11] The head is believed to have been burnt, ironically, during an exhibition in Bristol when the city was partially destroyed by rioters over the Reform Bill agitation of 1831–2.

What are we to make of Despard's desperate enterprise? In his sentencing, Lord Ellenborough said

> the objects of your atrocious, abominable and traitorous conspiracy were to overthrow the government and to seize upon and destroy the sacred person of our august and revered Sovereign.

There was little doubt of that. The *Newgate Calendar* concluded:

> it was certainly the most vain [futile] and impotent attempt ever engendered in the distracted brain of an enthusiast [fanatic]. Without arms or any probable means, a few dozen men, the very dregs of society, led on by a disappointed and disaffected chief, were to overturn a mighty empire; nor does it appear that any man of their insignificant band of conspirators – Colonel Despard alone excepted – was above the level of the plebeian race. Yet a small party of this description . . . brooding over their vain attempts at a mean public house in St George's Fields, alarmed the nation.[12]

So futile did the whole business seem that many men at the time and several historians since have concluded that Despard was mad. This is patently not true. As we have seen, seducing the London-based garrisons (Wood and Francis were privates in the Grenadier Guards) was the right way to go, especially as these regiments were closest to the king, both physically and in terms of their historical relationship.[13] Seizing the Bank of England also made sense. It was after that that the plan fell apart. Many historians have overlooked the importance of the Gordon Riots of 1780 when a charismatic leader, like Despard, had not only incited murder and mayhem but got away with it.

Incensed at the Catholic Relief Act of 1778, which was actually the government's cynical attempt to raise Catholic troops for the armed forces in the teeth of the American crisis, George Gordon was accompanied by a mob of several thousand to the Commons on 2 June 1780 to demand the Act's repeal. He broke off from his speech to the House to harangue the crowd from an upstairs balcony and an estimated 60,000 of them went on the rampage, burning down the houses of judges like Lord Mansfield and magistrates like Sir John Fielding before attacking the Bank of England and destroying as many prisons as they could. The gin distilleries in Holborn were blown up and large parts of the city reduced to rubble. As the dust settled, there were 235 dead, 173 wounded and 139 arrested.

Gordon's trial was a farce. The authorities deemed, inexplicably, that there was no direct evidence against him as having caused the violence and he was acquitted. Twenty-five others in the dock were found guilty of high treason and executed.

The key to the whole thing was the 'dregs of society', the 'plebeian race' who provide the cannon-fodder in any revolution. Today, we tend to dismiss this rank and file as unimportant. We look to the leader of revolt, from Spartacus to Castro, and measure their worth against some rational yardstick that we have invented. But there is little rational about revolution. It plays to the deepest emotions in man. If a mob could terrorize the largest city in the world for six days; if a mob could topple the ancien regime – then anything was possible.

Where Despard got it wrong was in not gauging the mood of the people properly. George Gordon was a blue-blooded aristocrat, a member of the House of Lords. Edward Despard was merely an ex-officer and an Irishman to boot, made bitter and resentful by the treatment he had received from authority. And he intended to kill a king, never on Gordon's agenda. In the end, the 'dregs' did not rise in his support and he paid the price.

Chapter 5

'A Plot, a Plot! How they Sigh for a Plot!'

In the year of Despard's planned insurrection, the first edition appeared of William Cobbett's *Weekly Political Register*. Knowledge was power and one prerequisite of knowledge was literacy. Without an ability to read, a man could not understand the arguments for which he faced the barricades. Without the ability to write he could not put his name to a petition demanding reform. The government knew this perfectly well and was in no hurry to educate the masses. Education was not only expensive, it was dangerous.

We know that all the men who faced trial over the Cato Street conspiracy were literate, at least up to a point. Richard Tidd's letter – 'Sir I Ham a very Bad Hand at Righting' – sounds like a Dickensian character's efforts, but it makes sense and no doubt proved the government's point; Tidd had murderous designs in his heart but how much of that was fostered by the incitements of the radical press? It is likely that the majority of men among the working class had basic literacy skills (this was far less true of women) because of the increasing number of schools. Sunday schools (like the one where William Davidson briefly taught) were available from 1780, although they did not take everyone. Their founder, Robert Raikes, insisted for example that all children wore shoes. Dame schools, at a penny a day, offered very basic education, but their numbers were growing. In 1810 and 1812 the National Schools were set up by Andrew Bell (for the Anglicans) and Joseph Lancaster (for the Dissenters). 'Calendar men', 'Number men' and ballad-singers hawked their written wares in working-class areas, including the 'dying speeches'[1] of men like Despard. They sold political tracts too.

The radical press's circulation fluctuated with the country's mood. The years after Despard and before the assassination of Spencer Perceval were relatively quiet. Most eyes were focused on the Channel as Bonaparte prepared the army of Boulogne for an invasion. Nelson effectively destroyed that opportunity at Trafalgar (October 1805) and thereafter, England was safe, at least from invasion. Admiral Earl St Vincent's boast of 1801 – 'I do not say they [the French] cannot come. I only say they cannot come by sea' – was now a proven fact. As the war began in Portugal and dragged on in Spain however and the bite of the Industrial Revolution was felt, the Midlands and the North saw the first outbreaks of Luddism and machine-wrecking. And when the war ended, the radical press had a field day.

Cobbett's *Twopenny Trash* was a clear winner. Between October 1816 and February 1817 it sold up to 60,000 copies a week. London dailies, like *The Times* and the *Observer* sold under 7,000 each. Thomas Wooler's *The Black Dwarf* had reached 12,000 by 1819. Freedom of the press – what could and could not be published – became a big issue. Fox's libel law of 1792 meant that juries had to decide on what was libellous and this often ran counter to advice given them by the Bench. One of the victims was the bookseller William Hone who upset Liverpool's government in 1817 by writing parodies on the Lord's Prayer, thereby neatly offending both church and state:

> Our Lord who art in the Treasury, whatsoever be thy name, thy power be prolongued, thy will be done throughout the Empire . . . Turn us not out of our places; but keep us in the House of Commons, the Land of Pensions and Plenty; and deliver us from the People. Amen[2]

Under Justice Abbott (who would preside over the Cato Street trials) Hone was acquitted. Under Lord Ellenborough (who had tried Despard) it happened again, despite the most appallingly illegal interruptions from the judge and a summing up of disgraceful partiality. This was the last time such a prosecution was brought and it was Ellenborough's last case. Men said he never recovered from being laughed at. There were 115 prosecutions brought in the two years before Cato Street, but after that, things quietened down. The reason is best summed up by the poet John Keats in a letter to his brother in September 1819:

> He [the bookseller and printer Richard Carlile] has been selling devotional pamphlets, republished Tom Paine and many other works held in superstitious horror. After all they [the authorities] are afraid to prosecute. They are afraid of his defence; it would be published in

all the papers all over the empire. They shudder at this. The trials would light a flame they could not extinguish.[3]

Even so, men like Cobbett, Carlile, Hone and the rest did serve time in prison, especially during the suspension of habeas corpus when no such trials took place. Joseph Swann, a Macclesfield hat salesman and newsvendor was gaoled for a total of four years and six months for selling seditious literature in 1819:

> Off with your fetters; spurn the slavish yoke;
> Now, now, or never, can your chain be broke;
> Swift then, rise and give the fatal stroke.[4]

This was inflammatory material and for every man who read it – or had it read to him – and muttered into his cups in a tavern, there were others (few, maybe – but that was the question) who were prepared to take it seriously and do something.

What emerged from the trial of Despard – and would emerge again in the Cato Street affair – was the number of radical centres, almost always public houses, where seditious meetings took place. In London, which would, of course, be the recruiting ground for Cato Street, the Two Bells, the Flying Horse, the Ham and Windmill, the Bleeding Heart, the Coach and Horses, the Brown Bear and the Black Horse were all places where like-minded gentlemen could hire a back or upstairs room for whatever purposes they wished. Few if any questions were asked and such pubs were perfect for the cross-pollination of grievances. Here the disaffected Irish could nudge elbows with hard-bitten soldiery, out of work canal 'navvies' and anybody else increasingly unhappy with their lot.

The acceptable face of working-class reform meetings were the Hampden Clubs formed in 1812 by the 'good, grey Major', John Cartwright. The clubs themselves were named after John Hampden, Oliver Cromwell's cousin who had defied the arbitrary government of Charles I by refusing to pay tax called Ship Money in 1637. Cartwright was originally a naval officer with estates in Lincolnshire and his title derived from his post in the county's militia. A sane and sensible critic, he sided morally with the Americans in the War of Independence and wrote the definitive democratic book *Take Your Choice* in the year that Thomas Jefferson produced his Declaration of Independence. It advocated parliamentary reform, universal male suffrage, equal electoral districts, annual parliaments and a secret ballot – almost everything in fact which the Chartist movement (1836–*c*.1850) stated as their aims.

Seen as too much of an extremist, Cartwright failed to get into parliament three times and in 1805 came to London to contact other radicals at both ends of the social spectrum – Francis Burdett, the baronet, and Francis Place, the tailor.

From 1812 much of Cartwright's life was spent travelling, establishing Hampden Clubs in the provinces. His insight into welding middle-class ambition and working-class muscle seriously worried the authorities and he was arrested in Huddersfield in 1813. Three years later, the first club outside London was formed by William Fitton at Royden in Shropshire and in Lancashire the weavers Samuel Bamford and John Knight formed others, as did the semi-literate doctor, Joseph Healey, at Oldham and the brush manufacturer Joseph Johnson in Manchester itself. By the year of Cato Street there were at least twenty-five such clubs across the country, all of them talking various shades of revolution.

The whole question of what happened at Cato Street depends on our definition of three words. Arthur Thistlewood and others at the 1820 trials talked of reformers. The *Shorter Oxford Dictionary* defines 'reform' as 'the removal of faults or errors esp. of a moral, political or social kind'.[5]

The problem was – how was the removal to take place? Much later in the century, the group of intellectual socialists calling themselves Fabians took their name from the Roman General Quintus Fabius Maximus, who avoided pitched battles but wore down his opposition gradually. This group worked slowly and patiently for change, always through legal means, by discussion and reason rather than violence.

Radical is the next word we have to understand. Again, the *Shorter Oxford* says 'Advocating thorough or far-reaching change, representing or supporting an extreme section of a party' – and immediately, we must ask another question – how extreme? The Press in 1811–20 is usually termed radical and some men were imprisoned both for writing and reading it. Tom Paine is usually referred to as a radical, so are William Cobbett, Francis Burdett and Colonel Despard.

At what point, then, does radical slide inexorably into the last of the 'three Rs' – revolutionary? The *Shorter Oxford* is downright disappointing

61

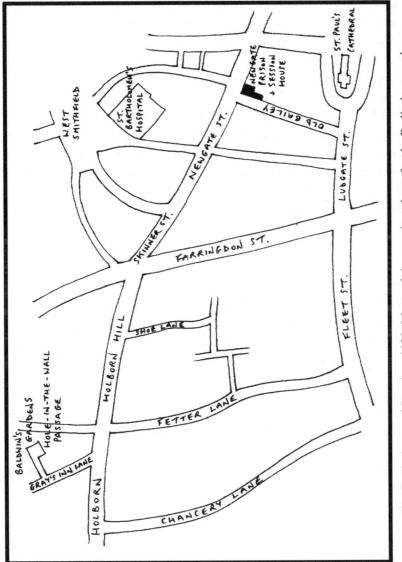

The Radical map of London, 1820. Many of the meeting places for the Radicals were along Holborn and the streets adjoining.

here: 'Pertaining to, characterized by, or of the nature of revolution, involving or constituting radical change.' In other words, we have been thrown back to the earlier word, as if 'radicalism' and 'revolution' are interchangeable. If we look up 'revolution' itself, we get 'alteration, change, mutation'. In terms of history, however, there is little doubt that revolution implies something sudden, swift and violent. Reformers may take years to effect change; radicals want to sweep away existing systems; revolutionaries arm themselves with swords, guns, hand-grenades and are prepared to die in a hay-loft or on the gallows.

What looked like a revolutionary act took place in May 1812. On that day, John Bellingham walked into the lobby of the Houses of Parliament and shot the Prime Minister, Spencer Perceval, dead. Perceval remains the only holder of the office to die in this way, despite the efforts of Thistlewood and the men of Cato Street eight years later. 'If it had not been for that horrid incident,' wrote George Malcolm Thomson, his tongue firmly in his cheek, 'Perceval might be remembered today as the smallest Prime Minister . . . or the prime Minister with the record number of children . . . or the one with the prettiest wife . . .'[6]

Spencer Perceval was a modest man with much to be modest about. In the portrait by G F Joseph, he has large, kind eyes, a receding hairline and a smirk hovering around his thin lips. He looks like a man a bit too eager to please. The offspring of a second marriage, he had to make a living at the Bar and for a while lived with his young wife above a carpet shop in Bedford Row. As time went on, he veered towards politics and obtained minor posts which boosted his income. Astonishingly, he was 'reckoned' by William Pitt, as the man most likely to succeed him and 'most able to cope with Mr Fox'. This is all the more surprising when his maiden speech was little short of a disaster. He became first Solicitor-General, then Attorney-General in Henry Addington's misnamed Ministry of All the Talents before moving on to the Exchequer and by 1809 he was First Lord of the Treasury – Prime Minister.

On paper, Perceval was actually a natural target for revolutionaries. 'An honest little fellow' he may have been, but he was also deeply reactionary, opposed to Catholic emancipation and any kind of reform. He only agreed to serve under Pitt in 1804 as long as the issue of Catholic emancipation was not raised. When the Luddite unrest broke out across the North, Perceval's immediate reaction was to send troops to the trouble spots. Parts of Yorkshire and Lancashire were under martial law by the end of May 1812 with arbitrary arrests, threats and even various forms of torture to find the mysterious – and non-existent – organizer of the machine-wrecking, General Ludd. There were bread riots in Leeds, Sheffield, Barnsley, Carlisle and Bristol.

Sydney Smith summed up the problem admirably – and it applied to all those men who should have been around the table at Lord Harrowby's in February 1820 just as much:

> I say I fear he [Perceval] will pursue a policy destructive to the true interests of this country; and then you tell me he is faithful to Mrs Perceval and kind to the Master Percevals . . . I should prefer that he whipped his boys and saved the country.[7]

On Monday 11 May, a committee of the Commons was in earnest discussion over Orders in Council relating to trade. Napoleon's Continental System was still in place, although Portugal and Russia had both refused to accept his decrees for port closures and continued to trade with Britain. Lord Brougham realized that Perceval was not present and sent a servant to find him. It was on his way across the lobby that the assassin struck. Accounts differ as to exactly where John Bellingham was hiding, but it was either behind a door or a pillar. He stepped out and fired his pistol at point-blank range into Perceval's body. The Prime Minister fell backwards, gasping, 'I am murdered!' as astonished MPs looked on, unable to grasp what had just happened. Bellingham simply stood there, his one shot spent, and waited to be arrested.

'My name is Bellingham,' he said later that day in response to questioning. 'It's a private injury. I know what I have done. It was a denial of justice on the part of the Government.'[8] In claiming he knew what he had done, Bellingham was signing his own death warrant. As we have seen, it would be nearly another half century before a definition of legal insanity was reached and Bellingham took his place in the dock like any other murderer.

When news of Perceval's death reached the provinces, there was general jubilation among the working class. 'A man came running down the street,' said a witness in the Potteries, 'waving his hat round his head and shouting with frantic joy "Perceval is shot, hurrah!"'[9] In Nottingham, there were flags and drums and street parties. In London, immediately after the outrage, a crowd quickly gathered and some of them cheered as Bellingham was led away. Polite society was appalled, ignoring the fact that in Lancaster that same month eight people were sentenced to death for rioting and thirteen transported to Botany Bay. At Chester, fifteen faced the rope and eight were transported. This was the England Spencer Perceval had governed. In the eyes of many people, his death was entirely justified.

'This is but the beginning,' the poet Coleridge heard someone mutter at Bellingham's execution. But in fact, ironically, the Prime Minister's murder had nothing to do with politics at all.

John Bellingham was an unstable businessman whose business took him to Russia. It all went wrong for him and he ended up in a Russian prison. With his money gone, he turned to the British ambassador in St Petersburg who was less than helpful. So too was the Consul-General. On his release, Bellingham came home, rented rooms in rundown New Millman Street and began to bombard the government with letters demanding redress. Since Bellingham had brought his disasters on himself and broken Russian law at a time when it was in the government's interests to keep Russia sweet against the common foe, Napoleon, nothing could be done for him.

At his trial between 13 and 15 May it was decided that Bellingham did indeed know right from wrong and he was sentenced to death. To the government, whatever the specific motivation on Bellingham's part, the plans of Despard, the riots of the starving, the machine-wrecking of the Luddites and the insanity of John Bellingham were all merely the jutting ugly tips of the same terrifying iceberg and the ship of state was on a collision course with it. No one was in the pardoning mood and Brunskill, the executioner, was sent for again.

Outside Newgate with a large crowd jostling and cat-calling it was clear that the condemned man was a hero. 'God Bless you!' they roared and such was the noise it was probably only Brunskill who heard Bellingham's last words: 'I thank God for having enabled me to meet my fate with so much fortitude and resignation.'[10]

At his trial, Edward Despard had referred to the Cabinet of Henry Addington as the 'man eaters'. As is clear from Sydney Smith's comment on Perceval the family man versus Perceval the Prime Minister, each of the Cabinet had his soft, loving side. Collectively, they could be said to be guilty of murder.

Essentially, by 1812, the men who would be the targets of the Cato Street conspirators had metaphorically taken their places around that dining table at Lord Harrowby's. The only conspicuous absentee was Arthur Wellesley, then beginning the second phase of his war in Spain, taking the fortresses of Badajoz and Cuidad Rodrigo. All the others were already there.

Oddly, in the whole of the 430-page account of the Cato Street trial by George Wilkinson, there is scarcely a mention of the Prime Minister, Lord Liverpool, who took over a nation, at once stunned and euphoric, on the death of Perceval. This is hardly surprising. The politician who would be dubbed years later 'the arch-mediocrity' by Benjamin Disraeli hardly emerges as a firebrand. Castlereagh, Sidmouth, Eldon – these were the black, reactionary heart of the Cabinet as far as the men of Cato Street were concerned; Liverpool was almost an irrelevance.

Robert Banks Jenkinson was 50 at the time of Cato Street. The portrait of him by Sir Thomas Lawrence shows a rather bland face with a slight twinkle around the eyes, a large, prominent nose and decidedly thinning hair. He was the son of a Tory country squire and was educated at Charterhouse and Christ Church, Oxford. It was rather unfortunate that he went on the obligatory Grand Tour (to soak up the classical sites and fleshpots of Europe) in 1789 as all Hell broke out in Paris. He personally witnessed the fall of the Bastille and for him more than most, this was a defining experience of terror that never left him.

At 21, the political borough[11] mongers were at work arranging for his seat for the pocket borough of Appleby in Yorkshire. Shy, awkward and rather serious, his maiden speech in the Commons was awful, especially as it was in answer to Samuel Whitbread's attack on Pitt's ministry over naval expenditure. Whitbread was a hugely popular Whig MP, as well as a brewer and promoter of ingenious contraptions; his bright yellow curricle was one of the sights of London. As a pacifist, he objected to anything pro-war. Dubbed 'England's greatest and most useful citizen' by the radical editor of *The Times*, Thomas Barnes, Whitbread was pro-Burdett and parliamentary reform.

Unaccountably, Pitt was impressed with Jenkinson's speech and gave him a junior post on the India Board. He visited French émigrés in Coblenz and became even more convinced that all things reformist were actually revolutionary and therefore dangerous. When Louis XVI was executed, Jenkinson was all for a declaration of war on France.

When war was actually declared, Jenkinson did his patriotic bit and became colonel of the Cinque Ports Fencible Cavalry, one of the many units raised in the 1790s to protect hearths and homes. In reward for loyalty, Jenkinson was made Master of the Mint and his father, also in politics, the Earl of Liverpool. On Pitt's resignation over the issue of Catholic emancipation, Jenkinson became Foreign Secretary in Addington's ministry. His father's elevation to the peerage made Jenkinson Lord Hawkesbury and when Pitt returned in 1804, he was Home Secretary, still only 33.

Pitt's death in 1806, largely through overwork and port wine, led to something of a panic to find a replacement. George III, increasingly ailing and out of touch, offered the premiership to Hawkesbury but he lacked the confidence at that stage to accept. He served under the Duke of Portland however, along with three other men who in various ways are central to the story of Cato Street – Perceval, Castlereagh and George Canning. The last two detested each other and fought an inconclusive duel. Duelling was illegal in England and the incident helped bring down Portland's government. Spencer Perceval stepped into the breach and Hawkesbury, now the Earl of Liverpool on his father's death, was made Secretary for War and the Colonies. As such, the war in Spain was his responsibility and to his credit he gave Wellington the free hand and equipment he needed.

Perceval's death saw Liverpool entering Number Ten. Now, he was ready, with wide experience in key Cabinet posts. A man who twitched under stress – George Canning called him 'Blinkinson' – he would be eclipsed by the 'new' men of 1822: Robert Peel, William Huskisson, Canning and, a long way behind in terms of ability, Frederick Robinson. Liverpool's strength was in choosing good men of talent and steering a middle course through turbulent times. Tell that to the men of Cato Street.

'Shed a tear for Henry Addington!' wrote George Thomson. 'There he is, poor man, a thin and not very succulent sliver of premiership between two thick slices of Pitt.'[12] The future Lord Sidmouth, whom the Cato Street conspirators loathed, was the son of a doctor, born in London in May 1751. He was at school in Winchester, at university at Brasenose, Oxford, and practised law in London until Pitt persuaded him into politics. In 1783 he became Tory MP for Devizes in Wiltshire and six years later, largely because of his diplomacy and understanding of procedure, Speaker of the House. He was a hard worker, but no orator and had absolutely no sense of humour.

The resignation of Pitt put George III in a difficult situation. He had appointed 'Master Billy' way back in 1783 and against all predictions the man had proved to be brilliant. But he would not be shifted over Catholic emancipation. The Act of Union of 1801 was Pitt's brainchild but a vital clause in it involved giving political parity to Catholics. As a stubborn reactionary who was also head of the Church of England, George could not accept this and Pitt resigned. Addington therefore had greatness thrust upon him. The king had watched the man going through his paces in command of his yeomanry regiment and was impressed by his leadership qualities! 'Addington, you have saved the country,' the king told him with rather lofty optimism.

In fact, the new Prime Minister lacked international experience and was a miserable speaker. With Pitt a hard act to follow, Addington had to contend with the waspish Canning – 'Pitt is to Addington as London is to Paddington' – as well as the fact that his relatively humble origins did not quite square with the Tory squirearchy. 'He was not', wrote William Wilberforce, 'well fitted for the warfare of St Stephen's.' He worked out the Peace of Amiens but must have been well aware that it was only actually a breathing space for Napoleon to manoeuvre himself.[13] As always in a peace, the government immediately (and stupidly) slashed income tax and reduced the naval establishment from 130,000 men to 70,000. The army was reduced to 95,000. Not only was this hopelessly short-sighted, but it unleashed on the country bitter ex-servicemen who found their old jobs already gone and themselves surplus to requirements. Such men may have joined Despard as their counterparts in 1820 may have joined Thistlewood.

Addington was a tolerable peace minister, but he was not a war leader. Napoleon's virtual invasion of Switzerland saw hostilities start again and the Prime Minister's first speech to rally Parliament was one of his worst ever. His government fell on 10 May 1804 and Pitt was back. In January 1805, Addington himself, now Lord Sidmouth, returned as Lord President of the Council. With Pitt's death a year later, Sidmouth joined the

'Ministry of All the Talents' as Lord Privy Seal and then as Lord President again under Perceval and finally as Home Secretary under Liverpool. By the year of Cato Street, Sidmouth had served for thirty years in six administrations. Canning, as always, had the last word – 'He is like the smallpox. Everybody is obliged to have him once in their lives.'

As Home Secretary, internal law and order was Sidmouth's particular concern. In the years that led to Cato Street, he stood out as a grim symbol of repression.

Had the Harrowby dinner actually gone ahead, one of its more dazzling members was George Canning. He was one of those larger-than-life characters who easily outshone most of his colleagues. Like Sidmouth, his origins were not of the blood as far as the Tory party was concerned. His father was an Irish squire who died in debt having tried to make some money out of journalism. His mother was a failed actress who produced a string of half brothers and sisters for little George. Luckily for the boy (the family was now living in London) his uncle, Stratford Canning, was a City financier and he paid the fees for Eton and Christ Church, Oxford. His mother continued to haunt the theatre and the linen drapery business and for the rest of her life he worried about her, swinging a secret pension for her when he took office.

Enormously popular, with a ready wit that often got him into trouble, Canning became head boy at Eton and wrote a school magazine which was so successful he sold it to a publisher for £50! He won Latin prizes at Oxford and played at law in Lincoln's Inn but his vanity and flamboyance made him a natural for politics. At first pro-Whig and pro-French Revolution, the outbreak of the Revolutionary War saw him change his mind and join Pitt's Tories. Such turncoats are rarely trusted and Canning carried the stigma of this for the rest of his life. It did not help that he was so proud of being Irish at a time when Ireland was usually regarded as one of the outposts of Hell. By 1792 he was contributing to the fortnightly *Anti-Jacobin* and, under Pitt's influence, became MP for Newport, Isle of Wight. His Commons speeches were theatrical and his acerbic wit won him enemies. As one opponent said, Canning was a 'light, jesting, paragraph-making man'. He would have been at home today among sound-biting politicians. By the late 1790s, he regarded democracy as 'tyranny and anarchy combined'.

In 1799 he was a member of the India Board, resigned with Pitt over Catholic emancipation in 1801 and delighted in attacking Pittites, like Jenkinson, who had joined Addington's administration. On Pitt's return, Canning was made Treasurer of the Navy, a post which bored and disappointed him. Under Portland in 1807 he became Foreign Minister at a time when European affairs were critical. This was the high water mark of Napoleon's power. He controlled Europe from the English Channel to the river Niemen and his Treaty of Tilsit with the Russian Tsar seemed to make his position unassailable. Well informed as he was by his spies abroad, Canning took a bold decision and ordered troops to Denmark to prevent the fleet from falling into French hands. He did the same with the Portuguese fleet.

It was now that Canning decided that the War Minister, Lord Castlereagh, must go. Wellington's early victory in Spain was effectively wiped by the interference of a more senior general, Sir Huw Dalrymple and the Walcheren expedition of 1809 was a disaster. Canning blamed Castlereagh for both. Castlereagh grew tired of Canning's opposition and wrote him a three-page challenge to a duel. As dawn broke on 21 September 1809, two of His Majesty's Government faced each other in the mists of Putney Heath and aimed pistols at each other. Canning's ball pinged a button off Castlereagh's coat; Castlereagh's ball took a chunk out of Canning's thigh. Both men had to resign.

Canning refused to serve under Perceval, hoping that he might have been sent for instead. It would also have meant serving with Castlereagh, which he was not prepared to do. In 1812 when he was offered the Foreign Office he again refused because Castlereagh was Leader of the House. In that year of Perceval's assassination he won the seat for Liverpool on the anti-slave trade vote and briefly, two years later, became ambassador to Portugal. In June 1816 he returned to take up the post of President of the Board of Control, which effectively ran Indian affairs and it was in this capacity he was still serving at the time of Cato Street. Perhaps more than anyone who should have dined with Lord Harrowby, Canning was a mercurial enigma. On the one hand he was a disciple of Burke and yet saw the need for constitutional change. As perhaps the most dazzling of the 'Liberal Tories' in the 1820s, he championed the underdog in foreign affairs, always put England first and outwitted the machinations of the

European superpowers. But in 1820, in terms of the rising popular clamour for reform, he was as unrelenting as Sidmouth.

Or as Eldon. John Scott was born in Newcastle in 1751, the son of a coal merchant. As with other Cabinet members, his relatively humble background is perhaps surprising, but, like others, it was overlaid with an Oxford education and a career in the law. His elopement with a banker's daughter at the age of 21 was the last wild thing he ever did and he was called to the Bar in 1776. True to form, seven years later he became MP for Weobley, a rotten borough in Herefordshire. Scott was virulently anti-French Revolution and watched the growing discontent of the British masses with a mixture of contempt and fear. He was Solicitor-General in 1788 and, as Attorney-General five years later, was able to use all the viciousness of the Bloody Code against sedition of any kind. As Sydney Smith wrote, 'Lord Eldon and the Court of Chancery sat heavy on mankind.' In 1801, under Addington, he became Lord Chancellor, the supreme arbiter on matters of law. His take on reform was extreme. Eight years after Cato Street he referred to the Bill to repeal the 300-year-old Test and Corporation Acts (which would enfranchise Catholics) as 'bad, as mischievous and as revolutionary as the most captious dissenter would wish it to be'.[14] His views on education were that learning to read would send 'a hundred thousand tall fellows with clubs and pikes against Whitehall'. One of his judgements in 1805 meant that certain schools were allowed to teach nothing but Latin and Greek. He and Sidmouth regarded themselves as the 'last of the old school' and as long as they dominated the Cabinet (Eldon was a favourite of both George III and George IV) these dinosaurs were unlikely to accept the sort of concessionary changes which would have made Cato Street unnecessary.

As always, the private man was different. He was cheerful, he was kind, he liked his port (usually two bottles a day) and he did say in one memorable moment, 'If I were to begin life again, damn my eyes but I would begin as an agitator.' But Lord Eldon did not begin again as an agitator. He just hanged those who were.

Of all the men who should have dined with Lord Harrowby, the one that most carried the scorn and contempt of the working class was the strikingly handsome Robert Stewart, Marquis of Londonderry, but always known by his earlier title of Viscount Castlereagh. Shelley's cold and damning line still hovers over the man's reputation – 'I met Murder in the way; he had a mask like Castlereagh.' It was his head in particular that butcher James Ings wanted to hack off at Lord Harrowby's and he carried his butcher's knife for the purpose.

Stewart was born of a Scottish-Irish family in County Donegal in 1769. A graduate of St John's College, Cambridge, his Grand Tour enabled him to hear a debate in the Constituent Assembly in Paris. He sat in the Dublin parliament from 1790 and in the Westminster Commons from 1794 to 1797 as MP for the pocket borough of Orford. When the Dublin parliament was disbanded under the Act of Union, Castlereagh was one of the hundred MPs to join Westminster, representing County Down, and refused an English peerage which would have taken him to the Lords.[15]

His was the unenviable task of Chief Secretary for Ireland in the year of Wolfe Tone's rebellion. The vicious handling of this rising was not Castlereagh's decision; in fact he complained about it bitterly, but the Irishman's memory is long and he was regarded in the provinces as little short of a monster. They conveniently forgot that he resigned in 1801 along with Pitt over George III's refusal to accept emancipation for the Catholics.

In July 1805 Castlereagh was made Secretary for War and the Colonies. With the exception of Pitt, now becoming increasingly ill, he was the only Cabinet minister in the Commons and this was to take its toll on the man's health and sanity in the years ahead. Out of office during the 'Ministry of All the Talents' he was back under Portland in his old job and at a crucially testing time. His reorganization of the appallingly amateurish militia was sensible and creative. His personal choice of Sir John Moore to command the Light Infantry was brilliant and even the decision to land at Walcheren to destroy the French fleet was a perfectly good one. Unfortunately, Moore was killed at Corunna and the commanders on the ground at Walcheren dragged their feet, losing half their command in the process. Not everyone pointed the finger of blame at Castlereagh, but he felt responsible nonetheless.

He bounced back quicker than Canning after the unfortunate business on Putney Heath and was at the Foreign Office before Perceval's assassination. It is perhaps a little over the top to accept Geoffrey Treasure's verdict that Castlereagh was 'perhaps the greatest foreign minister that this country has ever had'. The diplomatic shenanigans that were the Congress of Vienna of 1814–15 and the subsequent congresses are beyond the scope of this book. Castlereagh, with his wide command of languages, his feel for European attitudes and his personal friendship with Prince Metternich, the Austrian Chancellor, made him a natural for all this. But he was also secretive and a difficult man to love. Though he dismissed the ambitions of the Holy Alliance of European superpowers as 'a piece of sublime mysticism and nonsense', it took him eight years to realize that British interests were not being considered by anyone else and had to leave it to his old nemesis Canning to do something about that.

The average Englishman – and certainly the disgruntled labourer or would-be Jacobin – merely saw Shelley's Castlereagh, the cold unfeeling supporter of reaction that could cheer the yeomanry's bloody work at Manchester and frame the Six Acts to muzzle any attempts at reform. The problem was that, from 1812, Castlereagh was the *sole* Cabinet minister in the Commons, and therefore bore the brunt not only of awkward questions from the Whig opposition, but the uncertainty of some of his own party too. A strike by Glasgow weavers in March 1813; the opening of a Jesuit college in County Kildare in May 1814; Corn Law riots over the price of bread in London, March 1815 – all this and much more came Castlereagh's way and he was supposed to provide answers. Actually, none of it was his responsibility at all. But James Ings wasn't listening.

The other men who should have dined in Grosvenor Square were small fry. Harrowby himself was Lord President of the Council and was elevated to the higher ranks of the peerage as an earl in 1809. Dudley Ryder had been Viscount Sandon and Baron Harrowby before that. His grandfather had been Lord Chief Justice on the King's Bench in the 1750s and died the day after he had been offered a peerage by George II. The house on the south side of Grosvenor Square was merely the earl's town house. He also owned considerable estates in the Midlands – it was at Sandon Hall near Stafford that William Davidson, Cato Street's 'man of colour', worked for Harrowby on his furniture and fittings.

Nicholas Vansittart was 54 at the time of Cato Street and has the distinction of being the longest serving Chancellor of the Exchequer in British history and one of the worst. The son of the governor of Bengal, Vansittart was born in Bloomsbury and educated at Christ Church, Oxford. Called to the Bar, he began his political career as a pamphleteer for Pitt and stood as MP for that most rotten of boroughs, the 'accursed hill' of Old Sarum, near Salisbury. He held a succession of posts under Pitt and Addington and was making a name for himself as a financier. He became Liverpool's Chancellor of the Exchequer in May 1812 and embarked on a series of incredibly convoluted tax reforms to tackle the huge national debt brought about by the long years of war. He became very unpopular in the country at large and by 1820 his financial credibility had come under fire from William Huskisson in his own party, as well as the classical economist David Ricardo.

Henry Bathurst was the son of a former Lord Chancellor. An MP from 1783, he inherited his father's earldom eleven years later and was shunted rapidly through a range of government departments including the Treasury, the Admiralty, the Board of Control (India), the Board of Trade and the Foreign Office. Whereas the *Australian Dictionary of Biography* describes him as a 'capable minister and a Tory of moderate opinions',[16] it has to be asked how much in-depth experience he actually gained in any of those areas. As Colonial Secretary in 1820 he had little to do with internal events in this country, although he was concerned that transportation to Botany Bay (the fate of the more fortunate Cato Street conspirators) was not really working in any meaningful sense.

Charles Grimble wrote:

> [Frederick] Robinson is an excellent Minister in days of calm and sunshine, but not endowed with either capacity or experience for these strange times.

Historian George Thomson goes further: Robinson was a man 'with a plump, dimpled face, pleasant manners, a vein of unconscious humour and not much else.'[17] A contemporary[18] said: 'Why Fred Robinson is in the Cabinet I don't know.'

Frederick John Robinson was born to a titled family in Yorkshire, went with the usual monotony to Harrow and Cambridge and was MP for Ripon at the age of 25. As Chancellor of the Exchequer under Liverpool, his name is forever associated with the hated Corn Laws of 1815, *the* symbol of the greed of the landed interest. To be fair, the man was far from happy about the legislation, but a London mob attacked his house in Old Burlington Street and slashed valuable paintings. There was already a military guard there and two people were killed. In relaying all this to parliament,

Robinson broke down in tears and earned the nickname 'the blubberer'. He was Treasurer of the Navy by the time of Cato Street.

Nice men, with wives and children, families and friends. Adolf Hitler liked dogs and children and he worried about killing lobsters. The same man (although there is famously no hard evidence for this) advocated the murder of every Jew in Europe.

It is unfair to link Liverpool's Tory Ministry of 1820 with the monster of the twentieth century, but we have to see these men from the perspective of the Cato Street conspirators. To them, the Ministry itself was a conspiracy; one bent on punishing the poor for being poor, of keeping the cost of bread artificially high; of imprisoning, transporting and hanging those who complained.

And on its part the government saw conspiracies everywhere. 'A Plot! A Plot!,' wrote Cobbett of them. 'How they sigh for a plot!'

It was on its way.

Chapter 6

Pig's Meat

If His Majesty's Government wanted a plot, they needed look no further than the ideas of Thomas Spence. Whereas most members of the London Corresponding Society dreamt of universal suffrage, a free education and some vague notion of a better deal in life, it is likely that some of them were prepared to go further.

Spence himself seems a straightforward man, but his legacy is confused. Because he operated latterly almost exclusively in London and one of his supporters was the Cato Street conspirator William Davidson, we have to evaluate his contribution to the most brazen assassination plan in British history.

Spence was born in Quayside, Newcastle, in June 1750. The city was one of the rapidly growing industrial centres of the North, with coal and iron challenging the older, still medieval work of the woollen and worsted weavers. Spence's family came originally from Scotland and his father was a net and shoemaker who sold hardware in a booth on the Sandhill. Young Spence had eighteen full and half brothers and sisters, and his father taught him to read and write sufficiently well for the boy to become a schoolmaster.

In his twenties, Spence became fascinated by a land dispute in Newcastle over common rights and he wrote a pamphlet which was hawked around the city, advocating his ideas which, many years later, came to form the basis of Spencean philanthropy. Since land was the currency of conquerors and the symbolic cornerstone of power, Spence decided that it should be distributed in a different way. Based on the parish, long the centre of social life, land must be returned to the people. In fact, his tract of 1800 was called just that – *Restorer of Society to its Natural State*. Inevitably, Spence's proposals did not end there and he had a rather rosy, optimistic view of how easily it would all happen:

The public mind being suitably prepared by reading my little Tracts and conversing on the subject, a few Contingent parishes have only to declare the land to be theirs and . . . other adjacent parishes would immediately follow the example . . . and thus would a beautiful and powerful New Republic instantaneously arise in full vigour.[1]

All land would be held in common by each parish and profits from rents would be ploughed back into the parish to build and sustain schools and libraries. Each parish would send a delegate to a national assembly and every adult male would be a member of the militia.

Spence produced these ideas on paper in 1775, the year that the American colonies broke away, claiming that land which actually belonged to Britain was rightfully theirs. As long as Spence remained in a political backwater like Newcastle, there was little harm done,[2] but in 1792 he moved to London.

Now it was a different place and a different time and phrases like 'national assembly' had an alien and terrifying connotation. The Terror began in France that year and war was imminent. Cashing in on the latest bestseller Spence revamped his 1775 pamphlet with the title *The Real Rights of Man*. He sold Paine's original alongside his own and let men take their choice.

Spence first operated out of a shop in Chancery Lane, but found himself arrested almost immediately for selling Paine. Accordingly, he kept on the move, hiring premises in High Holborn, Little Turnstile, Oxford Street and eventually selling from a barrow in the street. He also sold medallions embossed with the scales of justice and saloop, a cheap coffee made from sassafras or medicinal bark. Francis Place, living and working in his tailor-shop-cum-lending-library also sold Spence's tracts and wrote of him:

He was not more than five feet high, very honest, simple, single-minded, who loved mankind and firmly believed that a time would come when men would be virtuous, wise and happy. He was unpractical in the ways of the world to an extent hardly imaginable.

Throughout the 1790s Spence continued to write and disseminate his tracts, the best known of which, between 1793 and 1796 was called *Pig's Meat or Lessons for the Swinish Multitude* (Burke's phrase of 1790). Chalked slogans – 'Spence's System' – began to appear on London's buildings and in December 1794 he was imprisoned in Newgate under the suspension of habeas corpus and once more in 1801 (this time for twelve months) for the release of the *Restorer* pamphlet which the government regarded as seditious. By now Spence had invented a Utopian state – 'Spensonia' – in which not only his land reforms, but his idealized society with its own phonetic language³ would be a reality. On 3 January 1795 Spence wrote to the *Morning Chronicle* complaining that over a three-year period he had been dragged four times from his door by law officers, three times hauled before grand juries, three times sent to prison and once indicted at the Bar. He put his case in writing – something Despard would never be allowed to do – 'The case of Thomas Spence, bookseller, who was committed for selling the second part of Paine's *Rights of Man*'.

'Spence's just plan for everlasting peace and happiness, or in fact, the Millennium' was all rather idyllic and a tiny knot of supporters remained loyal to the strange little man until his death in 1814. Quite large crowds turned out for his funeral and the Jacobin medallions he made were distributed to everyone there.

The jury is still out on Thomas Spence. He could be regarded as a harmless crank, but in view of what happened two years after his death, this is probably too simplistic a view. It goes without saying that Spence's ideas, which many see today as forerunners of socialism propounded half a century before Karl Marx, ran totally counter to Britain's ruling elite at the time and were regarded by them with a mixture of disbelief and horror. Even Spence's original pamphlet in 1775 led to his being disbarred from the Philosophical Society.

It did not help that he was likened to the French revolutionary François 'Gracchus' Babeuf whose plot was discovered in 1796 and written up extensively in the *New Annual Register*. Babeuf was a hot-headed ex-servant who ruffled feathers from the time of the Revolution to his execution in 1797. His rallying cry was 'insurrection, revolt and the constitution of 1793' and his song – 'Dying of hunger, dying of cold' – could be heard in the cafés of Paris by the mid-decade. Probably psychotic, Babeuf believed that the appalling September massacres had not been appalling enough and the only remedy was to destroy the Republic's government which consisted of 'starvers, bloodsuckers, tyrants, hangmen, rogues and mountebanks'.

It all sounded like an incitement for Despard and the men of Cato Street, but was there any link with Thomas Spence? No hard evidence exists, but there were rumours of weapon collecting and drilling in connection with the man's followers and, after all, Spence himself used underground revolutionary techniques – handbills, pub meetings, possibly the orchestration of bread riots in 1800 and 1801. In 1803 little children were arrested on the orders of Lord Portland, the Home Secretary, for selling Spence's tracts. Certainly, the government continued to believe that Spence's was one of the 'hidden hands' behind unrest. Francis Place on the other hand believed that Spence and his followers were harmless people 'next to nobody and nothing'. But Place often misread his contemporaries and was prone to pretend that working-class reform revolved around him alone.

But whatever the involvement of Thomas Spence himself in plans for revolt, there is no doubt that, after his death, his followers certainly were involved. Calling themselves Spenceans or Spencean Philanthropists they took to the streets of London in 1816 as the nucleus of what was intended – and might have become – open rebellion.

Meeting in a variety of public houses, they were focusing their thoughts on what might be termed agrarian communism with their slogan 'The Land is the Peoples' Farm'. The leading lights of this group were more properly Jacobins or Painites – 'old Jacks' – many of them republicans. There was no overall leader, but Dr James Watson and his son Jem (James junior) were perhaps most prominent. Watson senior is a shadowy figure, possibly 50 at the time of Spa Fields, 'a medical man and a chymist' who had been involved in radical politics for years. He was a friend of fellow surgeon John Gale Jones, a great believer in freedom of the press and of the mass demonstration as a means of squaring up to the authorities, 'the free and easy' as it was called. On 4 December 1816, the Lord Mayor of London said, 'I always considered the Watsons – both of them – the bravest men in England.' As always, Francis Place had a different view; the elder Watson was 'a man of loose habits . . . wretchedly poor', the younger was 'a wild, profligate fellow'.

The other father and son team in the Spencean leadership were Thomas Evans and his son, also Thomas, the elder being the group's librarian. Place paints a picture of an eccentric, wandering from pub to pub with a Bible under his arm. In fact, Evans's *Christian Polity the Salvation of the Empire* written in that year advocated socialism in a rural, agricultural setting and proved very popular with London working men, especially the shoemakers (the occupation of two of the five men hanged after Cato Street).

Thomas Preston, a master shoemaker, said when examined by the Lord Mayor in December 1816:

> I have seen so much distress in Spitalfields that I have prayed to God to swallow me up – I have seen a fine young woman who has not been in a Bed for nine months . . . I have ruined myself. I have not £1 . . .

Other leading members of the group were the labourers John Hooper and John Keens.

But there is one name that stands out in the context of this book: Arthur Thistlewood. Virtually everything we know about this man, unquestionably the leader of the Cato Street conspirators, comes from the information at his trial in the spring of 1820 and given some additional purple phraseology by George Wilkinson. Thistlewood was born in Horncastle at the foot of the Wolds in Lincolnshire where the Bain and Waring streams meet. The place was best known for its great horse fair, described by George Borrow in *The Romany Rye*. Borrow was the son of a regular soldier who served in the Napoleonic Wars and he became fascinated with the 'travelling people' to be found at fairs like Horncastle.

Thistlewood's father was a bailiff or steward to 'an ancient family' in the area and the boy, probably from the age of 8 (1778), was privately taught with a view to becoming a land-surveyor. At a time of increasing enclosure and when ownership of land was still the cornerstone of wealth, such a career was respectable and potentially lucrative. In his teens however the lad 'manifested idle and unsettled habits' and became something of a trial to his family until he obtained a commission in a militia regiment at the age of 21. It was now 1791 and the shock waves of the French Revolution were being widely felt. The militia were on standby in the event of war and invasion, but Thistlewood had other conquests in mind. Even in the militia, an officer had to purchase his commission and was expected to live a certain lifestyle, with expensive uniforms and an indulgence in the social round of balls, soirees, point to point races, drinking and gambling. Where and how he met 'a young lady of the name of Bruce' is not recorded, but she was worth £300 a year on account of the property she owned in Bawtry in the West Riding of Yorkshire, a little south-west of the Great North Road.

Thistlewood promptly resigned his militia commission and settled down to the life of a kept man, but he hadn't read the small print. The financial deal, in an age when men dominated the world of money and inheritance, was that the new Mrs Thistlewood received the interest on her fortune for her lifetime only. When she died sixteen months later in child-bed, the cash reverted and Thistlewood was broke. It seems from later events that the baby died too, so an unencumbered Thistlewood obtained a second commission in a 'marching', i.e. regular regiment. How he was able to do this without a purchase price is unclear, but it was 1793 and Pitt's government was desperate for officers and men to fight the 'blue-water' colonial war he believed would beat the French.

Because there is no record of Thistlewood's regiment, we cannot trace his whereabouts in these months. General Carey's tiny army of 7,000 men took Martinique, St Lucia and Guadeloupe, as well as Tobago, but large numbers of men became ill and died from dysentery and yellow fever without even seeing a Frenchman and Thistlewood quickly grew bored with this, resigned his commission and sailed to America.

The United States was a new nation with no love for the British and Thistlewood did not stay long. We have no idea exactly where he was although of course, at that stage, the westward extent of white settlement was still effectively the Allegheny mountains. Thistlewood then obtained a passport for France and reached Paris soon after the overthrow of Robespierre. By now, it was the end of July, Thermidor in the new Revolutionary calendar, and France was licking her internal wounds after two years of the Terror. If relations may have been strained for Thistlewood in America, they must have been doubly difficult in France for an Englishman whose country was at war. 'In France,' says Wilkinson, 'his evil genius still followed him.' There were irregularities in his passport and, despite the fact that 'he became initiated in all the doctrines and sentiments of the French Revolutionists',[4] found himself imprisoned by the French police. This was clearly not in Paris, but exactly where is unrecorded. Eventually an order for Thistlewood's release arrived from the capital along with that for a fellow Englishman called Heeley, who had been imprisoned for the same reason. When Heeley was cheeky to a gaoler, the officer hit him with his cane and Thistlewood retaliated with a fist. Both men were placed in solitary confinement as a result.

The storyline now becomes even more improbable. Professing himself a 'hater of oppression and injustice', Thistlewood finally obtained a real passport and went to Paris where he 'entered the French service [i.e. army] and was present during the perpetration of numberless atrocities by the French troops'. It seems odd that the man should stay in the only country that had so far shown any oppression or injustice to him, but it does confirm the general opinion that Thistlewood was at best a dangerous sociopath and may even have been deranged. 'He had considerable knowledge of military tactics,' wrote Wilkinson, 'was an excellent swordsman and always fearless of death.'

The atrocities referred to can only mean in 1795 the control of bread riots in Paris. If that is so, then Thistlewood, the wannabe *sans-culotte*, was on the wrong side. The fall of Robespierre saw a general sigh of relief across the country, with moderation creeping back and even the church gaining some renewed acceptance. By May, however, the old disorder returned among a starving population and the mob invaded a meeting of the Convention and stuck the head of a deputy on a pole. Elsewhere in the country the White Terror began, a counter-revolution by royalists hell-bent on restoring the Bourbons.

At some point, probably in 1797, Thistlewood joined a French grenadier regiment. The Revolution had effectively swept away the titled officer class and there was no purchase system in the army. By now Lazare Carnot's reforms were having some effect and the ragged army of the Republic was winning victories against the massed ranks of the ancien regime. Wilkinson also tells us that Thistlewood fought at Zurich, but he clearly did not know the name of the French commander. It was André Massena, later to become a Marshal of France and one of the 'souls of iron' under Napoleon. There were actually two battles of Zurich and it is possible that Thistlewood fought them both.

In the first, between 4 and 7 June 1799 Massena was driven out of the city by an Austrian force under Archduke Charles, but he pulled back to the river Limmat and fortified his position on the Zurichberg, settling down to a stalemate. By the end of September, the Austrians had been replaced by their Second Coalition allies, the Russians, under General Korsakov. Massena's attack was masterly. Outnumbered two to one, with a second Russian army and an Austrian force arrayed against him, he smashed first one army, then the next, in true Napoleonic style. It helped that his wing commanders were Generals Oudinot and Soult, both brilliant men in their own right. So Arthur Thistlewood could say, in all modesty, that he had saved France from invasion and helped destroy the Second Coalition as Russia withdrew days later.

Infuriatingly, Wilkinson refers to 'a variety of adventures in France and on different parts of the Continent' for Thistlewood but gives no more details. By the Peace of Amiens, however, it was time for the adventurer to come home. Returning to Horncastle where his father and brother ran farms, Thistlewood courted a local girl, Miss Wilkinson. The impoverished soldier was in funds again, not this time because of his new wife but because he had inherited 'a considerable estate' from a relative. He sold this for £10,000, a vast sum at the time, to a gentleman from Durham, but not outright. Instead, he took an annuity bond which gave him an annual income of £850. This was a risky venture and in eighteen months the purchaser went bankrupt, leaving Thistlewood relatively high and dry.

The narrative now gets confusing. The Thistlewoods moved to London along with a son, James, 'a natural child' (who the boy's mother was is not recorded). An attempt by Thistlewood's family to get Arthur settled on a Horncastle farm failed – he was paying more in rent and tax than the farm earned – and with what remained of his legacy he went south. He either got in with a bad crowd – 'all the vices and dissipation of the metropolis' – composed mostly of army officers richer than he was or he drifted into radical politics. Perhaps it was both. He lost over £2,000 to a card-sharping ring in a 'Hell' in St James's and was unable to recover the loss. Bitter and broke, he found the Spenceans, especially the Evanses, and still seems to have had enough cash to travel with the younger Evans to France where the pair stayed for almost a year.

From this moment, George Wilkinson believed, Thistlewood's only goal was to overthrow the constitution. Certainly when the adventurer reached London the place must have been buzzing with talks of Despard and Thistlewood had seen for himself in France how dangerous a mob could be. Get the London mob on your side, arm them, give them a leader and a cause and the rest would be history.

The end of 1816 was the perfect time, although we have no clear idea of what Thistlewood was doing in the fourteen years preceding it. Distress had reached an all-time high and the London Corresponding Society in particular was galvanized into action. The Spenceans wrote to possible national leaders to front a mass meeting on 15 November at Spa Fields. Today, Spa Fields in Islington is easy to miss. It is a small park bisected by a path and when I visited it the major concern was what sort of adventure playground locals wanted for their children. What would the revolutionaries of 1816 have made of that? To be fair, it was always a place for the people. Known as Ducking Pond Fields in the mid-eighteenth century, crowds came from all over London to watch bull-baiting and duck-hunting, to wager on the outcome of bare-knuckle prize fights, like the female match won by Bruising Peg in 1768. At Whitsuntide, it was the scene of Welsh or Gooseberry Fair with donkey races, cudgel play and gurning[5] competitions. In the 1770s the Methodist Lady Selina, Countess of Huntingdon, had a chapel built and by the time of the 1816 disturbances, a large graveyard occupied the two acres behind the building. It remained a notorious haunt of footpads however and only slowly did respectable streets develop across it. When the Spencean letter arrived, William Cobbett, in one of his more timid moments, declined, but Henry 'Orator' Hunt accepted.

Hunt would go to the opening of an envelope. Easily the greatest demagogue of the radicals, he was powerfully built, a crack shot, excellent boxer and fine horseman. He had a knack for public speaking and the crowd loved him. When speaking, the weaver Samuel Bamford noted, Hunt's grey-blue eyes became

> blood-streaked and almost started from their sockets . . . His voice was bellowing, his face swollen and flushed; his griped hand beat as if it were to pulverise.

He loved danger, he loved attention – and wore a white wideawake hat to make sure he got it in a crowd. If anyone could rouse the London mob, it was Henry Hunt.

What made Hunt so successful was his gentlemanly pedigree and conduct. Despard was popular for the same reason. Across the Channel in the early days of the Revolution, so was the Marquis de la Fayette. The radicals may have railed against privilege and power, but they were delighted when someone with those qualities agreed to lead them. They were, after all, part of a centuries-old hierarchy; actual equality was unknown to them. So Hunt was a loyalist, raising a troop of militia in his native Wiltshire, but man-of-the-people enough to challenge a colonel of yeomanry to a duel and to assault a gamekeeper; both gave him a prison record.

By 1806 Hunt had joined the radicals, standing unsuccessfully as MP for Bristol in that year. He also had a reputation as a 'bit of a lad', living in sin with a Mrs Vince in Brighton in open emulation of the Prince of Wales at the Pavilion up the road. The rather more scrupulous Cobbett had his doubts – 'Beware of him; he rides the country with a whore.' Hunt would write later of a letter from Arthur Thistlewood, 'requesting me, when I came to town, to favour him with a call, as he had to communicate to me matters of the highest importance connected with the welfare and happiness of the people'.

Hunt did not reply, but a second letter from Thomas Preston, specifically inviting him to address a mass meeting, had the desired effect.

It was not possible, or intended, to keep the Spa Fields meeting a secret. And the government was scared. A note in Sidmouth's Home Office read:

> The meeting in Spa Fields is aware of the Collection of Soldiers in this vicinity. The appearance of Troops will occasion the destruction of London. Twenty thousand Englishmen can set any city in such flames as no Engines can extinguish.[6]

The basic Spencean plan for Spa Fields was not particularly revolutionary. The idea was to hear prominent radical views and for a show of hands (the only means of voting until 1872) to elect Hunt and Sir Francis Burdett to take a petition to the Prince Regent. The petition asked for relief from distress and the reform of parliament.

Sir Nathaniel Conant had other ideas. He was a magistrate of Bow Street and as such, in command of the most dynamic police force in London.[7] But his men were not prepared for the size of the crowd. Some 10,000 people jostled in the open space outside the Merlin's Cave pub to listen to Henry Hunt. Some of them had just witnessed a hanging, so they were in jovial mood and Hunt was on fine form. His own white hat was prominent on that November day, but so too were the older symbols of revolution waved from the window behind him – the French tricolour and a cap of Liberty; perhaps one of those was waved by Thistlewood.

Hunt's speech was measured, demanding reform while at the same time not condoning violence. He spoke of mental rather than physical force, aware as he must have been of the Bow Street patrols and the scarlet-coated troops ringing the Field, but he did tease the authorities –

Arthur Thistlewood, 'on the day sentence of death was passed'. Was 'T' deranged or a hero of the people?

James Ings, the Portsmouth butcher, promised to cut off e heads of Lords Castlereagh and Sidmouth.

Richard Tidd, radical and conman, endeared himself to the crowd watching his execution.

William Davidson, the 'man of colour' who stood guard outside the Cato St stable with a carbine. He tried to play the race card by claiming that, to whites, all black men looked alike.

John Thomas Brunt, the conspirator who took a pinch of snuff before he died.

Robert Adams, the ex-cavalryman who betrayed the men of Cato St by turning king's evidence.

Thomas Hyden, the cow-
keeper who claimed to have
approached Lord Harrowby
with a warning.

John Monument, the
diminutive waverer whose
evidence helped to hang the
conspirators.

Robert Stewart, Lord Castlereagh, was the most handsome, and the most hated, cabinet minister of his day. Taken from a contemporary portrait by Thomas Lawrence.

Henry Addington, Lord Sidmouth, was the Home Secretary who ran a network of *agents provocateurs* to infiltrate radical groups. Taken from a bust by William Behnes, 1831.

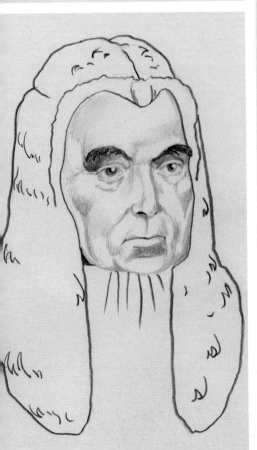

John Scott, Lord Eldon, Chancellor of England and a sworn enemy of reform. Taken from a bust by Frederick Tatham, 1830.

(*Left*) The Cato St stable as it looked in May 1820. The double doors to the left were to house a carriage. Note the grille over the centre door for ventilation for cattle. Huge crowds of sightseers visited here in the days and weeks after the conspiracy was uncovered. (*Right*) The stable today, a private house to the right of a new block of flats, ironically named Sidmouth Court. (*Photo: Author*)

The plan of the hay-loft in Cato St marking the spot where Smithers, the Bow St Runner, died.

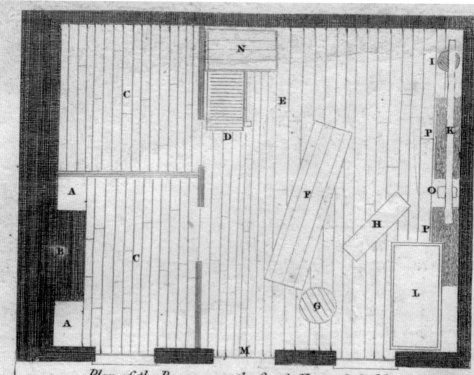

Plan of the Rooms over the Coach House & Stable.

A *Cupboard*	F *Carpenters Bench*	L *Hammock*
B *Chimney*	G *Tub*	M *Hay Loft door*
C *Rooms over the Coach House*	H *Chaff Cutter*	N *Carpenters Tool Chest*
D *Desending Steps to the Stable*	I *Corn Measure*	O *Stone*
E *Smithers Killed*	K *Plank of Wood*	P *Aperture for Hay*

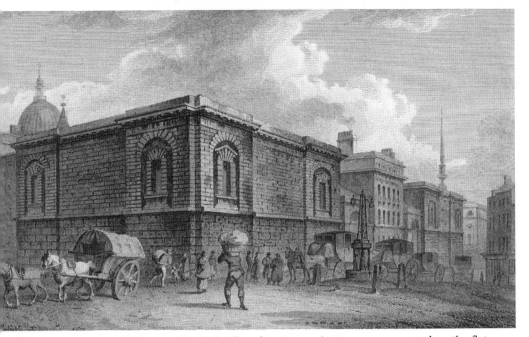

e old Session House and Newgate Gaol: the Cato Street conspirators were executed on the flat f.

e Central Criminal Court now stands on the site of the Session House and Newgate Gaol.
oto: Author)

Excavations into the Victorian drains outside the Central Criminal Court. The Cato St conspirators are buried some feet way to the right of the picture. (*Photo: Author*)

Execution day, 1 May 1820. On the scaffold, the hangman's assistant, James Foxen, holds up the first head – 'this is the head of Arthur Thistlewood!' The masked headsman, probably Tom Parker, is moving on to the second victim for decapitation.

Those who resist the just demands of the people are the real friends
of confusion and bloodshed . . . but if the fatal day should be destined
to arrive, I assure you that if I know anything of myself, I will not be
found concealed behind a counter or sheltering myself in the rear.[8]

Conant cannot have missed the fact that the greatest cheer came from
Hunt's 'fatal day' reference. Thistlewood would have caught that too.

Large numbers signed the petition, demanding universal male suffrage,
annual general elections and a secret ballot. It was voted unanimously that
Hunt and Burdett should present it to the Regent, but Burdett turned the
proposal down. This led to a quarrel between the radical leaders which
weakened the movement and delighted the authorities. While Hunt's
accusations of cowardice flew, he twice begged an audience at Carlton House
and was twice refused.

Accordingly, a second meeting was called at Spa Fields on 2 December,
to protest at the arrogant disdain shown to Hunt. It is difficult to imagine a
less impressive figurehead than the Prince Regent. A gambler, a womanizer
and spender of other people's money, George had no real understanding of
the political issues of his day and lived in such a cloud-cuckoo land that he
talked in military circles as if he had been present on the field of Waterloo.

Hunt was late for the second meeting and was told while rattling along
Cheapside in his carriage that a riot had broken out and that the mob had
taken control of the Tower of London. At Spa Fields, the hustings wagon
in the centre was draped with tricolours and a banner reading 'The brave
soldiers are our friends' – precisely the sort of notion that makes revolutions
happen. On the wagon stood the Watsons, Thistlewood, Hooper and the
other leading Spenceans of the Cock and the Mulberry Tree.

As far as the authorities were concerned, the last straw came when Jem
Watson quoted the speech made by Camille Desmoulins before the storming
of the Bastille:

If they will not give us what we want, shall we not take it? Are you
willing to take it? Will you go and take it? If I jump down amongst
you, will you come and take it?

This was clearly incitement, each sentence punctuated by ever louder cheers
and John Stafford, Conant's number two, ordered the arrest of the leaders
and the confiscation of their flags. From now on, everything became chaotic.

There were at least as many people at Spa Fields at this second meeting as at the first and Jem Watson jumped down from the wagon and snatched up a tricolour. In the symbolism of the day, the flags meant everything. On a field of battle, for centuries, the flag was a sacred token; it must not be allowed to fall into enemy hands. On the other hand, the tricolour on London's streets must have been to the authorities like a red rag to a bull.

With a vague, Despard-like plan in the leaders' heads, the mob marched towards Newgate with the probable intention of destroying the place for the second time in forty years and freeing the prisoners. Some of them broke off in the direction of the Royal Exchange to grab whatever gold lay there and the bulk moved against the Tower of London. On the way, to give them a fighting chance against the garrison, they looted gunsmiths' shops on Snow Hill. There is no doubt that for many of the mob, looting was the sole aim of the day (the crime would resurface, oddly, in the Cato Street trials) and when a looter got into a row with Jem Watson, the radical shot him in the stomach at point blank range.

Then, it all fell apart. At the Exchange Alderman Shaw and a mere seven constables staged a showdown with the mob, arrested three leaders and the rest went home. At the Tower, disappointed to discover that the soldiers were not after all their friends, a rioter climbed onto the railings below the walls, brandishing a cutlass, urging the garrison to join the mob. There is every likelihood that that rioter was Arthur Thistlewood. The garrison didn't move and, again, everyone went home.

In some ways, Spa Fields was the British equivalent of the attack on the Bastille and the differences are blinding. In one case, a desperate mob destroyed an object of tyranny and went on to overturn the world order, at least in Europe. In the other, the mob tired of the game, got bored and melted away into the alleys of London. This was partly because of how the second Spa Fields, in particular, was organized. When a man met Henry Hunt in Cheapside to tell him the Tower had been taken, he was not just spreading one of those aspirational rumours that flies at events like Spa Fields, he was deliberately making it up.

His name was John Castle and he was a spy.

Chapter 7

Oliver the Spy

Early September 1997 and an estimated one million people, united in grief and anger, were milling outside Buckingham Palace and along the Mall. Days earlier Diana, Princess of Wales, had died in a car crash in a Paris tunnel and the crowd was incensed that the royal family was failing to react properly to Diana's death. There was no flag flying over the palace because the Queen was away in Balmoral on holiday. There should have been a flag, the crowd thought, and it should have been at half mast.

Author and broadcaster Richard Belfield wrote:

> Should [the crowd] choose to march in any direction the only way they could be stopped would be to bring the army out of its barracks, an unthinkable act in peacetime, which would also result in heavy loss of life. An anxious civil servant asked if there was a precedent and was told 'Yes, Paris 1789.'[1]

It sounds incredible that such a mood and such a scenario could exist in the late twentieth century, but the royal family in particular had totally misunderstood the nation's mood. How was that possible? For 'crowd' read 'mob', for 'death of Diana' read 'Corn Laws' and we have an action replay of the decade after 1810. Today, because of the intrusion of the mass media, we know what our politicians look like. Up to a point we know what they say and do. They, in turn, with opinion polls and think tanks and MPs' surgeries, do their best to keep in tune with voters' needs and concerns.

In the early part of the nineteenth century, Cabinet ministers only appeared as crude cartoons, if, in the opinion of a Gilray or a Cruikshank, they deserved to be lampooned. The vast majority of politicians were faceless. They only appeared to their constituents (the equivalent of less than an eighth of the population) every seven years on election day. Their anonymity may have been a strength, but it contributed to the frustration of the people in that they had no peaceful and acceptable means of redress.

This again was a two-way street; the government and the politicians had no way of knowing the mood of the nation, especially its unenfranchised elements, unless someone told them.

That job was given to the *agent provocateur*, the spy. Arguably, the creator of a secret service in Britain was Francis Walsingham, the devoted servant of Elizabeth I and a member of her Privy Council. At a time of religious and political upheaval, when a rampant Spain was threatening the stability of Europe, there were at least five assassination plots against the queen. Walsingham's job was to keep the woman – and the country – safe by whatever means at his disposal. To this end, he employed a number of 'intelligencers' and 'projectioners', including university men like playwright Christopher Marlowe, to listen at keyholes and report to superiors. Robert Cecil, who effectively became the queen's first minister on the death of his father, Lord Burghley, continued the practice and not only foiled the Gunpowder Plot of 1605, but orchestrated it throughout.[2] With the help of his informer, Cecil knew exactly how far the plot had progressed, almost on a daily basis, and made life easier for the conspirators in order to catch them red-handed. Such Machiavellianism continued into the Protectorate of Oliver Cromwell and beyond.

The debonair fiction of the spy rests today on the suave figure of James Bond. Shaken but never stirred, Bond is a creation of the Cold War of the late twentieth century, even if he is partially based on Sidney Reilly (Sigmund Rosenblum) who was a triple and possible even quadruple agent for the British shortly before and during the First World War. The spies who operated in Georgian England were of a very different character. They were usually, but not always, literate and came from varied walks of life. They rarely reported direct to anyone in the corridors of power in Whitehall, but to magistrates, police officers and mill owners at a local level. The case of Colonel Despard and the case of Cato Street were different.

There is no doubt that William Pitt used a spy network and there is equally no doubt that, in liberal society and among the labouring poor, the use of such men was detested and smacked of the French Terror at its worst. There, neighbours were encouraged to inform on neighbours. Tittle-tattle and old grievances led directly to the guillotine. This policy extended right through from the Jacobin 1790s to the bread-deprived years two decades later. Committees of Secrecy met in the lobby rooms of the Commons in

1801, 1812 and 1817, turning pale as they heard anecdotal evidence of insurrection. In the 1790s, it was French agents working for the good of the Revolution across the Channel; twenty years later it was the work of Luddites and unbridled democrats. In both instances, the target was the same: the reactionary, retrenched and uncaring government.

E P Thompson sums up the situation superbly:

> The line between the spy and the *agent provocateur* was indistinct. The informer was paid by piece-rate; the more alarmist his information, the more lucrative his trade . . . At a certain stage, it is impossible to know how far they [the government] were themselves deluded by conspiracies which their own informers engendered . . . These years reveal such a foul pattern of faked evidence, intimidation and double agents . . . If the Cato Street conspirators had achieved their object in the assassination of the Cabinet, the Cabinet would have been slain by conspirators whom their own repressive policies had engendered and their own spies armed.[3]

The problem lies in the value of the evidence provided by *agents provocateurs*. Moderate reformers, like Burdett and Whitbread, poured scorn on the wilder stories. The social historians the Hammonds, writing in the middle of the twentieth century, tended to believe the bulk of what they read. E P Thompson, ever the defender of the forming working class, veered towards Burdett and Whitbread. Our dilemma, 200 years after the events is that we cannot *know* the extent of planned insurrection. All we can do is to see it in action.

In July 1817, five months after somebody threw a stone at the Prince Regent's carriage as he rattled past towards Westminster, the satirical cartoonist George Cruikshank drew a piece which encapsulated the honest man's view. Around a table littered with radical threats, Castlereagh, Canning and Sidmouth, conspirators against the people, are plotting to give titles and honours to the best known spies of the day – John Castle and W J Richards, who usually used the alias Oliver. In the background, John Bull, the upright, working Englishman, looks on appalled. 'Poor starving John', said the caption, 'is to be ensnared into Criminal Acts and then the Projectors and Perpetrators are brought forward as principal evidences.'

It was one of those projectors and perpetrators who met Henry Hunt along Cheapside on 2 December 1816. John Castle was a shady character, very much part of London's criminal fraternity. He was a 'bully', as pimps were called, and met some of the reformers while serving time in the Fleet prison. E P Thompson analyses the two types of informer and Castle fits both. He could have done his work at Spa Fields in exchange for immunity from arrest and punishment; or he could have been working just for cash. Can we therefore trust the word of men like Castle? No, but again we cannot dismiss his evidence out of hand. Employers, magistrates and the government employed several men in the same area, so Castle would have no way of knowing whether he himself was being spied on, a sort of quality control of what he had to sell.

In his semi-literate hand, he wrote to Mr Litchfield, solicitor for the Treasury at the trial of James Watson in March 1817:

> sir thear is one thing that I am not certain weather I menshened but I have thought it most properest to cumenecate to you thear was to have been small Detachments plased at Diferant Enterenses in and out of London to prevent Government for sending despatches to haney part of the Cuntrey as thear was only one hors soulger sent with them . . . proposed by young watson and thisilwood and a greed to by all.[4]

We cannot be sure exactly when Castle joined the Spenceans but by October 1816 he was on the committee of six with the Watsons, the Evanses and Thistlewood. The report above has the ring of truth because working–class meetings (even secret, underground ones that plotted revolution) had formal proceedings, including a revolving chairman, proposals, seconders and so on. It also makes sense because it proves a degree of planning not actually apparent from the events of the day.

In his memoir of 1822, Hunt wrote that, at the first rally, on 15 November, Castle had loudly proposed a toast over dinner at the Bouverie Hotel – 'May the last of Kings be strangled with the guts of the last priest'. Watson and Thistlewood were appalled by this and visited Hunt the next day to apologize. Neither of them seems to have realized that Castle was going over the top in an attempt to seem at one with the cause. At the meeting on 2 December, Castle was seen stashing weapons into one of the hustings wagons on its way to Spa Fields and told the court at Watson's trial that he had been tasked with making pikes.

The *agent provocateur* had done his job well. Sidmouth at the Home Office could now move against the reformers. The charge was treason and

Jem Watson made a run for it, shooting his way out of trouble with police officers at Highgate before boarding a ship in London docks disguised as a Quaker, his face disfigured with caustic, according to the *Independent Whig* of 27 July 1817. His destination? America, a safe haven where nearly everyone had committed treason forty years before.

The others were caught and Watson senior, Thistlewood, Preston and Hooper were put on trial at the King's Bench on 9 June. Previously the grand jury of Middlesex had decided there was a case to answer and Mr Justice Bayley told them they were to deliberate on 'the highest crime that can be committed – the crime of high treason'. There were four counts (which were to be repeated three years later in the Cato Street trials) and fourteen 'overt acts' mostly perpetrated on the second Spa Fields meeting on 2 December. A vast 228 possible jurors were whittled down to twelve men and true. One was a gentleman (Thistlewood's status); the others variously a buttonmaker, woollen draper, lottery office keeper, anchor-smith, carpenter/undertaker, capillary maker, ironmonger, shoemaker, carrier and druggist. What no one appears to have asked these men was their take on radical politics. We can, perhaps, draw our own conclusions, because after five days of evidence, another biased summation by Lord Ellenborough, the principal judge and a bottle of wine and some sandwiches, they found James Watson not guilty.

Ellenborough, Bayley and the other two judges, Abbott and Holroyd, must have been appalled. The prosecution decided to try each of the four Spa Fields leaders separately. This was a risk because if the first was acquitted, as was the case, then all of them would walk. On paper, the evidence against Watson senior looks strong, but the authorities made the mistake of relying on John Castle and his evidence occupied the whole of the third day. He was at the Bar for between eight and nine hours in which he outlined in great detail the insurrecting plans of the Spenceans and how he, Watson and Thistlewood had spent days talking to discontents in pubs across London to persuade them to join the rising. This was nothing to the next day however, when he was mauled by Mr Wetherell for the defence.

'Your memory was very good yesterday,' said the lawyer, '. . . seemed as good as an almanac, but today you do not recollect anything.' He ripped into his man, forcing him to admit that he had previously betrayed fellow criminals which resulted in those men's deaths; that he had done time for attempting to smuggle French prisoners-of-war out of the country, for money; that he was a forger; that he had committed bigamy; and that he was a 'bully' for a lodging house in King Street, Soho, where Mother Thoms hired out her rooms for half an hour at a time – or even, something the jury found amusing, for five or six minutes.

In his summation, Wetherell went further than the actual evidence would allow by implying that Castle was a government spy. The Attorney-General and the judges were outraged, but there is little doubt that Wetherell was right. Despite this, there is a sense that the Spa Fields four got off lightly. There were parties in London to celebrate their victory, with flags flown and toasts drunk. Perhaps it gave Arthur Thistlewood a sense of immortality, an optimism, which overcame his disappointment at how easily his revolutionary army had collapsed. It also meant that, for the rest of his life, he was a marked man.

But if the authorities had fallen down badly in placing their faith in Castle, worse was to come that year of 1817 and many miles to the north. E P Thompson makes the point that, if the weavers of Lancashire, Yorkshire, Nottinghamshire and Derbyshire had bought their banners to Spa Fields, then Watson's and Thistlewood's revolution might have worked.

On 1 March, Liverpool's government again suspended habeas corpus in the face of a growing number of riots across the country. On the 10th, starving spinners and weavers set off from Manchester to walk the 165 miles to London to see the Prince Regent. It was all part of the working man's naive faith in the hierarchy of Old England. However wicked, corrupt and uncaring the king's ministers were, the man himself (or in this case, because of George III's increasing infirmity, his son) was somehow approachable, fair and kind. Men believed the same of Charles I before, during and even after the Civil War. So did the Russian peasants who marched behind Father Gapon (another spy) to the Winter Palace in 1905. The spinners were called Blanketeers because they carried blankets over their shoulders to use as sleeping bags. In the event, after eleven miles, they were halted at Stockport by the army, who arrested the leaders and dispersed the rest.

One of the great question marks over this period of British history is the links between London and the provinces. Some provincial leaders, like Joseph Mitchell, a journeyman printer from Lancashire, visited the Spenceans in the Cock along Grafton Street and, as we shall see, events in

Manchester in the summer of 1819 had a direct bearing on Cato Street. It was on one of his visits to London that Mitchell met William Oliver, who sometimes called himself Oliver Williams and who had just been released from debtors' prison at the Fleet. Oliver's freedom had been arranged by the Jacobin shoemaker Charles Pendrill, who had been an associate of Colonel Despard.

Like many *agents provocateurs*, Oliver's exact occupation is uncertain. He has been described as a carpenter, builder, surveyor or clerk, but by the March of 1817 he suddenly became involved in radical politics, pestering Pendrill and others about the existence of Associations in London. On the surface, Oliver appeared to have the right credentials. Portraits of Cobbett, Burdett, Horne Tooke and Charles James Fox hung in his rooms, but relative country bumpkins like Mitchell didn't think to ask where the money had come from to buy such artwork. It came, in fact, from Sidmouth, whom Oliver had gone to see on 28 March.

No written evidence exists from the meeting, but it seems likely that Oliver's brief was to gauge the extent of planned insurrection in the North and if there was none, to do something about it. With a completely trusting Mitchell in tow, the spy set off on a whirlwind twenty-three-day tour that took in the majority of the Midlands and North's industrial centres and most of the working-class leaders there, pretending that the London societies were just waiting for the word. A provincial rising was mooted for 26 May. Oliver's reports to Sidmouth made it clear that it stood no chance of success. In the event, Mitchell was arrested on 4 May, travelling in disguise as a weaver and under an assumed name and Oliver returned to London.

With Watson and Thistlewood still awaiting trial at that point, there were an unknown number of scattered provincial leaders waiting for the green light from a government spy. The rumours grew wilder. There were plans afoot, Sidmouth was told, 'to make a Moscow out of Manchester'[5] but the 'fatal day' was postponed until 9 June (by coincidence the last day of the Watson trial) on the advice of Oliver. The nights would be darker because of the moon's phase and the authorities of course had all the more time to be ready. Sheffield was poised; so was Nottingham. Oliver was sent north again.

Cleverly pretending that the next county was already well ahead in its preparations (essentially the same ploy Castle had used when he told Hunt that the Tower was already taken) he spurred on the others. He laced the information with plausible detail. Thomas Wooler's *Black Dwarf*, he said, was printing the proclamations of a Provisional Government; in Wolverhampton the working men were poised to take Weedon barracks.

Nottingham was one of those areas with a long reputation of rebellion. The leading light in the spring of 1817 was Thomas Bacon, a framework knitter who had been known since 1791 as a Painite. He also had land reform ideas on the lines of the Spenceans. Another informer, Henry Sampson of Bulwell (probably unaware of Oliver's real identity) reported that 'a London delegate' (Oliver) had told local leaders that 70,000 men were poised in the capital and that Birmingham was ripe for rebellion too. Among the men Oliver spoke to was Jeremiah Brandreth, a newcomer to the area who may have hailed originally from Exeter and who lived with his wife Ann and three children in Sutton-in-Ashfield. An unemployed stocking frame knitter, it is likely that Brandreth had been involved in Luddite activity in the years before 1817.

Happy to leave the area in the hands of the 'Nottingham Captain', Oliver rode to Yorkshire and was there between 1 and 6 June. On the 4th, he held a secret meeting with Major-General John Byng who commanded troops in the area and tipped him off about a radical meeting at Thornhill Lees near Dewsbury that was scheduled for the 6th. Byng's soldiers arrested those present with the aid of a magistrate and Oliver conveniently escaped.

But it was now that Oliver's luck deserted him. He was spotted talking to one of Byng's servants in a hotel in Wakefield and received a tough grilling from the revolutionaries back in Nottingham, from which he was lucky to escape with his life. All this, however, was too late for Brandreth who had left two days earlier to raise the men of Pentrich and to collect others on their way to Nottingham.

Together with William Turner, a stonemason, George Weightman whose mother ran the White Horse pub in Pentrich, Isaac Ludlam, a stonegetter and about fifty others, the Captain went from village to village and house to house, demanding weapons and followers. Anyone who refused was threatened with violence. By 9 June, Brandreth had perhaps 300 followers. He wore an apron like a belt, was known to almost everyone as 'the Captain' and Turner was his 'Lieutenant'. At his trial, the Attorney-General built up Brandreth's military role even more by calling him 'generalissimo'. The plain fact is that when an officer and eighteen troopers of the 15th Hussars stationed at Nottingham faced the mob, the Captain-General was among those who threw down their weapons and fled.

It was raining and dark by the time the Pentrich rebels reached Codnor. Here they were refused entry to a house by its feisty mistress, Mrs Hepworth, and in fury, Brandreth fired his pistol through the window, killing a servant, Robert Walters. For a while, Brandreth's rhetoric and promises kept the band together. The plan was to storm the Butterley Iron Works, one of the biggest employers in the area, and make pikes and other weapons from the stock there. The owners would object; the owners would be killed. Each village was 'to kill its own vermin' and Brandreth even had a marching song for them, much quoted at his trial –

> Every man his skill must try,
> He must turn out and not deny;
> No bloody soldier must he dread,
> He must turn out and fight for bread.
> The time is come you plainly see,
> The government opposed must be.

'The Marseillaise' it was not, but its lyrics were revolutionary enough to see Brandreth hanged. He promised his followers, because Oliver had promised him, that the entire country would rise. One witness at his trial talked of 'the Northern clouds, men from the North would come down and sweep all before them and every man that refused would be shot'.[6] And in London, the Tower had already been taken and the keys handed over to the local Hampden Club. None of this, of course, was true; the men of Pentrich were on their own.

And some of them (who had not already crept home on that mad, wet night) may have been genuinely amazed to find that there was no Provisional Government already set up in Nottingham. On the contrary, there was just the army and the insurrection fizzled out.

A total of forty-six men were rounded up over the next few days and put on trial at Derby by special commission in October. In accordance with the usual procedure, each of the alleged four ringleaders – Brandreth, Turner, Ludlam and Weightman – was tried separately, the same jury (by and large) deciding all four cases. As in the Watson/Thistlewood trial, the big guns were brought in, both on the Bench and for the prosecution. Lord Chief Baron Richards presided, along with Mr Justice Dallas, Abbot and Holroyd.

The Attorney-General and Solicitor-General led a team of eight as opposed to the defence's meagre two, Denman and Cross.

The defence did their best and much of the argument, as in Watson's case, revolved around the semantics of what was an insurrection and what was a riot. Cross in particular tried hard to put the whole thing in perspective – 'Now there, Gentlemen, ends the history of the war against the great king of England in the year of our Lord 1817' – but the jury weren't buying it. They found Brandreth guilty in twenty-five minutes. One by one, Turner, Ludlam and Weightman followed suit, the deliberation period getting less and less each time. In the case of the others, they were advised to plead guilty and did so, receiving sentences of anything from transportation for life to six months' imprisonment, depending on their actual role in the rising. In a rare moment of humanity, the court took pity on the last group sentenced. They were very young and mostly siblings of the more serious offenders. 'Go home,' snarled the judge, 'and thank your God for His mercy.'

The defence put out dark hints during the trial of William Turner. 'One assumes', said Cross, and no one took him up on it, 'that Mr Oliver is at the bottom of this.' In the trial of Isaac Ludlam, he said:

> the leader [Brandreth] himself was deceived and he was also in other hands. Why is a veil still spread before the mysterious machinery which sets the lower agents in motion?

In Turner's trial, Denman raised a similar note, that there was someone 'behind the curtain' – 'Who and what is he who set the machinery in motion? Gentlemen, there is something hid in mystery.'

There was – his name was W J Richards aka Oliver the Spy. On the gallows, as Brandreth waited to die, he had the sangfroid to shout to the Derby crowd, 'God be with you all and Lord Castlereagh.' William Turner, with the noose around his neck growled, 'This is all Oliver and the Government.' The editor of the *Leeds Mercury* exposed Oliver as early as June and it may well be that the jury in the London Watson case, having read all this, were influenced to find for the defendant, especially as the other spy, John Castle, was so blatantly a rogue.

Earl Fitzwilliam, the Lord Lieutenant of Yorkshire, wrote, fuming, to Sidmouth, stating plainly that without Oliver there would have been no trouble on his patch at all. Sidmouth, of course, in the time-honoured tradition of central government, denied that Oliver was anything but a reporter of events and that, in fomenting insurrection, he had exceeded his brief. Few people believed him then and fewer still today. What is different is the contemporary reaction to men like Castle and Oliver. The whole notion of undercover and preventative forces was alien and repugnant to Englishmen of every social class. When Robert Peel's government introduced a plain clothes detective branch at Scotland Yard in 1842, there was a huge outcry; the whole thing was so sneaky, dishonest and un-British.

Oliver was not called at the Derby trials because the government realized that Castle's appearance in court had been so lamentable; they would follow the same policy in the Cato Street affair three years later. A whole rash of acquittals followed as a result of Oliver's exposure. The radical editors Wooler and Hone were acquitted on charges of seditious libel. Would-be revolutionaries in Glasgow and Folley Hall likewise won their freedom. A charge of sedition brought by the Lord Advocate, Alexander Maconochie, collapsed in July with lenient sentences, acquittals and counter-charges of bribery to secure a government verdict. This did not prevent Cruikshank producing his brilliant 'Liberty Suspended' cartoon, showing the pale, dead body of a female dangling from a gibbet on which the officials of church and state are pontificating. Around the gallows is a ring of the Life Guards with swords drawn.

Most worryingly for the government, the 'singular baseness, the detestable infamy' of Oliver drew the moderates and extremists together. The editor of the *Gorgon* wrote on 27 June 1818:

> They who passed the Gagging Act . . . were such miscreants that could they have acted thus in a well-ordered community they would all have been hanged . . .

When, in 1820, Brandreth's defence counsel, Mr Denman, was asked why he had not called Oliver as a *defence* witness, he admitted that his evidence would have been too incriminating and that he could not cross-examine in the usual way. Most radicals in the country believed that Mr Cross had been bought off by the authorities *not* to introduce Oliver into the proceedings.

Before her husband's execution, Ann Brandreth wrote to him in a letter he never saw: 'If you have (which is the general opinion) been drawn in by that wretch Oliver, forgive him and leave him to God and his own conscience.'

Jeremiah Brandreth, the Nottingham Captain, became a martyr to the people after all, the very thing the government had feared. Radicals like Hunt and Cobbett hailed him as a hero; so did Shelley, writing some of his bitterest poetry at this time. Oliver became synonymous with corruption and government intrigue, with everything that was wrong with the country in the years after Waterloo.

But worse was to come.

Chapter 8

Bloody Fields

They came in their thousands, from Lees, from Saddleworth and from Moseley. The discontented and the dispossessed, spinners and weavers from Middleton, Boarshaw, Hopwood, Chadderton and Back O' the Brow. Men, women and children, wearing (if they owned such a thing) their Sunday best, even though it was Monday.

It was 19 August 1819. For eleven of them, it would be the last day of their lives.

If we look, as we must, for a motive behind the Cato Street conspirators' bizarre enterprise, we should see it in part as an act of revenge. Because, in the short term at least, and in the area where it happened, there was no revenge.

Manchester, by the hot, dry summer of 1819 was huge. Together with nearby Oldham it boasted over 95,000 inhabitants, the poorest the Irish who lived in water-logged cellars on the edge of still open spaces like St Peter's Fields. Nearly a third of that population – half of the able-bodied adults – worked in the city's sixty mills, most of which were given over to spinning. The fastest growing of the English industrial sprawls, Manchester was on its way to becoming the cottonopolis, a centre of rich magnates and civic pride. It was also acquiring a reputation, along with Nottingham, Sheffield and London, as a dangerous radical centre. Later in the century, the hugely influential Anti-Corn Law Association would be born here, as would the Trades Union Congress.

If the Manchester spinners were already wage-slaves, working sixteen hours a day in stifling, unsafe conditions and living in unhygienic slums which would soon kill thousands of them, the weavers were in a more desperate situation. About 40,000 handloom weavers lived and worked supposedly as independents in the outlying villages, but as we saw in Chapter 2, their day had gone. Whole families were now subsisting on 12 shillings a week and yet the Corn Laws kept the cost of their staple diet sky high. The old Poor Law simply could not cope.

The radicals in the area understood their plight and as elsewhere, were doing their bit to alleviate distress. As we have seen, the first Hampden Club outside London was set up at Royton in 1816; this was only nine miles from Manchester. The grand old man of local radical politics was John Knight, who was arrested in 1812 for holding a seditious meeting. The thirty-nine men involved got off, but it was a warning shot over the bows in a cold war between radicals and loyalists that was about to get hot.

Samuel Bamford was another local leader, better known than the others because of his brilliant memoirs which inform our knowledge of the place and time. A weaver from Middleton, Bamford was highly articulate (though not much of a poet) and well educated. Like many of his contemporaries he was a devotee of Cobbett's *Political Register* and a man with his finger on the pulse of local grievances.

There were all shades of reformers in Manchester, from the mild tinkerers with outmoded medieval by-laws to Spenceans who probably advocated outright revolution. Most men – and there was a strong female voice in Manchester too – opted either for trade union activity or parliamentary reform. Both of these were likely to be slow and unsure, but increasingly, as the summer of 1819 arrived, the authorities in the area became convinced that *every* working man was bent on revolution.

Ranged against the radicals in Manchester were the cotton magnates and they were spearheaded by largely high Tory, largely Anglican magistrates like James Norris and the Reverends William Hay and Charles Ethelston. The extent of Ethelston's Christianity can be gauged by a line from one of his sermons: 'Some of the reformers ought to be hanged and some of you are sure to be hanged – the rope is already round your necks.'[1]

Arguably the real power in the city was Joseph Nadin, from 1803 Deputy Constable in charge of sixty men. The only portrait of him shows a bull-necked, broken-nosed man with a permanent sneer. The people hated him. 'Nady Joe' was one of the last in a long line of thief-takers who walked a tightrope between legality and illegality. In a microcosm of what the central government was doing with its spies, stirring up and entrapping otherwise honest men, Nadin would regularly plant stolen goods on people and arrest them. He had virtually unlimited powers of arrest and took a rake-off from the city's forty-seven brothels. His language appalled many, even those not of Manchester's chapel and church going fraternity. He was corruption writ large and has been immortalized in a song of the time.

> With Hunt we'll go, we'll go,
> With Hunt we'll go, we'll go,
> We'll bear the flag of liberty,
>   In spite of Nady Joe.

The radicals of Manchester watched events in London closely and, after Spa Fields, activity in the area quietened down for a while, although the city did get its most fearless radical newspaper the following year in the form of the *Manchester Observer* run by Joseph Johnson, a brushmaker, and John Saxton, from the cotton trade.

Simmering under the surface was the Ardwick conspiracy, which broke at the end of March. Taking a leaf out of Watson's and Thistlewood's book, the plan was to burn the city, rescue prisoners from the New Bailey gaol and to join with other groups that, it was generally believed, would be doing the same thing across the country. The *Leeds Mercury* described this as 'a paper insurrection' in that there was no actual trouble. Even so, Nadin arrested Samuel Bamford and Dr Healey and they, with six others, were taken by coach in leg-irons to Coldbath Fields in London. No charges were levied, but since habeas corpus was still suspended, this hardly mattered.

In a fascinating glimpse of 'us v. them', Bamford and Healey were interrogated by the Privy Council. Bamford found Sidmouth very affable, with 'mild and intelligent eyes'. He was 'much more encouraging to freedom of speech than I had expected'. For all Bamford was an impressive figure, a man of courage and resolution, he was also at heart a weaver. It does not seem to have occurred to him that Sidmouth was being affable and encouraging in the hope that Bamford would say something self-incriminating which might hang him. When Healey's heavy Lancashire accent was incomprehensible to their Lordships they asked him to write his name down. Virtually illiterate, he couldn't, so he gave them his medical card instead. Some wag had filled in what was actually a prescription form with the words '200 tablespoonsful each 2 hours'. The Privy Council had a 'great titter' at this and Healey laughed too. A moment's reflection should have assured him that he was being laughed *at* and not *with*.

In January 1818 habeas corpus was restored, but the government quickly passed the Indemnity Bill so that no one who had been held during the suspension of habeas corpus could sue for redress. As always the oligarchy of gentlemen who ruled the country had hedged themselves in with total legal protection. In Manchester there was a wave of strikes among the spinners and, although no rational man could doubt that was an economic issue, the local magistrates saw it differently. 'The lower classes are radically corrupted,' wrote Ethelston. 'Their aim is revolution.' And Sidmouth, neither as mild nor as intelligent as Bamford believed, agreed.

> It is impossible for the Secretary of State to contemplate with indifference the danger likely to result . . . from the existence . . . of large bodies of men, exposed to the harangues of disaffected demagogues.

What struck the authorities at the local level was the excellent behaviour of the strikers. 'The peaceable demeanour of so many thousand unemployed men is not natural,' observed Major-General Byng, believing that some sinister Machiavellian force was behind this new-found obedience and organization. When women joined the increasing number of mass meetings, this too was taken as a sinister front, not unlike Watson's and Thistlewood's use of girls to distract the garrison of the Tower.

Early in 1819, the local radicals wrote to Henry Hunt inviting him to speak on distress, the Corn Laws, universal suffrage, his usual themes, on St Peter's Fields on 18 January. This time Hunt suggested that a Remonstrance rather than a futile Petition be sent to the Prince Regent. About 10,000 turned up, the meeting was peaceful and at the dinner which followed, at the Spread Eagle, the toasts included 'The Rights of Man . . . the immortal memory of Tom Paine . . . the venerable father of reform, Major Cartwright . . . our banished countryman William Cobbett' and, rather incongruously, 'the beautiful Lancashire witches'.[2]

There was a little trouble that night when Hunt attended the Theatre Royal. When the crowd recognized him he was given a standing ovation and found himself thrown out into the street by officers of the 7th Hussars, stationed in the city. The fact that Hunt was a gentleman who had raised his own militia company counted for nothing. By appearing as the darling of the mob he was lumped together, like all radicals as a 'libellous, seditious, factious, levelling, revolutionary, republican, democratical, aetheistical villain'.

By the summer of 1819, tensions were growing in the area. In June, at Stockport, 20,000 people attended to hear Sir Charles Wolseley, who had witnessed the storming of the Paris Bastille, say, 'and Heaven knows I would assist in storming the English Bastille'. It was not the first (or last) time that oratory got a little out of hand. *Some* people in the crowd may have taken Wolseley's words literally; all the authorities did. Magistrates, led by Norris, stepped up police patrols. Nadin's men seemed everywhere, listening at doorways, rummaging for hidden stashes of pikes[3] and particularly reporting on the increasing amount of drilling that was going on on local heaths and moorlands. There was actually nothing sinister in this. Anxious to avoid the image of a shifty, restless mob, many of the working class had followed the dictum of Bamford and others, to march briskly on and off the chosen meeting venue and to stand silently to attention while listening to speeches. Schoolchildren, after all, were drilled in the same way. But so, too, were soldiers. And if Nadin's men could not see any weapons, they were only prepared to put the worst configuration of what they were witnessing.

While the panicky authorities sanctioned the setting up of the Armed Association for the Preservation of Public Peace, composed of the magistrates, the borough reeves and the constables, the radicals invited their darling again for 9 August.

In fact, a whole series of mass meetings served to unnerve the magistrates. On 12 July an estimated 30,000 met at Newhall Hill in Birmingham to listen to Major Cartwright and Thomas Wooler of the *Black Dwarf*. A week later, at Hunslet, near Leeds, another meeting was held, well attended despite the fact that this was lunchtime on a Monday, when most loom and jenny operatives should have been hard at work. At Smithfield, London on the 21st, Hunt addressed a large crowd and terrified the authorities by saying that

> from and after the 1st day of January 1820 we cannot, conscientiously, consider ourselves as bound in equity by any future enactments which may be made by any persons styling themselves our representatives, other than those who shall be fully, freely and fairly chosen by the voices and votes of the largest proportion of the members of the state.

This was unbridled democracy, to all of the authorities the most appalling scenario imaginable. It is very likely that Arthur Thistlewood and some at least of his Cato Street conspirators were present at this meeting.

Back in Manchester, by August, the magistrates were now thoroughly rattled. The *Observer* advertised Hunt's meeting of the 9th and the authorities, on Home Office advice, cautioned people not to attend in that the meeting was illegal.[4] There was, of course, nothing illegal about meetings of that type. Only if a resolution was passed that Manchester should select its own MPs (in 1819 they had none) could the meeting be declared illegal, speakers arrested and the crowd dispersed. Until that happened, no law would have been broken.

In the event, Hunt's meeting was postponed until 16th, a Monday, which effectively gave both sides time to prepare. The loyalist and radical press attacked each other in print. 'They began this way', warned the *Manchester Mercury*, 'in the French Revolution . . . they ended, by sinking into a tyranny more galling than that which they had endured.' Hunt, for the radicals, wrote of the forthcoming meeting:

> Our enemies will seek every opportunity, by means of their sanguinary agents, to excite a Riot, that they may have a pretence for spilling our blood . . .[5]

Prophetic words.

The morning of Monday 16 August was dry and bright. Between 8 and 9, all over the outlying parishes, thousands of men, women and children, with hand-embroidered banners streaming overhead, made their way to the agreed assembly points and began the march to St Peter's Fields. Some flags were white, others green and red with inscriptions like 'Universal Suffrage', 'Election by Ballot', 'Liberty is the Birthright of Man'. The grimmest – and no doubt the one the authorities eyed most carefully – was Dr Healey's from Saddleworth – a black square with the stark white letters 'Equal Representation or Death'.

'There is no fear,' Bamford roared to his own Middleton contingent, 'for this day is our own.'

The Stockport column reached the field first. Perhaps 1,500 strong, they carried a cap of liberty and two banners. Eye-witness John Smith, watching the events from Mount Street that led onto the Fields, felt easier when he saw little children in the crowd, walking quietly with their parents.

When Henry Hunt arrived, famous white hat gleaming in the sun, in an open-topped barouche, a huge cheer went up. With him was Mrs Fildes of the Manchester Female Reformers and a huge procession. The band from Royton struck up 'Rule Britannia'.

By a little after midday everyone was ready. The estimates vary. Hunt, who had never addressed so large a meeting as this, assumed there were 200,000 there. Magistrate Thomas Tatton believed 30,000 nearer the truth. *The Times* later reported between 80,000 and 100,000. Today, the general consensus is 60,000 – an astonishing one-sixth of Lancashire's population and this probably did not include the mildly curious who had followed the processions out of sheer nosiness from the Exchange and Deansgate.

We will never know how inflammatory Hunt's speech was going to be or whether the huge crowds would have lifted his oratory to new heights, because he never made it. To one side of the Field, on a balcony of a house belonging to a Mr Buxton in Mount Street, the magistrates watched the growing spectacle with little short of terror. They did not see the women, the children, the lack of weaponry. They missed entirely the patriotic airs of the bands and the holiday atmosphere. All they saw was the mob.

All weekend they had been psyching up for this moment and made the fatal decision to arrest Hunt and the others now mounting the hustings in the centre of the Fields – John Knight, John Saxton, Mrs Fildes, Richard Carlile (up from London for the occasion) and, if they didn't get out of the way in time, various journalists up there with them. The chain of command was shaky. The magistrates scribbled a quick affidavit, signed by thirty loyalists at Buxton's house, to give them carte blanche to arrest Hunt. This was passed to Edward Clayton, the borough reeve, who in turn summoned Joe Nadin. The thief-taker told him flatly that it was impossible to arrest Hunt from the podium, especially with the untrained special constables he had with him that day. It was probably a sensible decision from a police point of view. Nadin was well aware how hated he was. The sight of him pulling Hunt down from his pedestal would probably have provoked a riot immediately. But it now meant that the magistrates had to resort to the army.

The build-up of tension in the area over the previous weeks had given the magistrates plenty of time to call up the military, but again the chain of command broke down. The ever-sensible Sir John Byng was at York, so his number two, Lieutenant-Colonel Guy L'Estrange, was left to command at Manchester. Under him were: eight troops of the 15th King's Hussars who had arrived at the end of July; both battalions of the 88th Foot and six companies of the 31st. He had a detachment of the Royal Horse Artillery under Major Dyneley, a die-hard psychopath, with two six-pounder guns. He also had all troops of the Cheshire Yeomanry Cavalry and three of the most local unit, the Manchester and Salford Yeomanry (MYC).

And that was the problem. The *Manchester Observer* had written scathingly of this unit:

> The yeomanry are generally speaking the fawning dependants of the great, with a few fools and a greater proportion of coxcombs who imagine they acquire considerable importance by wearing regimentals.

They were middle-class men (they had to be able to afford their horses and uniforms) who detested the working class and used every opportunity to keep such riff-raff in their place. On the other hand, they were appallingly part-time, without the training or skill to handle the kind of sensitive crowd control needed for a day like this. Ostentatiously, the regiment had sent its sabres to be sharpened only the previous week.

It may have been an unintentional over-reaction, but a separate note was sent to Major Trafford of the MYC independent of the one sent to L'Estrange. Accordingly, Trafford ordered *his* number two, Captain Hugh Hornby Birley, to mount his troops and get to the field to arrest Hunt. The first fatality of the day occurred off the field in fact. Alone of all the troops positioned at various places in Manchester that day, Trafford had allowed his men into pubs and the unit that left Pickford's Yard was late. One of them, who may have gone off to relieve himself, found the Yard empty and galloped off down Cooper Street, hoofs clattering on the cobbles, accoutrements jingling and sent Ann Fildes[6] and her child flying. Two-year-old William's skull was smashed on the cobblestones.

It was 20 to 2 when the yeomanry arrived on the field. Various accounts, both modern and contemporary, refer to them galloping, but this is unlikely, given the size of the crowd and the space involved. Later radical cartoons all showed racing horses, one in particular with the MYC portrayed as overfed 'Piccadilly butchers' wielding axes.

In fact the MYC carried the 1796 pattern Light Cavalry sword, heavy and curved. It was 33 inches long and weighed 2 lbs 2 oz. Designed for use from the saddle, in the right hands it was every bit as murderous as an axe.[7] The Manchester and Salford men wore dark blue Light Dragoon uniforms with white facings and black leather shakos. One of the men who came in for particular opprobrium that day was the trumpeter Edward Meagher, partly no doubt because he was so visible. Trumpeters wore white uniforms and rode grey horses.

There was only a narrow avenue through the crowd to the hustings and the conventional cavalry advance was conducted in line abreast. Unfamiliar with this situation, the MYC tried to follow Nadin and his constables down the avenue and found their formation broken. Panicking, with a sea of disbelieving and then hostile faces around them, the yeomen began to hack with their sabres, their horses whinnying and rearing in complete confusion. Captain Birley got to Hunt first and tried to arrest him. Hunt was polite, but firm and refused to be arrested by anyone but a civilian officer. At the same time, he was trying to shout above the rising screams of hysteria, to defuse the already desperate situation. 'Stand firm, my friends. They are in disorder already. This is a trick. Give them three cheers.'

With the yeomanry and the constables forming a dense mass around the hustings, Hunt came down the steps of his own accord. Others were not so lucky – Joseph Johnson was dragged off by his ankles and Mrs Fildes, whose dress got hooked on the wagon's nails, was hit across the body by (luckily) the flat of a yeomanry sword.

With dust eddying all around them on that sweltering day, the MYC now hacked about them in all directions. 'Have at their flags!' somebody shouted and with the constables intent on getting the speakers away, the unit began to rip down banners and smash the hustings.

At about this point, it looked to the watching magistrates as if the crowd was attacking the yeomanry – and probably by now, in self-defence, it was.

'Good God, sir,' Magistrate William Hulton screamed at L'Estrange. 'Don't you see they are attacking the Yeomanry? Disperse them.'

In the dust and confusion, Bamford recognized the 15th Hussars forming up at the far end of the Field. There was blood and chaos all around him. 'Nay, Tom Shelmerdine,' he heard an old woman say as she came face to face with a yeoman in the melee, 'thee will not hurt me, I know.' She had nursed him as a child. He rode over her.

'Damn you, I'll reform you!' he heard another bark and, 'Spare your lives? Damn your bloody lives.' Men were scrambling to get their women and children to safety, but nowhere was safe.

Briefly, a cheer went up when others saw the Hussars. These were no local bully-boys with class warfare on their minds, but the heroes of Waterloo, fought four years earlier. Some accounts say the men of the 15th wore their Waterloo medals pinned to their yellow-frogged jackets. We have no clear description of this regiment on the day. The army hated 'aiding the civil power' and no one in the regiment would have felt much pride in what happened in Manchester. Almost certainly, the troops wore scarlet shakos and as it was high summer, grey pantaloons and no pelisses. One of the few artefacts to have survived from St Peter's Fields is a scarlet horsehair plume from the 15th.

Again, some modern accounts say that the Hussars charged. Again, there was no room. For cavalry to reach the gallop, they need to go through the 'walk, march, trot' phases first, their swords 'at the slope' on their shoulders with the trot. There simply wasn't the space on what was now a battlefield to manoeuvre in this way. They probably came on at a walk, perhaps rising to a trot, but the effect would have been the same. People panicked and ran, trampling each other in their blind terror, crushing people with their own body weight, hurling others down into the open cellars that ringed the field.

Outside the Friends' Meeting House, some of the mob had found loose pieces of timber and began bashing the yeomanry with improvised sticks. The yeomanry in turn slashed with their sabres. Lieutenant Hylton Jolliffe of the 15th knocked aside the swords of two of them and yelled, 'Gentlemen, gentlemen, for shame, forbear. The people cannot get away.'

In perhaps half an hour, it was all over. Samuel Bamford surveyed the field as his shattered people stumbled back through the Manchester streets to hobble the twenty miles home, numb, shocked, unbelieving.

> . . . the hustings remained, with a few broken and hewed flag staves erect and a torn and gashed banner or two drooping, whilst over the whole field were strewed the caps, bonnets, hats, shawls and shoes . . . trampled, torn and bloody. The yeomanry had dismounted – some were easing their horses' girths, others adjusting their accoutrements; and some were wiping their sabres. Several mounds

of human beings still remained as they had fallen, crushed down and smothered. Some of these still groaning – others with staring eyes, were gasping for breath and others would never breathe again . . .[8]

No official enquiry was ever carried out into what happened at St Peter's Fields. John Ashton, Thomas Buckley, John Lees and William Dawson died as a result of sabre wounds, all delivered, almost certainly, by the MYC. James Crompton, William Fildes, Mary Heys, Arthur O'Neill and Martha Partington were crushed to death. For the death of Sarah Jones and William Bradshaw, no actual cause is given. Joseph Ashworth was shot by the police in the dispersal of a near-riot later that same night as the mob returned, angry and vengeful. Thomas Ashworth was a special constable who had got in the way of the yeomanry at the hustings and suffered the same fate as the rest of the dead.

Of the 420 officially injured (and there are likely to have been many more with superficial wounds) John Baker was beaten with constables' truncheons and lost a great deal of blood. Margaret Goodwin was trampled by horses and was losing the sight of both eyes. Catherine Colman had three ribs cracked. Mary Jervis had her calf sliced off. William Butterworth had his shoulder blade smashed by a sabre and the wound would not heal. Many of them were too ill to work, including 18-year-old John Lees who had fought as a drummer boy at Waterloo. He died of his injuries over two weeks later, his back slashed in several places, his elbow bone sticking through the skin. The woman who helped lay him out said, 'I never saw such a corpse as this in all my life.'

The leaders of the day languished in prison before their trials and Dr Healey was added to the list on 24 August. Bamford was also in the New Bailey by the 26th. Hunt was sent to Lancaster gaol, escorted personally by Nadin (who, uncharacteristically, bought him a meal en route) and the few, but effective, legal champions on the radical side swept into action. Sir Charles Wolseley stumped up the ridiculously high £1,000 bail for Hunt and two solicitors, James Harmer and Henry Dennison, brought charges against members of the MYC.

At every turn, the local authorities made life difficult. They delayed inquests on those who had died, refused to accept evidence that did not suit them and did their utmost to stifle the radical press. They thanked the MYC officially for 'their extreme forbearance exercised when insulted and defied by the rioters'.

And what was worse – they had the backing of the government. To be fair, this was not unreserved, but even tacit *acceptance* of the magistrates' actions was seen by the people as tantamount to wholesale approval. Sidmouth had been holidaying in Broadstairs when the clash happened and expressed his lily-livered congratulations that casualties had been kept to a minimum.

The Prince Regent, in one of his particularly badly judged decisions, rattled off *An Important Communication to the People of England* aboard the royal yacht moored off Christchurch, expressing his satisfaction with the 'prompt, decisive and efficient measure for the preservation of public tranquillity' observed that day.

In the real world, of justice and sanity, the *Manchester Observer* was first into the fray. It noted that the 'bastard soldiers' of the MYC were particularly targeting the women on the Field and the paper used for the first time the name 'Peter Loo'. Not only the yeomanry but the magistrates were singled out for scorn – 'A Friend to Order' promised he would 'send a ball' to the head of Magistrate Hay in September and James Neville in the same month wrote from Liverpool:

> Shame! Shame! That a clergyman should head a band of privileged murderers and invite them to acts of bloodshed and massacre.

One hundred and fifteen miles to the south of St Peter's Fields a troop of the Warwickshire Yeomanry was clattering through Smith Street in the county town when a crowd developed, spitting at them and calling them 'Manchester butchers'. The radical cartoonists showed the MYC sabring the crowd and a little girl with her arms raised up under the flying hoofs crying, 'Pray, Sir, don't kill Mammy. She only came to listen to Mr Hunt.'

Bamford wrote:

> If the people were to rise and smite their enemies, was not this the time? Was every enormity to be endured and this after all? Were we still to lie down like whipped hounds, whom nothing could rouse to resistance? Were there not times and seasons and circumstances, under which the common rules of wisdom become folly, prudence became cowardice and submission became criminal? And was not the present one of these times and seasons?[9]

Arthur Thistlewood could not have read these words because Bamford would not write them for another thirty years. But he and the other men of Cato Street shared their sentiments and made their plans and took their chance.

Chapter 9

Men of Colour

On 15 September 1819, while he was still free on bail, Henry Hunt made a triumphal entry into London. The various associations and societies turned out in force with flags, bands and horsemen. One banner was white with a black crape border, inscribed to the victims of Peterloo. In a carriage behind Hunt's rode the heroes of Spa Fields – Watson, Thistlewood, Preston. John Keats wrote to his brother:

> It would take me a whole day and a quire of paper to give you anything like detail. The whole distance from the Angel at Islington to the Crown and Anchor was lined with multitudes.[1]

The authorities watched all this with unease. The Manchester magistrates, realizing they had been heavy-handed to say the least, now talked themselves into believing that they had been right. Magistrate Norris wrote of St Peter's Fields:

> They came in a threatening manner – they came under the banners of death, thereby showing they meant to overturn the Government.

And a Yorkshire loyalist wrote:

> I consider such meetings . . . to be nothing more or less than risings of the people; and I believe that these . . . if suffered to continue, would end in open rebellion.

There is a suggestion that Peterloo was one of those freak occurrences occasioned by a unique set of circumstances. This is nonsense. Such violence could have erupted anywhere in 1819–20 because the loyalists were terrified of the people and prepared to use excessive force against them. Some historians have tried to distance Sidmouth and the Cabinet, to imply that the Manchester authorities exceeded the 'spirit of the Home Office'. The 'spirit of the Home Office' was to keep working men in their place, especially if such men cheered their heroes like Hunt or Thistlewood; or if they carried any sort of banner demanding justice. In one of the most famous radical cartoons of the Manchester massacre the cherubic face of the Prince Regent floats above the slashing yeomanry with the words 'Cut them down, my brave boys!' This was the general attitude of the authorities, from the highest in the land to the Manchester Bench and below.

By the end of the year, many leading radicals, whether they had been involved in Manchester or not, were in gaol or awaiting trial on a variety of charges; Hunt, Bamford, Saxton and others who had been unceremoniously bundled from St Peter's Fields; James Wroe of the *Manchester Observer*; Burdett, Cartwright, Wolseley, Carlile.

What no one outside Manchester knew was that the heart had been ripped out of the local radical movement. Bamford wrote of men sharpening scythes and muttering in darkness about retribution. An ugly crowd milled for a night or two around the house of Edward Meagher, trumpeter of the MYC. But nothing actually happened. London, in particular, seemed unaware of this or perhaps they merely wanted to keep the open-air meeting alive. On 29 August there was a huge rally at Smithfield, at which Arthur Thistlewood was principal speaker. An even larger one took place the following week in Westminster, with Burdett, Cartwright and John Thelwall holding forth. And there were rumblings in the provinces too. In October and November there was talk of pike-production in smithies across Newcastle, Sheffield and Birmingham. Drilling was carried out in Halifax, Wigan, Bolton, Blackburn and Huddersfield.

It was in these weeks that Watson, Thistlewood and Preston began to plan their own revolution. Admittedly, the information came largely from an informer, John Williamson, but the authorities certainly believed it. The rising was initially planned to take place on the day of Bartholomew Fair, 28–29 August and the police were employed rummaging through agricultural baskets, oyster-tubs and sausage-stalls looking for pike-heads. The Life Guards and Royal Horse Guards were on stand-by just in case. By this time, it is clear that Thistlewood, not Watson, was the prime mover. He held secret meetings at midnight, made enquiries as to the number of cannon in certain London barracks and arranged for a crowd to cheer

Richard Carlile as he arrived for his trial at the King's Bench.

What prevented any rising at Bartholomew Fair (or anywhere else in London in these weeks) was an upswing in the economy, making the weavers of Spitalfields for instance less likely to get involved in dangerous politics. It didn't help that Watson, in particular, kept his plans a close secret in case of spies or informers, thereby confusing everybody, including himself. But the major reason, by November, was the passing of the government's Six Acts.

The term 'police state' did not exist in 1819, but the measures rushed through by the government after parliament reconvened at the end of November almost defined it. The Training Prevention Act prevented the unarmed, silent drilling which had so unnerved Byng and Nadin's constables. Anyone found guilty would be liable to transportation for seven years or imprisonment for two. The Seizure of Arms Act gave the authorities the right to search any premises or individual for illegal weapons, especially no doubt the dreaded pike. The disturbing point about this was that the oath of only one witness was necessary for this law to be put into motion. When that witness was a spy or the searchers were Nadin's corrupt, evidence-planting constables, the scope for injustice was huge. The Misdemeanours Act was designed to rush judgments through the courts. The longer men like Hunt were allowed to wander round on bail stirring up discontent, the worse a situation was likely to get. The Seditious Meetings Act prevented the holding of meetings of more than fifty people without the written consent of a magistrate or sheriff. Even with consent, such meetings could be dispersed within fifteen, as opposed to sixty, minutes and there were to be no banners, no outsiders and no semblance of drill. The government was also aware of the inflammatory potential of newspapers and journals, no doubt the *Manchester Observer* foremost among them. The Blasphemous and Seditious Libels Act threatened radical editors (and indeed non-radical ones like Thomas Barnes of *The Times*) with severe punishment including exile for articles likely to disturb the peace. The Newspaper and Stamp Duties Act, finally, hit journals like the *Black Dwarf* and *Twopenny Trash* with duties for the first time. This meant that cheap editions were now a thing of the past; editors had to deposit large sums of money against any fines that might be imposed.

It is true that habeas corpus was not again suspended, but it is difficult to imagine how much tighter the radical cause could have been hemmed in. At a stroke, freedom of the press was censored. The right of Englishmen to bear arms was destroyed. The open-air meeting, the most public expression of working-class and popular grievance, was savagely curtailed. None of this excuses what nearly happened in Grosvenor Square two months later, but it does place it in context. As long as men like Lord Ellenborough could see 'no possible good to be derived to the country from having statesmen at the loom and politicians at the spinning jenny', the only recourse open to the hard-liners of the radical movement was illegality and bloodshed.

In February 1818 the leader of the Cato Street conspiracy, Arthur Thistlewood, continued his headlong rush to self-destruction by challenging Lord Sidmouth to a duel. He published an open letter to the man, listing a whole variety of grievances, some personal, some national. As a result, Thistlewood found himself in prison, first at the King's Bench, then in Horsham. According to E P Thompson, Sidmouth paid for Thistlewood's time in gaol personally, but if he did, Thistlewood was singularly ungrateful, because on his release he not only sent a list of damages to Sidmouth, but had them published in pamphlet form. Thistlewood claimed he had been all set to emigrate with his wife and son to America and that Sidmouth owed him £180.

A rather miffed John Cam Hobhouse, Sidmouth's Under Secretary, told Thistlewood his demands were unreasonable. Thistlewood replied that he hoped Hobhouse

> thenceforth . . . will cast off [his] hypocritical saintlyness . . . and appear in no other character but [his] own, that of the willing tool of the vilest of mankind.

And he sent Hobhouse a list of belongings from his family that he wanted back – a coat, a pair of pantaloons, a waistcoat, three shirts, two pairs of stockings, a hat, a coat, waistcoat and trousers for his little boy, as well as the lad's bed, box of colours, inkstand, two writing books, music books and several goose-quills. Not to mention Mrs. Thistlewood's umbrella.

By the autumn of 1819, Watson, Thistlewood and the rest had organized the mysterious Committee of Two Hundred; mysterious, because when Thistlewood needed their support in Cato Street, they were nowhere to be seen. Some of them certainly can be named. John Gale Jones, the old Jacobin who had been active in London radicalism since the 1790s was there and apart from the old Spa Fields 'gang' of Watson, Preston and Thistlewood himself, Samuel Waddington had joined the throng. They were backed by various hard-line publications – the *Republican*, the *Medusa* and the *Cap of Liberty*.

Increasingly the centre of activities for Thistlewood in the weeks before Cato Street became the White Lion, in Wych Street, alluded to several times in the subsequent trials. 'Here of an evening,' deposed an eye-witness,

> a select committee assembled and no others were admitted. This was the room in which the most private transactions were carried on. Mr Thistlewood or Dr Watson always came out into the passage to speak to any person who called there on business. In a very large room upstairs . . . upwards of a hundred ill-looking persons have assembled of an evening; in it the open committee and loose members of the society met . . . Here their processions etc were arranged; their flags . . . kept while the more private business was carried on below in the parlour.[2]

It was as well, given the events of February, that Henry Hunt had already distanced himself from Thistlewood. He disliked Watson and John Gale Jones – 'You are a damned officious, meddling fellow' he told him – and felt generally that the hero of Peterloo should be accorded even more adulation in London than he actually received. While Hunt and others still advocated slow, peaceful means to secure change, ultra-radicals like Thistlewood were now, especially after the Six Acts, going their own way.

A national day was planned for mass meetings, with 1 November, All Hallows Day, as the target. All over the North plans were being made for this throughout October and it says a great deal for the murderous shift of inclination that Major-General Byng, keeping his ears to the ground in Yorkshire, should now believe that Thistlewood, not Hunt, was the key. In the event, only a few meetings actually happened, partly because Hunt officially washed his hands of it. In an unworthy moment – although it may have been to avoid bloodshed – he fell back on the old expediency of accusing Thistlewood himself of being a spy.

Throughout November, the radicals tore themselves apart in their own newspapers, the loyalists clearly delighted by this turn of events. In the first week of that month, William Cobbett came home from his exile in America, bringing with him the bones of Tom Paine. Cobbett *in absentia* was far more powerful than Cobbett in the flesh. He was never a hands-on rabble-rouser and he was out of the swim of the monumental events of a cold, wet November in England. Putting forward only one proposal after the Six Acts, he set up a fund for reform to be raised by the unions, but since only he would know how much was in it, only he would decide how it should be spent, the whole thing looked like the act of a man who was either deranged or needed to recoup personal cash fast.

There is no doubt that, at the end of 1819, there was a vacuum in the radical movement of this country. Into it, with both feet, stepped Arthur Thistlewood. Subsequent historians, building on ever more lurid accounts that appeared shortly after Cato Street, have branded the man as an 'atom-bomb traitor' (R J White), given to 'personal neuroses' (John Stanhope) and even 'Britain's first professional terrorist' (Clive Bloom). None of these quite fits the bill. We have already charted what is known of Thistlewood's career up to 1819, but what of his followers?

Richard Tidd was born in Lincolnshire, probably in 1775, and the first we hear of him he was apprenticed to a Mr Cante of Grantham. Apprentices normally began work with a master at the age of 12. Four years later he left for Nottingham. Again, apprenticeships normally ran for seven years, so it may be that Tidd never actually finished his 'probation' as a shoemaker. He would have arrived in Nottingham about 1791 when the town already had a reputation as a turbulent place prone to food riots. He stayed here for two and a half years, leaving at about the time when Jacobins were ducked in a local pond. We have no idea of young Tidd's politics at this time, but the thumbnail sketch provided by Wilkinson paints a picture of a dodgy character, on the run from *something*. By 1795 he was in London, presumably working as a shoemaker (a particularly radical profession at the time), and in 1803 'he thought it prudent to retreat into Scotland'.[3]

The reason for this flight was that there was a price on his head – £100 to be exact – because he had tried to vote illegally for Francis Burdett against Mr Mainwaring at the Middlesex election. Middlesex was famous as the most 'open' county (i.e. with the largest number of voters) but this did not apply to Tidd, who was not actually a freeholder and therefore had no vote.[4] Like all Wilkinson's summaries of the conspirators' lives, a great deal of the basic chronology is flawed. 'He was engaged in the conspiracy for which Colonel Despard suffered', Wilkinson writes and this, more than the Middlesex election, probably explains his rapid departure from London.

Where Tidd lived in Scotland is not recorded, but after five years he probably thought the coast was clear and came south again, living and working in Rochester for a further nine years. Wilkinson also records that Tidd worked a scam on and off for a number of years and this would have been made easier by the fact that he kept on the move. At a time when volunteers for the army were welcomed with open arms, Tidd enlisted in a number of regiments, took the king's shilling and the offered bounty. This was a cash inducement for likely lads to sign up. True, most of it was whittled away at the barracks for mysterious 'expenses' but for a short time it was in the volunteer's hands. This was Tidd's window of opportunity and he took it, working his way (according to Wilkinson) through half the regiments of the army under assumed names.

None of this *quite* accorded with Tidd's claim at his trial:

I always was a hard-working man, working sixteen and eighteen hours a day. I never had any time to spare, except on a Sunday.[5]

According to Wilkinson, Tidd was back in London by 10 March 1818, living at 4 Hole-in-the-Wall Passage, Baldwin's Gardens, near Brook's Market. He had a wife, Ann, a brother and a daughter, Mary Barker, who spoke for the defence at her father's trial. 'From that time on,' wrote Wilkinson, Tidd 'attended all Mr Hunt's meetings, public and private and was present at all the subsequent Radical meetings.'

Tidd denied this in court – 'I never attended any meeting after the acts to prevent illegal meetings' (November 1819) – but he did claim it was fellow conspirator George Edwards who told him he had it on the highest authority that meetings could go ahead as long as they focused solely on parliamentary reform.

For much of his life, the rather gloomy Tidd had a presentiment that he would one day be hanged. He was 'unhappily', wrote Wilkinson, 'too good a prophet'.

James Ings was born in Portsea of a family of 'respectable tradesmen' with a reasonable amount of money. Although at his trial he claimed to be 'a man of no education and very humble abilities', he could clearly write and became a butcher. Hit by poor trade in the vagaries of the war and peacetime economy, he had to sell up his tenements and move to London. By this time he had a wife and four children and, with the money he still had, set up a butcher's shop in the West End. This didn't work either, so he moved to the cheaper East End, setting up another butcher's shop in Baker's Row, Whitechapel. Ings tried to make a go of this 'from midsummer to Michaelmas', but the long, hot summer was against him. With no means of refrigeration, butchers' premises were particularly at the mercy of the weather and Ings moved around the corner to Old Montague Street where he opened a coffee-shop with the last of his money. He finally pawned his watch to be able to send his wife and children back to Portsmouth.

Coffee-houses, like pubs, were centres of radical politics and Ings began to read and distribute pamphlets like Richard Carlile's. Here, too, the men of Cato Street began to drift. Ings testified:

> After my wife had left me, there was a man who used to come and take a cup of coffee at my shop. I never had nothing to do with politics, but he began to speak about the Manchester massacre.

This was George Edwards and from then until 23 February, he rarely left Ings alone.

Abandoning the coffee-shop, the ex-butcher moved in January to Primrose Street, near the Fleet market. By now he was virtually destitute, trying desperately to sell his furniture. And so he was grateful for the bread and cheese Edwards bought for him in the White Hart and even more when Edwards provided a room in the house of John Brunt. What Edwards did not make clear, at least at first, was that there were strings attached.

John Thomas Brunt was a Londoner, born in Union Street, off Oxford Street, probably in 1782. Although his father was a tailor, young Brunt became apprenticed at the slightly elderly age of 14, to a Mr Brookes, maker of ladies' shoes, just down the road. When Brunt's father died as the boy reached 18, his mother bought him out of his apprenticeship and he effectively worked for her for some years. At 21 he became articled to a boot-closer and quickly excelled at the trade. For several years a window display in a Strand shop exhibited a prize-winning boot made by Brunt. Two years later he married a 'respectable young woman' named Welch who gave birth to their son on 1 May 1806 – by coincidence exactly fourteen years before the boy's father would die on the scaffold.

Brunt did not explain how he came to be in Paris shortly after the end of the war, but it was probably connected with the presence of Wellington's army of occupation, still of course requiring boots which Brunt made. While at Cambrai, Brunt met Robert Adams, who may still have been a serving soldier with the Royal Horse Guards. 'Adams worked for the officers', Brunt said at his trial, implying that this was in the leather trade in a private capacity. Jealous of the quality of his work, Adams threatened Brunt that he would kill him and Brunt took the hint and travelled to Lilsle to work for an English tradesman named Brailsford.

Clearly, Brunt had taken his son to France with him and on their return, found that his wife had 'lost her senses' and was in the asylum of St Luke's, believing that her husband and son had been murdered. She was released into his care and must have been extremely grateful for this. At the time, St Luke's had 300 patients and was in woeful need of upgrading. Its superintendent preferred chains to other forms of restraint and believed that the insane responded only to strict discipline. There were high windows without glass that were covered at night with iron shutters. Brunt returned to the boot trade, doing well enough by 1819 to have his own apprentice, a lad named Joseph Hale. This boy would testify against him in court.

The last of the men to be hanged for his part in Cato Street was William Davidson, the enigmatic 'man of colour', who so fascinated his contemporaries and, Thistlewood perhaps aside, remains the most complex of the men of Cato Street. He was born in 1786, in Kingston, the second son of the Attorney-General of Jamaica and a slave woman. Wilkinson described the father as a 'man of considerable legal knowledge and talent' and this sort of master/slave, black/white relationship was not uncommon. Young Davidson was technically a mulatto, a half-breed, but portraits of him show very definite African features. It was perhaps rather a bizarre decision to send the 14-year-old William to England to study for the law, but presumably Davidson senior had notions of the boy returning to Jamaica to practise. His mother was bitterly opposed to it, but lost that particular battle and the boy 'having learned the first rudiments of education' went to an academy in Edinburgh where he focused on mathematics. After this he moved to Liverpool with letters of introduction to his father's agent.

For nearly three years, Davidson worked as an articled clerk for a Liverpool lawyer. The work was dull (Benjamin Disraeli would tire of it equally quickly a few years later), the hours long and much time was spent laboriously copying legal documents with a quill pen. Born by the sea as he was, Davidson may have had a natural wanderlust and signed as a clerk on board a merchant vessel. Less than a day out from port, however, he found his duties consisted of scrubbing decks with the other hands.

Clearly, sailing in wartime carried its own risks. Davidson's ship was stopped by a British man of war and the crew impressed. At his trial, the 'man of colour' claimed to have 'ventured my life fifteen times for my country and my King' and if this was true, his time aboard the warship was the only possible opportunity for this. Six months later, he was back home and somehow managed to get out of the navy, sending begging letters to his father's friend. The upshot was that Davidson was now apprenticed to a cabinet-maker and all thoughts of the law seem to have gone out of the window.

Davidson rarely seems to have been without female companionship and was on the point of marrying a Liverpool merchant's daughter when her friends got wind of it and whisked her away. We have already seen the outrage caused by Colonel Despard's mixed marriage, to the extent that even subsequent generations of his family claimed that the woman was merely a servant. The loss of his bride-to-be was naturally a blow to Davidson, who decided to go back to Kingston on board a West Indiaman.

History repeated itself and Davidson was once again pressed into the navy. This time he deserted at the first opportunity and, cadging from friends, became a journeyman. Wilkinson's narrative becomes confusing at this point. Technically, desertion in wartime was a hanging offence, but there is no further mention of this and Davidson's mother now appears on the scene, paying the boy 2 guineas a week through her agent (presumably her husband's friend from Liverpool).

In Litchfield, Davidson was employed by Mr Bullock, a cabinet-maker who was impressed with the young man's high levels of skill, earning up to 4 guineas a week. With a total of 6 guineas a week at his disposal, Davidson began to pay court to the 16-year-old Miss Salt, who seems to have been a feisty girl who met the handsome mulatto secretly. Since the girl would come into an inheritance of £7,000 when she came of age, it was clearly worth Davidson's staying around. Mrs Salt reluctantly agreed to the marriage, keeping her husband in the dark. When Mr Salt discovered the truth, he lay in wait for Davidson in his garden and fired a pistol ball through the suitor's hat (presumably aiming for his head). Salt summoned a constable and Davidson was charged with attempted robbery.

An unusually upright magistrate believed Davidson's version of events, set the man free and imprisoned the girl's father. A deal was struck – Salt would allow the marriage if Davidson brought no charges. So far, so good, but a hidden clause was that Miss Salt could only marry when she came of age. Davidson was prepared to wait; she was not. When her father sent her to 'a distant part of the country' she found someone else and married him instead.

Davidson was heart-broken. He bought poison from a chemist in Litchfield and swallowed it. He lost his nerve however and told a friend who provided an antidote, thus saving the man's life. A kind of pattern develops in the lives of the Cato Street conspirators. Reversals, life's upheavals, downward paths – all play their part, leaving the men particularly vulnerable and disordered. Davidson let his business slide and had soon spent virtually all of the £1,200 his mother had settled on him in a London bank.

We have no time-line for any of this, but after the collapse of his Midlands business he came to London and worked for Mr Cox, a cabinet-maker in the Haymarket. At the same time he became a Sunday school teacher in a chapel in Walworth and for the first time we have a religious light thrown onto Cato Street. Among those condemned to death in April 1820, only Davidson turned to his God. In Walworth, the cabinet-maker fell foul of the law again. The exact details are unknown and Davidson mentioned them in the Cato Street trial in one of the earliest – and weakest – attempts to play the 'race card' on record. He was clearly in the habit of touching up not only his female colleagues in the Walworth Chapel Sunday School, but some of the girls as well. Wilkinson wrote:

> He habitually indulged in attempts of a gross and indelicate nature on the persons . . . way-laying them on their return home . . . from divine worship and taking improper liberties with them.

He was not the first or the last Sunday school teacher to abuse his position of trust and for a while, his targets put up with it. One of them finally reported matters to the committee who conducted an enquiry and kicked Davidson out. 'His habitual lying, prevarication and intrigue' had become as obvious as his 'brutal propensities'.

At the Cato Street trial, Davidson claimed that one black man looked very like another; that he had been wrongly accused in the Walworth case; and that he had found the real culprit and forced him to apologize to the young lady concerned. Since, at the time, Davidson was trying to pretend that he was an innocent bystander at Cato Street, a man in the wrong place at the wrong time and there were perfectly innocent explanations for his carrying a sword and carbine that night, it all merely underlines Wilkinson's obvious contempt for the man.

In 1816, Davidson went into business for himself in Walworth and married a widow, Mrs Lane, who had four small children. The year was a bad one for cabinet-makers as it was for everyone else and he lost trade, moving to Marylebone. It was here and it was then that his political activities began.

The men we have met so far were hanged for their involvement in Cato Street, but six others escaped the drop and a seventh never even appeared in court. The six are notoriously vague. Because they changed their plea to guilty after the trials of the five, they did not directly face the wrath of the court themselves, so our knowledge of them is limited. Usually, they appear as a collective group, huddled in a smoky tap-room muttering mutiny. We have no clear picture of them as individuals.

James Wilson was a tailor; Richard Bradburn a carpenter; James Gilchrist a shoemaker; Charles Cooper a bootmaker; John Monument a shoemaker and John Shaw a carpenter. Together with Ings, Tidd and Davidson, they were all arrested in the hay-loft at Cato Street or the area nearby. Cooper lived in Garden-Court, Baldwin's Gardens, and most of them were local men whose lodgings could be found in the rabbit warrens off Oxford Street and Holborn. On the warrant issued for arrest on the night of 23 February, in addition to some of the names above[6] were Abel Hall, a tailor, and John Palin, a child's chair-maker and former corporal in the East London Militia.

Not all the Cato Street conspirators were caught. Some got away from the notorious hay-loft and melted into the London underworld. But one who escaped deserved, perhaps, more than anyone to die. And he did not even appear in court, although his name was mentioned by every defendant and most witnesses. Among the 162 potential witnesses listed to attend at the Old Bailey Session House in April, one name stands out – that of George Edwards, modeller of Ranelagh Place.

In the trial of Arthur Thistlewood, the witness Robert Adams, a former conspirator who had turned king's evidence referred to Edwards sitting in the White Hart on 19 February. It took him a while for his eyes to acclimatize after the glare of the snow outside, but he saw the man there in the company of the others. And it was Edwards who, in the same pub on the next night, announced that a Cabinet dinner was due to be held at Lord Harrowby's in Grosvenor Square. On the 21st, Edwards was busy making 'fusees' (hand-grenades) along with Ings and Abel Hall.

Joseph Hale, Brunt's teenaged apprentice at Fox Court, remembered Edwards as a regular visitor to his master's house, more often indeed than Adams. He believed him to be an artist.

For the defence, Mary Barker, the daughter of Richard Tidd, remembered Edwards often visiting her father's house at Hole-in-the-Wall Passage and that he took away boxes she now knew to be ammunition: 'I do not know what Edwards was.' But Thistlewood's defence counsel, Mr Curwood, knew. The jury, he said, had heard of the name of Edwards in this case. This man, who lived at 166, Fleet Street, who afterwards lived at Ranelagh Place, why was this man not called? He was not an accomplice in any criminal degree, as must be inferred from the conduct of the Government in letting him go quite at large. Why was this man not called? They would then have the spy to support the testimony of the informer Adams. He could tell the jury why; because it was remembered what had been the effect of calling a witness of a similar description on a former occasion.

Curwood was of course conjuring up visions of John Castle in the Spa Fields trial of Dr Watson and the result was that he and his testimony were put out of court altogether and had no other effect on the minds of the jury, than to convince them that the whole was a fabrication. Did their Lordships, berobed and bewigged on the High Bench, squirm? Did they feel an atom of remorse? Of guilt? Of shame? Of course not. If they knew – and bearing in mind the fact that they so clearly were the establishment, they must have – then they believed that planting George Edwards in the heart of the Cato Street conspiracy was not only fair and just, but part of their duty. Castle, with his ineptitude in the dock and his long history of crime and misdemeanours, failed to hang Watson. Oliver, altogether cleverer and kept out of court, had helped to hang Brandreth.

Now, their Lordships merely waited to see what Edwards could achieve for the men of Cato Street, all of them, in their different ways, men of colour.

Chapter 10

'Dreadful Riot and Murder'

The plan was almost certainly Thistlewood's and it went like this. All the king's ministers were to be targeted and murdered in their town houses. The Duke of Wellington, as Master-General of the Ordnance, had his famous house at Hyde Park Corner with its grandiose address of 1 London. Lord Liverpool, the Prime Minister, of course resided at 10 Downing Street. Lord Castlereagh, the Foreign Secretary, lived in St James's Square, not a stone's throw from the haunt of prostitutes and gambling 'hells'. Lord Harrowby, President of the Privy Council, had his house at 39 Grosvenor Square. And so on. In fact, the only prominent address not whispered about in the half-darkness of some radical tavern in the early weeks of 1820 was Carlton House, the private residence of the Prince Regent. Perhaps he was considered such a nonentity that he was not worth killing. Or perhaps, taking a leaf out of the French revolutionaries' book, they intended to make the heir to the throne some sort of citizen-king.

The next decision to be made was – when? William Harrison, as an ex-Life Guards man, had been talking to one of his old comrades still in the service and gleaned some useful information. For such multiple assassinations to work, there would have to be minimal strike capability from the authorities – the police and the army. The death of George III provided the solution. On the evening of 29 January, the 'old, mad, blind, despised and dying king'[1] as Shelley called him, finally succumbed after years of mental and physical pain. On 31 January, the Prince Regent was proclaimed George IV and troops outside Carlton House cheered dutifully. It was a month of mixed emotions for George. On the one hand, he was king in name as well as deed after effectively ruling the country for nine years. On the other hand, his father had died only six days after his younger brother, the Duke of Kent. And the new king's mind was already bent to his first royal problem – what to do about his ghastly, estranged wife, Caroline of Brunswick.

The old king's funeral was scheduled for 15 February and Harrison's old comrade had assured him, in the course of an innocent conversation, that every London soldier would be at Windsor. Thistlewood reasoned, perhaps bizarrely, that they would be too exhausted to get back to London to handle a revolutionary mob on the rampage.

The killing of the ministers was to be decided by lot. The conspirators would be divided into units, each one led by an assassin. During these discussions, duly debated and voted on, in true democratic fashion, James Brunt seemed to be keener on total, unswerving loyalty than anyone else. 'Whatever man the lot fall upon', a witness quoted him at his trial, 'and fails, I swear by all that is good, that man shall be run through on the spot.'[2]

While all this slaughter was going on, John Palin's task would be to disable various army barracks by throwing grenades into the straw. In the case of cavalry barracks, like that of the Life Guards in Knightsbridge, the stables were built below the men's sleeping quarters so that the rising flames would be easily lit in the first place and would engulf the first storey. Men and horses would die, either from their burns or from choking on the acrid fumes. Whatever the outcome, the troopers would be too busy fighting fires and saving lives to worry about little things like insurrection.

Conspirator Cook's job was to secure artillery. There were a number of mini-arsenals in London, apart from the Tower and Cook's remit was to grab them before the authorities did. There were two field pieces at the Artillery Ground and more at the London Light Horse Volunteer barracks, both off Holborn. Thus armed, the revolutionaries and their by now growing cohorts would move east, placing their cannon in the Cornhill and next to the Royal Exchange and would call upon the residents of the Mansion House to surrender. This would become the headquarters of the new provisional government which would be set up under Thistlewood. The next target was the Bank of England and the decision was made to preserve the huge account books so that proof of the government's financial mismanagement and plain embezzlement could be shown.

Other members of the team were to patrol the routes out of London and still others to disable the telegraph so that the capital was essentially sealed off. Communication during the night would be by the call sign 'button'. One conspirator would whisper 'b-u-t' to another, who would reply 't-o-n' and messages could be sent in this way from street to street.

Part of this plan was lifted directly from the mish-mash of Spa Fields. Part of it smacked of Despard. None of it made any real sense. Unlike Spa Fields, Thistlewood does not seem to have worked on soldiers' loyalties, so the only reliance was on most troops being out of town for the king's funeral. In the days before the event, a number of conspirators were buying up weapons – the odd carbine, blunderbuss and sword. The money seemed to come mostly from Edwards who, oddly, went from the poverty of a model-maker with little work, to a man well dressed, able to buy weapons and stand drinks. The equipment obtained, powder and ball shot as well as the makings of hand-grenades, was stored at Brunt's house in Fox Court and Tidd's in Hole-in-the-Wall. There had to be a base for operations and this is where Harrison came in. He acquired a hay-loft over a cowshed or stable in Cato Street, off the Edgware Road, and everything seemed ready.

It was now, almost at the last moment, that the plan changed. The king's funeral idea was dropped, exactly why is unclear and on Tuesday morning, 22 February, Edwards brought news to the committee at Brunt's that the Cabinet dinners, cancelled in respect of the king's death, were to be resumed the following night at Lord Harrowby's in Grosvenor Square. Thistlewood sent out for a paper and sure enough, there it was, listed in the *New Times*. Brunt was delighted

> Now I will be damned if I do not believe there is a God. I have often prayed that those thieves [the Cabinet] may be collected all together, in order to give us a good opportunity to destroy them and now God has answered my prayer.

The new plan was now as follows. The conspirators had the time and place – Grosvenor Square shortly after 7. Everyone would be in the square by then, taking advantage of the buildings and trees as hiding places and Thistlewood would knock on Harrowby's door with the pretext of an urgent note. The servants would be eliminated first, threatened with pistols. If they refused to obey or showed any signs of fight, hand-grenades were to be lobbed in amongst them while the leaders went for the Cabinet. Ings in particular saw it all very clearly:

> I will enter the room first, I will go in with a brace of pistols, a cutlass and a knife in my pocket and after the two swordsmen [the ex-cavalrymen Harrison and Adams] have despatched them, I will cut

every head off that is in the room and Lord Castlereagh's head and Lord Sidmouth's I will bring away in a bag . . . As soon as I get into the room I shall say 'Well, my Lords, I have as good men here as the Manchester Yeomanry. Enter citizens and do your duty.'[3]

By Wednesday morning, Thistlewood was drawing up last- minute paperwork. Again in Brunt's house in Fox Court, he was drafting a manifesto when Adams arrived. He had written:

Your tyrants are destroyed. The friends of liberty are called upon to come forward. The provisional government is now sitting.

It had that day's date, 23 February, and was signed by James Ings, Secretary. And that, as far as anyone knows, is as far as plans for the revolution ever got.

'Cato Street is rather an obscure street,' wrote George Wilkinson in his preface to the trial transcripts, 'and inhabited by persons in an humble class of life.' It runs parallel with Newnham Street, joining John and Queen Street. It was virtually a cul-de-sac in 1820, open at one end for carriages and almost closed at the other by posts. The conspirators' headquarters was a dilapidated stable near the open end, belonging to a General Watson, who was away in Europe. Drawings made at the time show a two-storey, flat-roofed building with a set of double doors (for carriages) and a side door on the ground floor with one window covered with a shutter. There were two windows and a door on the first floor, the door presumably to allow hay to be lifted in and out from a wagon in the street below.

A single set of stairs led up to the loft which was divided into three rooms, one large, two small. Only one of the smaller rooms had a fireplace and on the night in question, as well as conspirators and their weaponry in residence for what Thistlewood called 'the West End job', there was a hammock, a carpenter's bench, a chaff cutter, a tool chest, a tub and a corn measure.

On the afternoon of 23 February, various people were seen coming and going into the stable, each time locking the door behind them. Sacking was nailed across the upstairs windows to minimize nosiness, but the conspirators had reckoned without the curiosity of their neighbours. George Kaylock at 22 Cato Street saw Harrison and somebody else going in about 5 o'clock. Kaylock spoke to him, to be told that Harrison had taken two rooms in the building and was going to 'do them up'. Between 5 and 7 at least

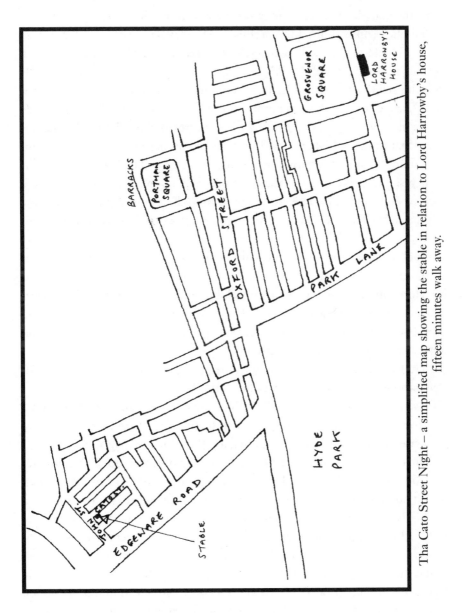

The Cato Street Night – a simplified map showing the stable in relation to Lord Harrowby's house, fifteen minutes walk away.

twenty 'decorators' were seen arriving. Richard Monday, living next door at number 23 saw Davidson standing under an archway at 20 past four. He knew the man, having seen him in company with Firth the cow-keeper, from whom Harrison had hired the premises. Monday had just come home from work. He had his tea and went to the pub (almost certainly the Horse and Groom across the road). On his return, he saw Davidson carrying a bundle into the stable and noticed he now had a pair of pistols and a sword at his belt. Elizabeth Westall, from number 1 (next door to the stable), had already seen a man carrying a sack entering the premises at about 3 o'clock. She was somewhat unnerved when Davidson knocked on her door to ask for a light. We cannot know now whether the woman was alarmed by Davidson's colour (which she mentions) or his brazen cheek. Nor can we know why Davidson seemed determined to draw attention to himself. The light was to light the candles in the hay-loft, but surely the conspirators could have brought their own.

Such was the level of secrecy – or perhaps the lack of planning – that not all the conspirators knew the stable rendezvous. Some were told to meet at the Horse and Groom, others to go to John Street and from there, they were taken to the hay-loft. Thistlewood, Ings and Wilson were already there and everybody was told to help themselves to the pistols, swords, grenades and home-made pikes littering the place.

Tidd was late, but Thistlewood calmed everybody down by pointing out that various key people were elsewhere and that not everybody was going to Grosvenor Square. About 7 o'clock the Lincolnshire man turned up with a relative newcomer, John Monument, and by this time there were twenty-five men crammed into that small loft, making their final preparations.

On the ground, Ings and Davidson were on sentry duty, the butcher armed with his knife. He had tied twine around the hilt so that the weapon would not slip as he went about his gruesome business at Harrowby's.

Across London, in Grosvenor Square, whoever was detailed to keep watch there noticed nothing amiss. Servants and deliverymen came and went as if in preparation for a dinner. A dinner that was never to happen. A dinner that only existed as part of an elaborate trap. It would have taken the Cato Street conspirators between ten and fifteen minutes to reach Grosvenor Square – 'at that hour when suspicion must be lulled asleep and when no apprehensions could be entertained of personal danger' – but other feet were on the move before theirs. They belonged to George Ruthven and eleven men of the Bow Street patrol.

This forerunner of the Metropolitan Police was set up in the house of a former magistrate, Sir Thomas de Veil, in 1739 but was effectively created in its best known form by the Fielding brothers, Henry and John, both magistrates, in 1751. The six original Runners had no uniform and no pay, but they were allowed the reward given to thief-takers and this was incentive enough. There were always two officers on duty, day and night, and, rather like the detective branch of Scotland Yard which replaced them, had a brief to investigate crime anywhere in the country. By the 1770s their reputation had grown enormously. These were not the lame and ancient 'Charlies', parish constables who patrolled the streets and called the hour, but fit, active men who could be relied upon to stop criminals in their tracks. They were now paid 1 guinea a week out of a Secret Service Fund. Any whiff of a paid police force would have outraged liberal society and riff-raff alike; there was something so *European* about it. From the abortive attempt on the life of George III in 1786 (when a woman had tried to stab him with a blunt fruit knife) two officers were permanently assigned to protect him. Doubtless they were in the royal box in May 1800 when James Hadfield tried to shoot the king.

Seven other police offices were opened in London in 1792, each one with six Runners attached. It was the very plain-clothes-ness of the Runners that made them so useful. Although they occasionally wore scarlet waistcoats, which earned them the nickname of 'Robins', Cruikshank's sketch of the arrest of the Cato Street men shows the officers in long top coats, double-breasted jackets, tan-topped hunting boots and breeches. The only things that mark them out of the ordinary are their pistols and cutlasses. Interestingly, Cruikshank's depiction of the moment of the murder of 'Smithers the Police Officer' sees him dropping his brass tipstaff. These were issued to every Runner and magistrate in London – some of them are still preserved at the London Museum and the Police College in Bramshill. It goes without saying, of course, that Cruikshank cannot resist propaganda. The police officers are clean-cut, well dressed (and, by definition, outnumbered) whereas the conspirators, even a gentleman like Thistlewood, are shown as scruffy, uncouth ruffians with desperate eyes.[4] Some of the less committed are already climbing up through the roof to make good their escape.

Because Ruthven's Runners could blend so well, the conspirators seemed unaware that their movements were being watched the whole day. Once Richard Birnie, the Bow Street magistrate, was sure that the Cato Street hay-loft was the focus of activity, he swore out a warrant for the arrest of Thistlewood, Brunt, Hall, Ings, Potter, Palin, Edwards, Shaw, Adams, Tidd, Wilson, Davidson, Harrison and Cook. There is some confusion over whether Ruthven actually took the paper with these names on it to the stable. His brief was to arrest anyone there and he was told to expect support from the Coldstream Guards from the Portman Street Barracks nearby.

It was probably half past 8 by the time Ruthven reached Cato Street and already something had gone wrong. There were no soldiers in place that Ruthven could see and from the conspirators' point of view, they themselves should have moved off at least forty-five minutes earlier. The first person Ruthven saw, armed with a sword and with a blunderbuss resting on his shoulder, was William Davidson. He saw someone else too, almost certainly Ings, but couldn't make him out in the shadows. He yelled at his men to grab these two and made for the stairs.

This was little better than a ladder and would only permit one person through the open trapdoor at a time. Putting his head over the rim, in the candle-light he saw twenty-four or twenty-five people squeezed into a room 15 feet long. He clambered up, followed by his colleagues Ellis and Smithers. The only man he recognized was Thistlewood, standing to the right of the carpenter's bench.

'We are officers,' Ruthven shouted. 'Seize their arms.'

Thistlewood retreated slightly into the doorway of one of the rooms behind him. He had a long, drawn sword in his hand (probably cavalry pattern although great play was made at his trial that this was of foreign manufacture) and, as Smithers crossed to him, Thistlewood lunged, driving the blade through the Runner's body. The man fell back, blood trickling over his waistcoat and fell against Ellis, gasping, 'Oh, my God! I'm done!'

Someone yelled, 'Put out the lights – kill the buggers and throw them down the stairs.' Thistlewood slashed several of the candles with his sword and in pitch blackness, all hell broke loose, everybody making for the stairs. With great presence of mind, Ruthven joined in the cry to 'kill them' and bolted down the steps in the guise of a conspirator.

The murder of Smithers happened in seconds and, in the confusion, men had different memories of it. James Ellis who had been right behind

Ruthven on the stairs was sure there were three men at ground level. Davidson, 'a man of colour', wore cross belts and was carrying a carbine, not a blunderbuss.[5] On the stairs, Ellis heard the scraping of feet and 'a noise like fencing with swords'. Had Smithers drawn his cutlass and did he attempt to outfence Thistlewood? Once on a level with the others, Ellis brandished his tipstaff. This was not only a symbol of office, but with its metal crown head, quite a nasty weapon. He called on Thistlewood to surrender or he would fire and pointed his pistol at him. As Thistlewood stabbed Smithers and the officer fell, Ellis fired, but missed. He did not record, at the trial, how he got to the ground floor, but presumably joined in the headlong rush to freedom with the others.

Other than the dead man, then, only Ruthven and Ellis were witness to the murder itself, but that was enough and at ground level, there was chaos. At last the soldiers had arrived, a detachment of the Coldstream Guards under Captain[6] Fitzclarence, an illegitimate son of the Duke of Clarence. Although he did not mention it at the trials, he had been incorrectly briefed and not only thought that the piquet was to fight fires but he had gone to the wrong end of John Street, 70 yards away. The sound of gunfire had brought him and his men to the right spot.

Here, Fitzclarence met Ruthven and by this time the conspirators were shooting their way out. It was of course pitch black in that cul-de-sac and most of the streets around would have been in darkness. Apart from the Coldstreamers, whose buttons and musket locks would presumably have reflected any available light, it was not easy to tell Runner from conspirator. Runner William Westcott had stayed on the ground the whole time and heard firing in the loft. Ings made a bolt for it and Westcott tussled with him. He obviously broke free because, the next thing Westcott remembered, Thistlewood was hurtling down the stairs firing at him. Instinctively, the Runner dropped to the ground, later to find three bullet holes in his hat[7] and a wound to the back of his hand where a ball had grazed him. Thistlewood hacked at Westcott with his sword before vanishing into the West End night.

Ruthven saw a man who turned out to be Richard Tidd making a dash for the door.

> I met Tidd grappling with one of the military. I secured him. I caught hold of his right arm, pulled him round and fell with him on a dung heap.[8]

He was taken, along with others, across the road to the Horse and Groom. Ellis heard a cry in the midst of the shooting and saw Davidson running along Queen Street, still armed with his sword and carbine. He grabbed him and helped with the arrest of four others during the night. William Brookes was not from the Bow Street patrol, but was pressed into service by Magistrate Birnie who was by now at the scene himself, directing operations in the middle of the fight. Immediately Brookes came face to face with Ings and someone else armed with a cutlass. Ings fired and wounded Brookes in the shoulder before running off in the direction of the Edgware Road. Although in pain and shock, Brookes gave chase and was probably relieved to see Ings throw away his pistol. In the event another policeman, Giles Moy, collared Ings and a disbelieving Brookes asked why he had fired at him. 'I wish I had killed you,' Ings grunted.

While Fitzclarence was confronting a swordsman at the bottom of the stairs – 'Don't kill me,' the conspirator blurted, 'and I will tell you all' – his men were doing stalwart service all around him. As another conspirator tried to escape, he was grabbed by a guardsman who slipped and the conspirator

> presented a pistol at [Fitzclarence's] breast; but as he was in the act of pulling the trigger, Sergeant Legge rushed forward and, whilst attempting to put aside the destructive weapon, received the fire upon his arm.

The ball scraped along his sleeve from wrist to elbow, but did minimal damage.

Davidson in particular put up a fight. He slashed at Fitzclarence with his cutlass but missed, and Private James Basey hauled him down, suffering only a cut finger. 'Fight on while you have a drop of blood in you,' Davidson shouted to the others still milling at the stable entrance, 'You may as well die now as at another time.'

Fitzclarence seems to have been the first up into the loft. There was gunsmoke all around him and the first thing the officer saw was the bloody body of Smithers and one of the conspirators kneeling beside him. Whoever it was was also soaked in blood, which turned out to be the dead man's. 'I hope they will make a difference,' he pleaded, hands in the air, 'between the innocent and the guilty.' Three men cowering in a corner were hauled out, one jabbering, 'I resign myself. There is no harm. I was brought here innocent this afternoon.'

With these four and three more the Runners had captured below, there were now seven men in effective custody. Perhaps the luckiest in the whole incident was Private Muddock of the Guards. Stumbling in the darkness of the hay-loft, he tripped over a conspirator who fired at him at point blank range. Fortunately, the gun misfired and the conspirator threw it away, shouting, 'Use me honourably'. The pistol was loaded nearly to the muzzle.

No one was asked or commented on how long the hand-to-hand fighting in Cato Street went on, but it cannot have been more than ten or fifteen minutes. While the police herded the prisoners into the Horse and Groom, the soldiery were employed collecting the weaponry from the loft – 'a great quantity of pistols, blunderbusses, swords and pikes, about sixteen inches long, made to screw into a handle'. There were also ball cartridges, powder flasks and a sack full of hand-grenades. The conspirator prisoners and their weapons were marched off to Bow Street, while the body of Smithers was taken down from the loft and laid out in a back room of the Horse and Groom. Magistrate Birnie interviewed four of Fitzclarence's men – John Revel, James Basey, William Curtis and John Muddock – before allowing them, with their captain (whose uniform was in shreds) to return to their barracks. For safekeeping, the ammunition and weapons went with them and were locked in Fitzclarence's quarters.

Now Birnie went to work on the Bench. Before him were: James Ings, Richard Bradburn, James Gilchrist, Charles Cooper, Richard Tidd, John Monument, John Shaw and William Davidson. Some of these men were already known dissidents. Inevitably, Davidson stood out. He sang 'Scots wha ha'e wi' Wallace bled'[9] while Runner Ellis clapped the cuffs on him and snarled, 'Blast and damn the eyes of all those who would not die for liberty.' Ellis recognized the man at once as one of the principal speakers at Finsbury Market a few months earlier and a black-flag carrying rabble-rouser in Covent Garden.

Wilkinson wrote:

Ings was a fearful ruffian, a rather stout man, apparently between 30 and 40, but of a most determined aspect. His hands were covered with blood and as he stood at the bar, manacled to one of his wretched confederates, his large fiery eyes glared round upon the spectators with an expression truly horrible.

If only half the description of the appearance and behaviour of Ings is acceptable, the man was the most deranged of the lot.

Each man in turn was asked if he had anything to say. Only Cooper and Davidson spoke, reminding the authorities present that they had instantly surrendered (which in the case of Davidson, was patently untrue).

At 9 o'clock on the morning of 24 February, Ruthven, Lavender, Bishop, Salmon and six other Runners were sent to pick up Thistlewood. There was of course a warrant out for the others, like John Palin and George Edwards. Most of these conspirators were never seen again. Wisely, Thistlewood had not gone straight home to Stanhope Street, but had holed up at 8 White Street, Little Moorfields.

The Runners divided their number, half at the front, half at the back, and Daniel Bishop got the key from the landlady, a Mrs Harris. He opened the door as quietly as he could and let his eyes become accustomed to the darkness. A head popped up from the covers and Bishop's pistol was already aimed at it. 'Mr Thistlewood, I am a Bow Street officer. You are my prisoner,' and he launched himself at the conspirator, pinning him to the bed. With the other Runners holding him, Thistlewood was handcuffed. He was still fully clothed and had ball cartridges and flints in his pockets.

By this time, news of Cato Street had spread throughout London and a mob had gathered at Bow Street, jostling Thistlewood as he was taken in to see Birnie. 'Hang the villain! Hang the assassin!' was the general cry. While waiting in an anteroom, Thistlewood admitted he knew he had killed one man and hoped it was Stafford, the chief magistrate. Birnie interviewed Thistlewood briefly and then the conspirator was sent to the Home Office, under close guard to be interrogated by the very men he had planned to kill.

Large numbers of eminent people came to gawp at him and his reaction was hardly surprising. 'His appearance', wrote Wilkinson, 'was most forbidding. His countenance, at all times unfavourable, seemed now to have acquired an additional degree of malignity.' He calmly drank some porter (beer) and asked the names of those who had come to see him. He asked what gaol he was to be sent to and hoped it was not Horsham.

At 2 o'clock, Thistlewood was placed, still handcuffed, before the Privy Council. Wellington was there, along with Harrowby, Liverpool, Westmoreland, Sidmouth, Eldon, Vansittart, Canning, Castlereagh, Wellesley Pole, Scott, Sir S Shepherd (ex-Attorney-General), Bragge

Bathurst and others. It must have been a surreal moment. Thistlewood, shabby and emaciated in comparison with his appearance at the Spa Fields trial, looking one by one at the men who, but for fortune, would now be dead. The heads of Castlereagh and Sidmouth were not on poles on London Bridge, but still on the shoulders of their owners. The Lord Chancellor told him that he would be charged with murder and treason. Asked if he had anything to say, Thistlewood declined at that stage. He was committed to Coldbath Fields in the custody of six officers, while the Privy Council looked in horror at the weapons of their own destruction which were now placed before them.

Large numbers of people flocked to the stable at Cato Street when an enterprising local, with no authority, started to demand a shilling entry. This was all part and parcel of the obsession with violence that would dog the rest of the century. When William Corder killed Maria Marten seven years later, virtually the whole of the Red Barn where her body was hidden was dismantled and taken away by souvenir hunters.

Earlier that day, Sidmouth had issued a statement to the Press. The *London Gazette* wrote:

> Whereas Arthur Thistlewood stands charged with high treason and also with the wilful murder of Richard Smithers, a reward of One Thousand Pounds is hereby offered to any person or persons who shall discover and apprehend . . . the said Arthur Thistlewood . . . upon his being apprehended and lodged in any of His Majesty's gaols. And all persons are hereby cautioned upon their allegiance not to receive or harbour the said Arthur Thistlewood, as any person offending herein will be thereby guilty of high treason.

'Gentlemen,' said Mr Bolland, junior counsel for the prosecution at the trial of Thistlewood. 'Thank Heaven that Providence which kindly watches over the acts and thoughts of men, mercifully interposed between the conception of this abominable plot and its completion.'

But Providence and Heaven had nothing to do with it. The Privy Council were up all night on 23 February and none of them – not even Lord Harrowby – was at Grosvenor Square. Even though Thistlewood was under arrest by the time the *Gazette* appeared, he was not when Sidmouth sent them his note. And when exactly did Sidmouth find out that it was Thistlewood who had killed Smithers? And whatever happened to that word 'alleged' which is enshrined in English law? In other words, Thistlewood's neck was in the noose before any legal decision had been made and twelve police officers and a piquet of the 2nd Coldstream Guards were despatched to a run-down cowshed in an obscure street . . . on the off-chance of preventing a revolution? And how was the Bow Street magistrate Richard Birnie able to swear out a warrant for precisely those men found in the hay-loft?

The real conspirators in the Cato Street story were their lordships of the Privy Council.

Chapter 11

'On a Charge of High Treason'

They held an inquest on Richard Smithers on Friday 25th. It would be another half century before coroners had their own buildings for inquest purposes and the Horse and Groom, where the Bow Street officer's body had been laid out, was used instead. With the usual pomp and ceremony, Mr Pyall, the beadle of St Mary-le-bone proclaimed proceedings open and the Middlesex county coroner, James Stirling, took his seat.

The police surgeon, Mr Fisher, talked the jury through Smithers's wounds. He had not been called until that morning, by which time the dead man would have been stripped and washed and rigor mortis would have come and gone. Smithers was 'a good-looking man, stout, about thirty three years of age'. The fatal wound, two inches long and half an inch broad, had been made between the fifth and sixth ribs on the right side to a depth of about twelve inches. The 'sharp instrument' had grazed the surface of the liver, cut the pericardium and pierced the right ventricle of the heart and the left lobe of the lung. The ribs on the left side had prevented the weapon passing right through the body. Death was caused by loss of blood. Other wounds to the body included a second sword cut under the shoulder blade and a pewter pistol ball imbedded in the shoulder to a depth of six inches. Unless Thistlewood hit him twice, it is likely that these wounds occurred in the chaos of darkness after Smithers fell.

George Ruthven was called next and explained events in the hay-loft, from the time he had received the warrant of arrest from the Marlborough Street magistrate, Mr Baker, to the end of the affray. He was very keen to underline the presence of Thistlewood – 'I knew him as well as I know my father' – and the fact that it was Thistlewood alone who offered violence in the hay-loft before the lights went out. This was the first time that the conspirators' names were used – John Shaw, 'a man named Blackburn [sic]', James Wilson, and Tidd, who 'fired at a sergeant' as well as at Fitzclarence.

It cannot have done the Runners' credibility much good when Ruthven admitted that, of the twenty-five men in the stable, only nine were taken into custody. He estimated that about twenty shots were fired, but some of these were probably just to cause alarm.

James Ellis gave his evidence next, giving his address as 22 Paradise Row, Palmer's Village, St Margaret's, Westminster, confirming that it was Thistlewood who stabbed Smithers and that he, Ellis, had fired at the man and missed. He also lamented that the short cutlasses that the Runners carried were useless against the longer weapons of experts like Thistlewood.

William Westcott came next, his address at 10 Simmons Street, Sloan Square, explaining how he had grappled with Ings, still wearing his butcher's apron, and how both he and Thistlewood had got away in the confusion.

Giles Moy, of 11 London Court, Marylebone, was a nightwatchman. He assisted Brookes in capturing Ings and took him to the watch house. The butcher had bullets in his pockets, gunpowder and a haversack (for the head of Castlereagh or Sidmouth).

Sergeant Legge of the 2nd Battalion the Coldstream Guards explained the turning out of the piquet 'usually employed on occasions when the military is required in aid of the civil power'. He showed the jury his ripped jacket sleeve where a pistol ball had torn the cloth, the pistol fired by Richard Tidd. Legge had time to check the hay-loft, find the body of Smithers and to return to Portman Street for reinforcements. Clearly, no one knew the extent of the insurrection or how many more armed killers roamed the streets. He mentioned the names of Monument, Cooper and Gilchrist.

The coroner reminded the jury of the law of joint culpability. It may have been Thistlewood who killed Smithers, but the law held that all his confederates were equally guilty.[1] At that point, a note arrived from Magistrate Baker referring to the original warrant he had sworn out. At that point in the inquest, it was still in the hands of the Privy Council.

The next witness has caused confusion. The text clearly calls him William Sarnon and he gives his address as the Edgware Road and his profession as tailor. He appeared to be merely passing Cato Street about 8 o'clock and got caught up in the fighting, being fired on at least twice. On the other hand, Ruthven refers to a Runner called John Surman who was with him that evening. The similarity of surname may be just a coincidence.

All this was enough for the jury, who pronounced Thistlewood and Davidson guilty of murder. They asked the coroner for clarification on the issue of joint culpability and whether surrendering without a struggle carried any weight. Told it did not, a murder verdict was brought against the rest of the prisoners 'and others unknown'.

During the day, Smithers's parents arrived to visit the body. They were 'so decrepit as scarcely to be able to get up the stairs'. Smithers's body was removed to his lodgings in Carteret Street and the funeral took place at 4 o'clock on Thursday 2 March. It was a moving and well attended ceremony, proof of the shock that Cato Street had caused to London's people. The Runner's widow was too distraught to attend, so the principal mourners, walking solemnly in deepest black behind the hearse, were Smithers's father and brothers and a large body of Bow Street Runners. John Lavender represented Smithers's earlier police office in Queen Square and Mr Armstrong and his son from Worship Street were there too. The upper windows of the cortege route were full of spectators, as the sad column wound its way from Tothill Street to St Margaret's church. Here, while the Reverend Rodber held the service, the churchyard was crammed with sympathizers, including magistrates, policemen and a contingent of the Coldstream Guards.

Days before this the machinery of the law swung into motion. Two of the conspirators, Robert Adams, 'late of the Royal Horse Guards' and the tailor Abel Hall, offered to turn king's evidence, a system which we would call a 'deal' today; they would live in exchange for all they knew about the others. Hall was not grabbed at Cato Street, but was arrested by Runners at a house in Seward Street. A quantity of weapons, presumed to be part of the conspirators' stash, was found in an old shed of a house in Regent's Park. On Monday 28 February, the Privy Council offered a reward of £200 for the apprehension of John Palin. Lavender and Bishop of the Bow Street office received information that he was holed up in the Battle Bridge area. When they reached the house, the bird had flown, but three men and 'a woman of somewhat suspicious appearance' were arrested. Since one of the men was lying in bed fully clothed and another was melting lead in a frying pan, police suspicions seem to have been justified, yet Magistrate Birnie let them go on the grounds that they were 'unknown'.

This issue makes it clear that various members of the radical underground were known to the authorities and were actually being watched. Ruthven testified that the reason he knew Thistlewood so well was that he had 'followed him for days together'. And since Thistlewood had been involved in Spa Fields, it followed that 'the notorious Preston, the cobbling politician' was up to his neck in it too. He was arrested on the 28th, his lodgings at 17 Prince's Street, Drury Lane, having been searched days earlier. He had told officers that his 'armoury could not boast of a swan-shot nor his port-folio of a scrap of paper of the slightest political interest'. He accepted arrest cheerfully as he'd been here before, but his daughters were furious at what today would be called an invasion of civil liberties. Moved from one watch house to another, Preston denied all knowledge of Cato Street and appeared before the Privy Council the next day. Here, according to the authorities, he 'behaved with his usual boldness and low insolence' in an interview lasting half an hour, before being taken to the Bridewell at Tothill Fields. Before he left the Council Chamber, Lord Castlereagh passed by – 'Aye, there he goes!' Preston called after him. 'I have talked more treason, as they call it, today than ever I did in my whole life before.'

One of the man's outraged daughters, Ann, wrote to Sidmouth and waited in the lobby of the Home Office for his reply, complaining of the treatment her father had received. Three days later, having been given the cold shoulder by Cam Hobhouse, she was allowed to give her father a change of clothes, but not to talk to him.

Another dissident who was rounded up was Samuel Waddington, known to be a placard-carrying trouble-maker who had tried to set up a rally on Kennington Common. He protested at the seizure of his books 'with ridiculous effrontery', claiming that he had done nothing which would merit a charge. All that was actually found was a full-length portrait of himself, blowing a horn and carrying Cobbett's *Twopenny Trash* under his arm! George Wilkinson, writing all this at the end of the year, was happy to report that no charges were brought against Waddington and that he had given up politics for the 'more quiet occupation of porter to a tallow chandler'.

On the day of Smithers's funeral, the Privy Council were to discuss legal proceedings. The great and the good of national politics were at the Home Office including Robert Peel and William Huskisson, both of whom would become prominent members of the Cabinet in two years time, and Viscount Palmerston, the 'terrible milord' who would dominate foreign policy for half a century after this point. The next day, Mr Adkins, Governor of Coldbath Fields, brought the prisoners before their Lordships under heavy guard. Other conspirators, still at this stage including Preston, were brought by Mr Nodder from Tothill Fields. With them was Firth, the Cato Street loft keeper, who was assumed to be part of the conspiracy.

Handcuffed together and facing their accusers, the prisoners had a wretched appearance and some were mere boys. Thistlewood looked 'jaundiced, nerveless and emaciated'. Davidson was cheerful enough. Preston was annoyed, but clearly enjoying the limelight. Again, a number of influential people trooped through the chamber to gawp at them.

One by one the prisoners were examined by the Council. Thistlewood put his hat on and refused to answer the charges of murder and high treason brought against him. Ings was sullen, but snapped, 'It is want of food which has brought us here. Death would be a pleasure to me . . . if I had fifty necks, I'd rather have them all broken, one after the other, than see my children starve.' Preston couldn't wait – 'If it is the will of the Author of the World that I should perish in the cause of freedom – his will, and not mine, be done!' He threw his arms about 'which savoured strongly of insanity'. Wilson, Davidson and Tidd laughed openly at the distinguished visitors, like Lord Westmoreland, who came to stare at them. Brunt, as Thistlewood's supposed second-in-command, put his hat on and said nothing.

At the end of the day Thistlewood, Brunt, Monument, Davidson, Harrison, Wilson, Ings and Tidd were sent under cavalry escort to the Tower, where Captain J H Elrington, the fort-major, was waiting for them. As they waited for the carriages to arrive, the conspirators chatted loudly, almost certainly for the benefit of their captors, about the spread of the conspiracy – 'Aye,' Harrison laughed, 'time will show all things.' As they pulled away in their carriages, Ings called to the crowd, 'Hurra, boys!' but the mob was grimly silent in return. They didn't even giggle at the ludicrous sight of the giant Harrison handcuffed to the diminutive Monument in his wide-awake hat. The mob followed them all the way to the Tower, no one making sympathetic noises at all. And this despite the fact that Ings continued to use the 'most revolting' language against the king's ministers and seemed to know, or pretend to know, various people in the crowd.

At the Tower, each man was accommodated separately and their cells guarded by Yeoman Warders. Thistlewood was placed in the Bloody Tower, possibly in the same cell that was the home of another 'conspirator', Walter Ralegh, for fourteen years in the reign of James I. Davidson and Ings were locked in a prison over the waterworks, Monument at the back of the Horse-Armoury, Brunt and Harrison over the Stone-kitchen, Tidd in the Seven-gun Battery and Wilson in the prison over the parade. The number of Yeoman gaolers was increased six-fold to sixty, just in case. After all, the Tower had been a focus of attack three years earlier and no one was taking any chances.

Bradburn, Shaw, Firth, Gilchrist, Hall and Cooper, probably always regarded as second-string conspirators, were taken under cavalry escort to Coldbath Fields. Simmonds the footman and Preston were sent to Tothill Fields and no warrant for murder was ever brought against them.

Sweeping up operations were still going on. Robert George was presumed to be a gang member. He was a haberdasher and tailor of Chapel Street, Paddington, and a little boy playing in the street had lost a marble that rolled into George's premises. Here, the lad saw guns and a sword and immediately told the authorities. George's son, who lived opposite, had disappeared on the night of Cato Street and he was traced by Runners Ruthven and Salmon[2] to the Dundee Arms, Wapping, where the ex-sailor was waiting for a ship to Gravesend. Despite nothing incriminating being found on him apart from a stick which *might* be used as a pike handle, he was placed in the House of Correction at Coldbath Fields on a charge of high treason.

The premises of all the conspirators were searched with a fine-tooth comb. Susan Thistlewood, 'a smart, genteel little woman', backed her husband's political stance 100 per cent. She was calm and dignified as officers turned her lodgings over and was patience itself when she visited her husband and was body-searched 'even to the removal of her stays and cap'.

Preparations for the trials began on 8 March with a Special Commission of Oyer and Terminer[3] set for the 27th. On that day, twenty-three gentlemen forming a Grand Jury met at Hicks' Hall at 9 o'clock. Lord Chief Justice Abbott explained to them the exact meaning of treason, a tedious recitation which would be repeated and argued over several times in the weeks ahead. Very properly, Abbott reminded the jury that they were to reach their conclusions on evidence only, not on the wild rumours which were no doubt flying all over the country by now.

A number of witnesses were called, Robert Adams the conspirator-turned-traitor sitting for three hours in the witness box before being returned to Coldbath Fields. John Monument from the Tower was very uneasy, 'pale and dejected', and generally seems to have been of a gloomy disposition. Several women and two boys were examined. The deliberations lasted for two days and at the end of them the Grand Jury decided that 'true bills' of high treason be brought against Thistlewood, Davidson, Ings, Brunt, Tidd, Wilson, Harrison, Bradburn, Shaw, Gilchrist and Cooper. These bills were not found for Robert George and Abel Hall. In the case of the Smithers's murder, true bills were brought against Thistlewood, Brunt, Tidd, Wilson, Harrison and Shaw. At first, Davidson was not included in this, but the oversight was corrected by an emergency session of the Grand Jury in which Davidson was accused of shooting at Runner Gill with the intent to murder him.

On Monday 3 April, a list of 227 potential jurors of the county of Middlesex was drawn up and the four-count indictment drafted. The first count of high treason was that the conspirators

> did compass, imagine, invent, devise and intend to deprive and depose
> our said lord the King of and from the style, honour and kingly name
> of the imperial crown of this realm.

This would have been achieved by eleven 'overt acts', including conspiracy to assassinate the Cabinet, seizure and manufacture of weapons, attacks on barracks and so on. In fact, a reading of the acts implies a great deal of repetition, as though the authorities were determined to bring these men to book by charging them with every crime under the sun.

The second count involved the intent

> to move and excite insurrection, rebellion and war against the King .
> . . and to subvert and alter the legislature, rule and government and to
> bring and put the King to death.

The same eleven overt acts were cited as proof, even though in the evidence that was to follow there was only one oblique mention of an attack on the life of George IV.

The third count consisted of an intent

to levy war against the King, in order by force and constraint to compel him to change his measures and councils.

The overt acts were cited here, as in the first two.

The fourth and final count makes mention of the fact that the conspirators had made war against the king, which was merely a continuation of the intent in count three. Later discussions explained to a confused jury that 'war' in this context meant rebellion.[4]

An astonishing 162 witnesses were called upon to be in readiness, although in practice only a third of those were actually called. Adams, the cordwainer-conspirator heads the alphabetical list. Several of Ruthven's Runners are there, as are magistrates like Birnie, Captain Fitzclarence and several of his piquet, Yeoman Warders of the Tower, witnesses to the Cato Street night and a scattering of His Majesty's Ministers.

On 14 April, the prisoners were transferred from the Tower and Coldbath Fields to Newgate, next door to the Session House where the trials would open the next day. Despite the secrecy which accompanied those plans and the fact that the move happened at 7 in the morning, a huge crowd gathered at the Tower to see the seven coaches with their Life Guard escort make the journey. At Newgate, a similarly vast mob had gathered and the gaolers fanned out, forming a half moon at the entrance to allow the felons in.

In Newgate Thistlewood was given a room of his own, complete with fire and the inevitable armed guard at the door. The other six were lumped together, but at least had a yard for exercise. The four lesser fry from Coldbath arrived in the afternoon without escort and by this time most of the crowd had gone home. The four were locked in one cell.

On the night before the trials began, friends and families of the accused got together to raise subscriptions. Clearly in the majority of cases, the men now in custody were the principal breadwinners and genuine hardship resulted from their removal from the workplace. Mary Brunt had one child; Ann Tidd eight; Amelia Bradburn eight; Mary Shaw had two; Charlotte Preston had three sisters; Susan Thistlewood had one son; Sarah Davidson six children and Caroline Harrison three. The 'Appeal to the British Nation' on their behalf was probably written by Mr Harmer, who, as we have seen, specialized in handling contentious radical cases like this.

At last, in the document, the word 'alleged' appears for the first time.

The families were merely asking for justice and did not enter into the details of the accusations. They did however point out that the word of the Bow Street Runners was by definition from interested parties and that such men have been known to have 'instigated . . . crime, that they might afterwards betray the delinquents and obtain the promised reward'. And the Press 'are notoriously guilty of loading their daily columns with the most scandalous falsehoods and misrepresentations'. In a veiled reference to Spa Fields, the Appeal went on that the conspiracy was 'nothing more than the artful invention of hired spies and secret Agents'.

Anyone who could offer cash for the suffering families should send direct to relatives or to the printer at Duke Street, Spitalfields, Mr Walker of Gun Street, Spitalfields, or Mr Griffin of Middle Row, Holborn.

Barristers Adolphus and Curwood were retained by Thistlewood, Brunt, Davidson, Tidd and Ings; Messrs Walford and Broderick for the rest. It is difficult to gauge the position of these men. By definition the products of a Classical education, graduates of Oxford or Cambridge or one of the London Inns of Court, they were part of the establishment which looked on Cato Street with abject horror. On the other hand, every man had a right to a defence and as the accused was not allowed to speak in his own defence, it was doubly incumbent on defence counsel to do a very difficult and valiant job. It was obvious to Adolphus and Curwood that those accused of murder would be found guilty by the overwhelming evidence against them. For that they would hang anyway. But the crime of high treason carried the ghastly penalty of drawing, quartering and decapitation and perhaps in deference to the families of the accused, they carried out a surprisingly effective damage limitation exercise to avoid that.

The Sessions House was an ugly, flat-roofed building alongside Newgate gaol along Old Bailey. It had a semi-circular wall around the entrance so that witnesses could be separated from the waiting crowds and a separate room so that they no longer had to wait in a pub opposite. Inside the courtroom was an angled mirror that threw light onto the faces of the accused on winter days when the daylight began to fade. With all the pomp and circumstance of the law the trial of Arthur Thistlewood opened at 10 o'clock on Saturday 15 April. As in the Spa Fields trial, it was agreed that each conspirator be tried separately, beginning with the conspirators' leader. Again, as in Spa Fields – and the Brandreth trial – the legal heavyweights of the day lent their presence to the proceedings, both to underline the gravity of the charges and to ensure that the men of Cato Street suffered the full penalty of the law.

Lord Chief Justice Abbott presided, along with Lord Chief Justice Dallas, Chief Baron Richards and Mr Justice Richardson, all of them pillars of the establishment and all of them with clear memories of Spa Fields and Jeremiah Brandreth.

The prisoners entered, without shackles, led by Thistlewood, who looked pale and dejected. He wore a velvet-collared black coat over a light waistcoat and blue trousers. One by one each man came to the bar, raised his right hand and swore to his name. A complication arose with Wilson who said, 'That is not my name.' His counsel, Curwood, explained that he would put in a plea of misnomer for this man, to be told that now was not the time. When it was the time, this quite legitimate complaint was simply ignored by their Lordships on the Bench.[5] Each prisoner then pleaded not guilty and answered the question as to how they would be tried 'By God and my country'. Ings, however, cut to the chase – 'I will be tried by God and by the laws of reason. The laws of reason are the laws of God.' Abbot instructed Mr Brown, the gaoler, to tell Ings to plead in the usual way and the butcher eventually agreed. The charges were read and the prisoners returned to Newgate in readiness for Thistlewood's trial on Monday.

The problem for Adolphus and Curwood was twofold. Thistlewood was a known agitator who had stood trial for high treason before. Because of Peterloo, the mood of the country was even more bitter towards the authorities now, but this was not apparent in the streets of London in the case now being tried. It was as though the men of Cato Street had crossed an invisible line in the struggle for liberty and the whole business left a nasty taste. Counsel for the defence had also to get past what appeared to be a bona fide case of cold feet from two of the conspirators who had turned king's evidence, to the reality of the situation – the spying of George Edwards on behalf of Lord Sidmouth. They made sure that as many witnesses as possible referred to Edwards, because they knew from discussions with their clients that he was the real instigator of the Cato Street plot. The problem was that Edwards was simply a witness (one, after all, of 162) and could not be found. In fact, he did not need to be, because Thomas Hyden and Robert Adams had come forward voluntarily.

On that Monday morning, the counsel weighed in for both sides. The prosecution consisted of the Attorney-General, the Solicitor-General, Mr Bolland and Mr Littledale. Before the whole thing got under way, a shabbily dressed man placed a hat in front of Thistlewood which was found to contain five oranges. These were removed as possibly containing poison, but later in the trials and again at the execution, oranges were permitted. It was usual for prisoners to stand at the bar but, because of the great length of the proceedings, Thistlewood was allowed to sit.

The 227 jurors were whittled down to twelve. Since Thistlewood's right was to a jury of his peers, five were called 'Esquire' and two more 'Gent'. The others were: a carpenter, a lighterman, a builder, an iron-plate worker and a cooper. At half past one the Attorney-General opened the case with a statement of events. Inevitably, it referred to all the other prisoners in court as well as Thistlewood and ran to twenty-nine closely printed pages. Then the witnesses were called.

Robert Adams was first and his evidence was damning. He outlined the way he had been inveigled into the plot by Thistlewood and explained the mechanics of how the insurrection was supposed to work. There were a few anomalies, as Adolphus later pointed out. At a meeting the week before 23 February, Thistlewood had told Brunt and Palin to check if a house near Furnival's Inn was suitable to set fire to. They reported it would 'make a d— —d good fire' but as defence counsel made clear, those buildings were brand new and far *less* likely to catch fire than most others in London.

On the second day, Eleanor Walker explained the odd comings and goings of John Brunt, her lodger at Fox Court, and Brunt's apprentice, Joseph Hale, told of the weapons that were stashed there and who visited – 'They used to call Thistlewood sometimes T, his initial'. And on the night in question, a ruffled Brunt came home late, his clothes dirty, telling his wife that 'it was all up'.

The watchmen, Thomas Smart and Charles Bissex, told the jury that they had seen four suspicious-looking men hanging around Grosvenor Square on the 23rd. John Morris, the journeyman cutler, remembered Ings arriving to have two swords sharpened. Edward Simpson, Corporal-Major of the Life Guards, explained that Harrison had served with him at the Portman Street barracks which looked out over Cato Street. James Adams, the pawnbroker, told how William Davidson had taken a blunderbuss out of pledge.

But it was the next witness that was the lynchpin of the prosecution's case, in the absence of the elusive Edwards. Thomas Hyden was a cow-keeper and had been a member of a shoemaker's club. A few days before 23rd, he met James Wilson who put a proposal to him – 'He asked me if I would be one of a party to destroy his Majesty's ministers' – and made great play of the fact that hand-grenades were ready and the target was probably Lord Harrowby's house. Hyden, horror-struck by the speed of events and what they meant, contacted Harrowby, who confirmed Hyden's version of events as the next witness called.

A week before the 23rd, Harrowby was riding alone 'among the young plantations in Hyde Park'. Near Grosvenor Gate, he was met by 'a person' who asked him if he was Lord Harrowby and gave him an urgent note for Lord Castlereagh. On the morning of the 23rd, Hyden met Wilson again and was told to meet him at the Horse and Groom at half past 5. Twenty or thirty men would be there, with others who would assemble at Gray's Inn Lane, together with the Irish in Gee's Court along Oxford Street.

When asked by the defence why Hyden had gone to see Harrowby, he explained that he could not contact Lord Castlereagh although he did pass his house three or four times to find him. All this must have struck defence counsel as decidedly 'fishy'. Even allowing for the fact that Wilson was a little foolhardy in trusting Hyden, a man he can't have known well, with the plan, how odd it was that Hyden, a cow-keeper, should not only recognize a government minister by sight, but that Harrowby should give the man the time of day and accept a note written to someone else. It was extraordinarily convenient, to say the least, that someone privy to such damning information should come forward in the way that Hyden did. And it was nothing short of bizarre that when Hyden got to Cato Street, at nearly 7 o'clock, he declined entry to the stable on the grounds that he had to buy some cream. Davidson, to whom he spoke, seemed quite happy with this and told him to be back by 8 or, failing that, to follow on to Grosvenor Square. It was Lord Harrowby himself who nearly let the government cat out of the conspiratorial bag when, under cross-examination by Mr Curwood, he told the court:

> I had some general knowledge of some conspiracy or something of the kind, going on before this . . . that some plan was in agitation, but we did not know the time at which it was to take place or the

particulars . . . I do not know a person named Edwards.

But Lord Sidmouth and his secretary, John Cam Hobhouse, did. They had employed him, urged him almost certainly to act the *agent provocateur*, gave him cash to buy weapons and made themselves accessible to receive his regular reports. None of this evidence was of course available to the defence counsel and the prosecution did not need it because they had Hyden, Adams and the next king's evidence witness, John Monument. Thistlewood had approached the shoemaker some weeks before the 23rd in the company of Brunt and told him 'Great events are now close at hand – the people are every where anxious for a change' and accordingly, Monument had gone to Cato Street. His next piece of evidence was rather strange. He told the court that, while handcuffed to Thistlewood on their way to the Privy Council, Thistlewood had told him to say that it was Edwards who had been the instigator of the plot. Monument refused, 'when I had never seen such a man as Edwards in my life'. Thistlewood had gone on to describe Edwards to him.

Curwood's defence tried to do what Watson's had in the Spa Fields trial, tear to shreds the testimony of men who had turned king's evidence:

> an accomplice was a necessary witness; but though necessary, he was
> not of necessity to be believed. The more atrocious the guilt in which
> he steeped himself, the less worthy he was of credit.

In other words, Adams and Monument should be disregarded – they had bought their lives with their testimony and that alone meant that the testimony was likely to be tainted. And then Curwood turned to the mechanics of the government's plot against Thistlewood and the men of Cato Street. Thomas Dwyer, an Irish brick-layer from Gee's Court, was another conspirator who got cold feet. Recruited by Davidson, he told Thistlewood he could raise twenty-seven men for the rebellion. His role on the night in question was to procure the weapons known to be stored (bizarrely) in the same building as the Foundlings Hospital. Dwyer had met virtually all of the conspirators, seen the pikes being tied to handles and the grenades prepared and promptly reported all this to a Major James who told him to report to Lord Sidmouth. On oath, Dwyer claimed he was an honest, hard-working man who had lived in Marylebone for fifteen years – 'and yet all of a sudden a band of traitors intrusted me with their traitorous designs'.

Curwood effectively destroyed Dwyer by calling Edward Hucklestone, who told the court, 'I do not think [Dwyer] is to be believed on his oath'. Dwyer made money on the side by blackmailing gentlemen in St James's Park. His brother had been transported for a similar offence. The scam worked like this; Dwyer would accost a man in the park, get him into as compromising a position as possible and then Hucklestone would 'catch' them and the blackmail would ensue. It was a money-spinner throughout the century and one of its unlikely victims was probably the Foreign Secretary, Lord Castlereagh, only months after Cato Street.

But Curwood was on a roll. Questioning Joseph Doane, the Court Papers Reporter, and Andrew Mitchell, printer of the *New Times*, it became obvious that the report concerning the forthcoming dinner at Lord Harrowby's appeared only in the *New Times* and not the other eleven papers it might have appeared in. How pat, then, that it was the *New Times* that Thistlewood should have sent for. But who had told the conspirators of the Harrowby dinner? Edwards. And how easy for Edwards to suggest that the *New Times* would carry the relevant details. He may even have volunteered to go out to buy a copy himself.

The third day opened with Curwood's summation on Thistlewood's behalf. He was not, he told the jury, going to dispute the fact that his client was a murderer; but that he was guilty of high treason rested heavily on the word of Adams and the fact that at *their very first meeting* Thistlewood entrusted his entire plan to him. The rest of Curwood's defence dealt with the implausibility of the plot:

> barracks were to be taken, cannons carried away, Ministers assassinated, government subverted, the Mansion House occupied, all by fifteen or twenty men.

Counsel asked where the money was to come from to make it all work. There had been talk among the conspirators of treating their followers and Brunt, though out of work, offered £1 for the purpose. Indeed, hunger had driven these desperate men to do *something* in the hope of plunder. As for the setting up of a Provisional Government, the conspirators did not even have access to a printing press, as the 'your tyrants are destroyed' lines were written by hand. As for the canvas bags carried by Ings for the heads of Castlereagh and Sidmouth, they were far too small for the purpose. 'Is it possible, gentlemen,' Curwood asked, 'to sacrifice human life upon evidence like this?'

Curwood slammed again into Adams, who had heard murder committed and waited for four days and his own arrest, before he 'disburthened' his heart. In the witness box, Adams repeatedly used phrases like, 'No, I have something else to say before I come to that' and 'No, I have not come to that yet.' Where did this arrogance come from? Although Curwood did not have the tangible evidence to prove it, it came from the backing of the Privy Council. With the information unsubstantiated and in some cases invented by Edwards, the Privy Council were able to coach Adams as to what to say. And to make sure it all went swimmingly, who should be directing operations but the two men now leading the prosecution, the Attorney-General and the Solicitor-General.

Next, defence counsel went for Monument, reminding the jury that his evidence and Adams's did not add up as to meeting times, places and people:

> Adams sees not what is done in Cato Street. Monument sees not Adams and is not seen by Adams. Dwyer sees neither Adams nor Monument on any occasion.

Curwood at last, thirty-five pages in, got round to the missing Edwards – 'Why was this man not called?' The trial transcript merely reports the dialogue. We cannot see the disapproving faces on the Bench, hear the howls of fury and annoyance from all quarters of the Court, but when Curwood said, 'They [the Prosecution] would then have the spy to support the testimony of the informer' we can imagine it would have been pandemonium.

The Solicitor-General followed, claiming that the testimony of Adams, Monument, Hyden and Dwyer was 'in all respects pure and uncontaminated' and other witnesses not involved in the conspiracy had reported on meetings, weapons-buying and grenade-making. The Attorney-General then took over, reminding the jury of all that damning, if circumstantial evidence they had heard over three days. And Lord Chief Justice Abbott delivered his summation.

When he had finished the jury retired, only to come back a few minutes later to have the law explained to them (again) on the exact definition of the four counts of high treason. About fifteen minutes later, the verdict was delivered – guilty on all four counts. Thistlewood, who had been totally composed during his trial, remained so now and was returned to his cell. He ate a little during the evening and asked Brown, the gaoler, for some wine.

Wilkinson seems to have believed that Thistlewood expected acquittal, perhaps on the basis of Spa Fields. But he had killed no one at Spa Fields and he was not having to contend with the 'missing mendaciousness' of George Edwards.

As dusk fell on that Thursday, the crowd outside the Sessions House, seen to contain faces familiar from Smithfield, Spa Fields and Finsbury, melted away.

Chapter 12

The Hand of Death

James Ings wore black for his trial that opened on Friday 21 April. They were probably the only clothes he owned, other than his butcher's apron, but it also spoke of a sense of foreboding. Like all the conspirators he had sat in court throughout Thistlewood's trial and unless there were to be extensive mitigating circumstances, it seemed likely that the guilty verdict would follow for them all.

After various challenges by both counsel, twelve men and true were sworn in as jurymen and the Solicitor-General outlined the case and explained the meaning of high treason as he had previously. He spoke for one hour and ten minutes before calling his witnesses. The published version of the trials that followed is no more than a summary, in the interests of space and tedium. The same witnesses were called and delivered the same testimony, although Robert Adams must have surprised the court by admitting that when the Prince Regent last attended parliament, Ings had gone to St James's Park, armed with a pistol intending to shoot him. Of all the conspirators, James Ings seems the most volatile and unstable.

The witness Robert Hyden cut a forlorn figure, explaining that he had been a gentleman's servant, but was now in the Marshalsea Prison with a debt of £18 hanging over him. John and Thomas Monument both stated that they went to Cato Street out of fear and intended to run away (from Lord Harrowby's) once the shooting started.

Throughout the day, Ings's behaviour was erratic. He followed the evidence closely at times, but at others seemed suddenly gloomy. The next day when his butcher's knife was shown to the jury, Ings called out as a reminder, 'It was not found upon me, my Lord.'

Curwood, in defence, also reiterated the meaning of high treason, but was rebuked by Sir Robert Dallas on the Bench for referring to Thistlewood's trial (of which, of course, the Ings jury had no direct knowledge). He delivered the same attack on Adams and Hyden that he had made previously and lamented the fact that Palin and Cook had not been found because they might well have made excellent defence witnesses. Curwood's first witness was Thomas Chambers, a radical who had attended a number of meetings with Ings, Adams and Edwards. He spoke of the *Black Dwarf* and *Medusa* and admitted that he had carried banners at Smithfield with the legend 'The Manchester Massacre' and, when Hunt arrived in triumph, another marked 'Trial by Jury' (which of course was what was going on now). Before Adolphus's summation, Ings requested a convenience break and returned sucking an orange 'with great composure'.

Following the same track as before, Adolphus discredited the king's evidence men but was clutching at straws when he tried to claim that because the Bank of England and the Mansion House were not the property of the king that no high treason had been committed.

Ings was then allowed to address the jury and most of the biographical details we have already heard came from this moment in the trial. He claimed to have been duped by Edwards and burst into tears when he said:

> I am like a bullock drove into Smithfield market to be sold. The Attorney-General knew the man [Edwards]. He knew all their plans for two months before I was acquainted with it . . . When I was before Lord Sidmouth, a gentleman said, Lord Sidmouth knew all about this for about two months.

As for Adams –

> That man . . . who has got out of the halter himself by accusing others falsely, would hang his God.

In a few sentences, the 'man of no education and very humble abilities' had summed up the crux of the problem of the Cato Street period. Sidmouth knew perfectly well about the conspiracy because he had installed George Edwards to stir things up and make it happen. And the practice of accepting evidence in terms of a plea bargain, where a man could spout any rubbish in the sure knowledge that he would walk free, speaks volumes for the corruption of the legal system and the government of the day. The jury however were in no mood to listen. It took them just twenty minutes to find James Ings guilty on the first and third counts.

John Brunt faced justice two days later, on Monday 24th. He was soberly dressed, pale and composed, with a sheaf of papers on which he had scribbled notes. The jury was sworn, eight of them having already served in Thistlewood's trial.[1] Bolland and the Attorney-General went through the motions as before, but when Adams appeared in the witness box, Brunt yelled, 'My Lords, can the witness look me in the face and look at those gentlemen (pointing to the jury) and say that I said this?' Adams assured him that he could. 'Then,' shouted Brunt,' you are a bigger villain than even I took you for.' The court, of course, immediately clamped down on what was fast becoming a circus. Adams, in fact, came across as a born-again reactionary – 'my mind was perverted by Paine's *Age of Reason* and Carlile's publication'.

The same prosecution witnesses trooped through the court throughout this day and the next and it was noticeable that the prosecution were becoming blasé. At one point, when a juror stood up and pointed out that there was no actual evidence that Brunt had ever had any ammunition in his house, the Chief Baron was forced to concede that that was true. To balance that, Adolphus had been 'unavoidably absent' during part of the trial and that 'might have led to some inaccuracies'. The reason for his absence is not given.

Brunt then spoke on his own behalf, denying that he had any knowledge of 'another Despard job' in Grosvenor Square. He poured scorn on Adams's testimony – 'Is it upon such evidence as this, that you will deprive a son of a father and a wife of a husband?' Clearly, he and Adams had issues going all the way back to Cambrai four years earlier, but Brunt slammed the treacherous John Monument too and spends four pages focusing on the mysteriously absent Edwards – 'Should I die, by this case, I have been seduced by a villain, who, I have no doubt, has been employed by Government.'

This time, the jury took half an hour to find John Brunt guilty, on the third and fourth counts. His composure did not slip. He bowed to the court and was taken away.

Richard Tidd and William Davidson elected to be tried together and the proceedings opened on Wednesday 26 April. Four of the jury had served already and the wranglings of the exact definition of high treason and the events of Cato Street must by now have been trickling out of their ears. It was noticeable that Adams was embellishing his testimony with every trial.

Bradburn, for instance, was ready to make a box to send Castlereagh's head to Ireland; and Adams swore he had never told anybody he intended to have 'wine and blood for supper'. Throughout the day, Davidson took careful notes and asked if he may have his wife visit him that night. The court, quite correctly, said it had no power to grant that request.

On the Thursday, Davidson had seen the light and carried a Bible with various passages marked. It was essentially the book of the establishment, in marked contrast to the godless literature of Paine and the radicals. A number of character witnesses for both men were introduced by the defence, but against the charges of Cato Street, they cut little ice.

Davidson's appeal to the court was the most grovelling of all the conspirators. He claimed never to mix with other blacks – 'because I always found them very ignorant' – as though being an honorary white man might save his neck. He was merely walking past Cato Street on the night in question when a man he knew named George Goldworthy (from Liverpool) 'an accomplice of Edwards', thrust a sword into his hand and was as astonished as anyone when the shooting started and he found himself under arrest. Contrary to the Runner's evidence, he swore he never offered any violence 'but gave myself up quietly'. He then trotted out the 'wrong man' story over the sexual harassment charges on account of his colour. Reaching for a glass of water, he said, 'My colour may be against me, but I have as good and as fair a heart as if I were white.' He gave the jury his family history. He quoted from scripture. He quoted from Alexander Pope, the eighteenth-century poet. And he ended, 'I hope my death may prove useful to my country – for still England, I call thee so.'

By comparison, Tidd's defence was short and to the point. Edwards had inveigled him into attending the Cato Street meeting and he even produced the spy's note of the address – the Horse and Groom, John Street – to prove it. He knew nothing of any plan in Grosvenor Square and ten minutes after his arrival at the hay-loft, found himself under arrest. The jury took forty minutes to find Davidson and Tidd guilty on the third count of high treason.

James Wilson now withdrew his misnomer plea and entered another of guilty. The five remaining prisoners – Bradburn, Shaw, Harrison, Gilchrist and Cooper – all appeared in court with the same plea. Their counsel, Walford and Broderick, had watched the previous trials and realized there was no effective defence left.

At 9.15 on Friday 28 April, eleven conspirators, all double-ironed,[2] shuffled before their Lordships in the Sessions House of the Old Bailey. Thistlewood, resigned to his fate and ill-looking, was allowed to address the court. He was very eloquent, contending that not even a Cicero[3] could deflect Sidmouth and Castlereagh from their vengeance.

'Justice I demand,' he roared at the Bench. 'If I am denied it, your pity is no equivalent.' He accused the court of inhuman treatment, of bending the rules to achieve a guilty verdict –

A few hours hence and I shall be no more . . . [I] died when liberty and justice had been driven from [this country's] confines by a set of villains, whose thirst for blood is only to be equalled by their activity in plunder.

He slammed Hyden, he slammed Dwyer; above all he slammed Edwards. And he said he had vowed vengeance on the heads of those who had caused Peterloo – 'when infants were sabred in their mothers' arms and the breast, from which they drew the tide of life, was severed from the parent's body'. The conspiracy against him, against all radicals, was perfect because it was carried out by the highest in the land, which included the Attorney-General and the Solicitor-General, with vast resources at their disposal. As for assassination, Thistlewood reminded the classically taught bench that Brutus and Cassius were praised for the murder of the tyrannical Julius Caesar and 'High treason was committed against the people at Manchester'.

The court was horrified and disgusted. They had expected Thistlewood to beg for mercy. Instead he attacked them, their corruption, their malice.

Davidson spoke next. Intriguingly, he brought up (although he didn't use the term itself) *diffidatio*, the medieval law enshrined in Magna Carta which allowed the citizenry to overthrow a corrupt government. This was not treason, he rightly claimed, but weakened his case by repeating his whinge about his being led astray by Edwards and Goldworthy.

James Ings also blamed Edwards, but, like Thistlewood, he wanted to go out in a blaze of glory. He was not part of a plan to assassinate ministers, but if he had been, assassination was not as appalling as the starvation men of his class faced every day. He cited Peterloo.

These yeomen had their swords ground beforehand and I had a sword ground also . . . I hope my children will live to see justice done to their bleeding country.

Brunt bounded forward, complaining he was given neither ink nor paper to make any notes. He pointed to the sword of justice on the wall and felt his 'blood boil in his veins' at the way justice was perverted and 'her sacred name prostituted to the basest and vilest purposes'. He was a Deist[4] and looking at the whole course of the trial, asked: 'Is this, then, Christianity?' He harangued the king's ministers – Castlereagh and Sidmouth had an antipathy against the people – 'is that high treason?' He had no ill-will against the king, but the king was ruled by a lawless faction, the robber-barons who made up the government. He was more than ready to die, a martyr for the good of his country.

Richard Tidd denied any involvement in the conspiracy. James Wilson said he had been dragged into the whole thing by Adams. William Harrison said everybody was lying. Richard Bradburn and John Shaw accused Adams of lying. Charles Cooper said there was no evidence of high treason against him. James Gilchrist, in floods of tears, went to Cato Street on the promise of food – he had not eaten all day – and continued to cry until the prisoners left the court.

They placed the black cap on the head of Chief Justice Abbott and one by one, he sentenced Thistlewood, Ings, Brunt, Davidson and Tidd to death.

> You and each of you, be taken from hence to the gaol from whence you came and from thence that you be drawn upon a hurdle to a place of execution and there be hanged by the neck until you be dead; and that afterwards your heads shall be severed from your bodies and your bodies be divided into four quarters to be disposed of as his majesty shall think fit. And may God in his infinite goodness have mercy on your souls!

The court crier intoned 'Amen' and the prisoners did not flinch. Thistlewood, with the sangfroid which never deserted him, took a little snuff and looked around the court 'as if he were entering a theatre'.

Over the next two days, events moved fast. The radical press went into overdrive, countered by the loyalist papers. There was no Court of Appeal for the condemned men – that would be set up in 1907 – and the Privy Council met the day after the passing of sentence to decide the execution date. Thistlewood, Brunt, Ings, Davidson and Tidd would hang and be decapitated, but the quartering of their bodies was remitted as it had been for Despard and Brandreth. The death sentence for the others was commuted to transportation for life and that meant Botany Bay.

That night, Brown, the governor of Newgate, broke the bad, but hardly unexpected news to the five marked for death. It was to be Monday morning, 1 May, a day that would live on in the annals of working-class freedom for ever. There was a silence, then Thistlewood said, 'The sooner we go, sir, the better.'

That Saturday, the five had been visited by the ordinary or chaplain of Newgate, the Revd Cotton, who begged them to make their peace with God. He tried again on Sunday, talking to each man in his separate cell and Davidson cracked. He asked for the services of a Wesleyan minister, a journeyman tailor called Rennett. In the event, the man was unavailable but a replacement was found in the 'person of Mr Cotton himself'. 'The rays of Christianity burst, as it were, through his dungeon's gloom' on the Sunday and Davidson wrote a letter to Lord Harrowby, to be delivered by the Under-Sheriff.

Sunday was the last day that the condemned men would see their families. Susan Thistlewood came with her son and the other wives and children. The gaolers themselves, long hardened to such gallows-side scenes, were very moved by the whole experience. Brunt alone remained stoical, claiming that his execution day would be the happiest of his life. Because all except Davidson called themselves Deists, the usual final service at Newgate was dispensed with. Apart from the families, the only person trying to see the prisoners was the radical Alderman and MP Mr Wood, who wanted the answers to three specific questions. He would have to wait.

Of all of them, Ings spent the worst night. Terrified of the morning, he rambled on to the others through the stone walls of his cell, expressing the hope that his body be sent to the king to make turtle-soup out of it. At 5 on Monday morning, Cotton tried for one last time to offer the last rites. Davidson prayed with him, but the others still refused. He and Brunt were the only two who drank a toast to the king's health. The contents of their last breakfast is not recorded, but their request to eat together was denied.

Outside Newgate, all was bustle. The day dawned bright and since Saturday, Sheriff Rothwell had been working with Sidmouth to finalize details. The Home Secretary was too well aware of the vast mob that would gather and dispensed with the idea of dragging the five to the scaffold on hurdles as per the death sentence. Throughout Sunday, carpenters' saws and hammers could be heard extending the platform outside the Sessions House to house all the prisoners and allow room for decapitation. A crowd had gathered and had to be dispersed by the police so that work could continue. Posts and rails were strung along the Bailey to prevent a repetition of the scenes that accompanied the hanging of Holloway and Haggerty in 1807 when the crowd panicked due to overcrowding and over thirty people were trampled to death.[5] Every approach to the prison, along Newgate Street, Giltspur Street, Skinner Street and Fleet Lane was, in effect, cordoned off. None of this deterred the crowd that had assembled as darkness fell on Sunday night. They stayed there, without food or shelter, waiting for the morning.

As always in cases of execution, but especially for the 'poor deluded wretches' of Cato Street, those with windows overlooking the yard charged a fortune for their views, but even with prices as high as two guineas[6] there were plenty of takers. People crowded against the barriers and young men dangled precariously from lamp posts and the top of the Newgate pump. A shout went up between 5 and 6 as quantities of sawdust were strewn on the scaffold platform and swathes of black cloth were tied around the uprights.

At 6.20, a detachment of Foot Guards took up position opposite Newgate and a second further east, towards the City, ready for any eventuality. Six light field guns were placed by the Royal Horse Artillery outside the livery stables near Christ Church and more Life Guard units picqueted Ludgate Hill and Bridge Street. The City Light Horse, whose guns John Palin and others were to have grabbed on the 23 February, were dispersed to key positions throughout the city. When John Bellingham was hanged, the authorities had posted placards warning the crowd not to push, but no such precaution was used now.

While Sheriff Rothwell inspected the gallows and the crowd were moved ever further back by a wall of constables, Alderman Wood was inside the gaol demanding to see the prisoners. He was told this was impossible, that Newgate was now under the control of Lord Sidmouth and not the City of London. That argument would not have surprised Thistlewood.

The crowd remained quiet and well behaved. Any rescue attempt of the five was probably impossible because the authorities had planned this day well. There were no banners, no weapons, no apparent *politics* at all, just a low murmur when something new happened. Just in case, however, and to prevent another Peterloo, a number of placards were ready outside the debtors' door with the legend 'The Riot Act has been read. Disperse immediately'. While the Life Guards, saddled and waiting outside St Sepulchre's church, helped police drag a bystander down from a roof by his heels, the crowd roared with delight. This, to the authorities, was all to the good – a happy crowd was less likely to go on the rampage.

Shortly after 7, the hangman appeared. This was the repellent illiterate James (Jemmy) Botting, who probably hanged 175 people during his time in the job. He was constantly complaining about the pay and working conditions, signing the letters that someone else wrote for him with a cross. He had been in post for two years by this time and was the first hangman to receive a regular wage (£1 a week) in addition to perks, such as handouts from undertakers and selling off bits of rope which were believed by some to have magical properties.

Botting supervised the bringing out of the coffins, assisted (although Wilkinson's account does not mention him) by James Foxen. The only difference between the pair was that Botting called his victims 'parties', whereas Foxen preferred 'gentlemen'. More sawdust was then thrown into the black caskets.

While the reprieved six jabbered their gratitude in another part of the prison – only Wilson and Harrison felt a sense of guilt – the procession of the great and bad out onto the scaffold began. Thistlewood emerged from the condemned cell first and bowed to the Sheriffs. He looked up at the sky. 'It appears fine,' he said and waited while his irons were knocked off. At last, Alderman Wood reached him to ask his questions and an unseemly quarrel broke out between Sheriff Rothwell, who claimed he did not want Thistlewood's peace of mind to be disturbed and Sheriff Parkins who insisted Wood be allowed to talk to him. Parkins and Wood won the day and the Alderman asked Thistlewood when and where he had met George Edwards. 'At Preston's,' Thistlewood told him. 'About June last.' Wood wrote the answers down.

Tidd emerged next, smiling, and when his anklets were smashed off darted across to Thistlewood. The pair shook hands. 'Well, Mr

Thistlewood,' Tidd said. 'How do you do?' 'I was never better,' his leader replied. Ings positively danced across the yard, dressed once more in his rough pepper-and-salt butcher's jacket and a dirty cap. His hysteria grew as the moments ticked by, laughing and shouting as he sat on the bench with the others. Brunt was composed as they tied his hands and removed his shackles. 'All will soon be well,' he told the others. Davidson, who had taken the sacrament at 6 (it was now 7.30) prayed fervently along with the chaplain. Cotton was still desperately trying to get the others to show remorse and repentance, but they still refused, each of them about to face their God in their own way.

When everything was ready, the five men shook hands and the 'yeoman of the halter' secured the pinioning. Cotton's voice could be heard across the silent crowd. 'I am the resurrection and the life' and St Sepulchre's bell in the morning tolled.

The chaplain climbed the scaffold steps first – the only one in that grim little procession who would come back down of his own accord. Thistlewood, an orange in his hand, looked out over the vast crowd, a sea of uplifted faces in the middle distance. Someone shouted 'God Almighty bless you'. The conspirator did not flinch. As Wilkinson put it – 'Thistlewood with the rope around his neck was the same Thistlewood that appeared so conspicuous at Smithfield.' He sucked the orange and assured anyone who could hear him that he died a friend to liberty.

Ings in the mean time was going to pieces. He tried to sing the old radical song, an inversion of the American revolutionary Patrick Henry's 'Give me Death or Liberty'. 'Aye,' Brunt shouted. 'It is better to die free than live slaves.' Tidd was brought forward next and with difficulty shook Ings's hand. The Lincolnshire man's eyes filled with tears – 'My wife and I . . .' but he could not go on. 'Come, my old cock o'wax' – astonishingly it was the crumbling Ings who spoke. 'Keep up your spirits; it will all be over soon.' When Tidd reached the scaffold, three cheers broke out from the crowd, impressed by the bold way in which he approached the drop. He bowed to the crowd on Snow Hill; he bowed to the faces towards Ludgate Hill. The people, briefly, loved him and more so when he angled his neck to make Botting's job easier, with the knot to the right so he would die quicker. Like Thistlewood, he refused a hood over his face.

When Ings was roped, he shouted, 'Remember me to King George IV;

God bless him and may he have a long reign.' He also asked that his other clothes go to his wife, so that 'Jack Ketch[7] should have no coat of his'. In a moment of gallows philosophy, he turned to one of the gaolers – 'Well, Mr Davis, I am going to find out this great secret.' He bounded onto the scaffold, 'Goodbye, gentlemen. Here go the remains of an unfortunate man.' The cheers he roared out to the crowd however fell hollow on the silent watchers. To Wilkinson, they were 'nothing but the ravings of a disordered mind'. By the time he turned to Ludgate Hill, he was jabbering a string of unrelated nonsense, still intermittently trying to sing the Death or Liberty song. Tidd quietly reproached him. 'Don't, Ings. There is no use in all this noise. We can die without making a noise.'

Ings refused Botting's hood and asked that his own cap be pulled over his eyes, but only at the last moment. 'Ah ha!' were his last shouted words. 'I see a good many of my friends are on the houses.' Davidson reached the platform, muttering prayers with Cotton. For the last few minutes he had stood apart from the others, divided by race, by colour, by prejudices that were entirely his own.

Brunt was last – and he complained about this. He looked terrible. His cheeks were sunk, giving a weird prominence to his chin, forehead and eyebrow ridge. When he saw the weak sun dancing on the breastplates of the Life Guards, he shouted, 'I see nothing but a military government will do for this country.' He nodded to people in the crowd. He took one last pinch of snuff.

'God bless you, Thistlewood!' a voice shouted and Botting went along the line, fitting the hoods. 'Now, old gentleman,' Ings said to the hangman. 'Finish me tidily . . . Pull the rope tighter; it may slip.' And, with the cloth over his eyes, called out to the chaplain, 'I hope, Mr. Cotton, you will give me a good character.' Davidson finally shook Cotton's hand and for a moment the chaplain stood alone with the condemned, intoning 'those awful sentences which have sounded last in the ears of so many unhappy men'.

The trapdoors fell with a crash. As the horrified spectators looked along the line from left to right, they saw Thistlewood's body writhe for moment, each kick fainter than the last and then twirl slowly on the creaking rope 'as if upon the motion of the hand of death'. Tidd thudded into eternity and scarcely moved. By sheer chance, his neck must have snapped in accordance with the scientific principles of hanging which were not yet established.

Ings, in keeping with his ravings of moments before, twisted and leapt in the air, Botting and Foxen grabbing his legs to finish him quicker. Davidson, after three or four heaves, hung silent and still. Brunt, like Ings, did not go quietly and the hangman had to wrestle with him too.

The crowd who had watched all this showed no sign of unease, which must have been a relief to the titled people watching from upstairs windows and to the cordons of police and cavalry. But worse was to come. It was one thing to hang a man – even five men – in public. That was the norm and for most it was 'bread and circuses', the organized butchery of a 'Roman holiday'. But hacking off a villain's head was something else and it was rare. Botting let the bodies hang for half an hour to ensure that life was extinct, then drew them up into a bizarre sitting position, taking off the hoods and ropes and one by one placing the rope-burned necks on the sloping edge of the block.

Thistlewood's face was mauve, but otherwise peaceful and the crowd expected Botting to wield the axe that was propped on the scaffold. In fact, he didn't move. What the mob did not know was that decapitation was a skill too far for Jemmy Botting and a second figure, with a small knife in his hand 'similar to what is used by surgeons in amputation' moved towards Thistlewood's corpse. Later commentators have assumed the headsman was dressed as a sailor, but in fact he wore a dark blue jacket, grey trousers and a slouch hat. His face was completely obscured by a black mask and a coloured handkerchief and from contemporary illustrations he is clearly a civilian.

The crowd at last reacted and shouted as the blade hit the neck. For a moment, the headsman hesitated, then hacked through muscle and bone to hand Thistlewood's head to Foxen. The mob hooted as the hangman's assistant held the trophy aloft to all four points of the compass and shouted, 'This is the head of Arthur Thistlewood, the traitor.' The howls of the mob grew louder. Botting and Foxen then 'reassembled' the head and placed it with the body in the coffin, sliding the block along for Richard Tidd. There is little doubt that, apart from the charisma of Thistlewood, the Lincolnshire man had won the hearts of the crowd and the sight of his purple, dead face galvanized the crowd – 'shoot that bloody murderer!' someone shouted. 'Bring out Edwards', and the cry was taken up. The headsman worked quickly, disappearing briefly as rubbish was hurled at him by the nearest spectators. Foxen held Tidd's head in both hands and went through the process once more. 'This is the head of Richard Tidd, the traitor.' The same followed for James Ings. And then for William Davidson, whose mouth was slightly open, but whose features otherwise showed no change. When Foxen held the head up however, blood dripped profusely from the severed neck, to the hisses and groans of the crowd.

Brunt's clothing had become trapped in the platform doors and there was a grisly struggle as Botting and Foxen wrestled to release the corpse. Brunt's face was bright purple with his hair hanging over his forehead in a terrifying manner. To make matters worse, the headsman fumbled this one, dropping the head on the sawdust. An hour and eight minutes after Thistlewood had walked up the scaffold steps, Foxen called out for the last time, 'This is the head of John Thomas Brunt, the traitor.'

The Cato Street conspiracy was over . . . wasn't it?

Chapter 13

'This is But the Beginning . . .'

The mob who watched the dispatch of the Cato Street conspirators had gone home by tea-time and the soldiery stood down. It was not all anti-climax however. The masked headsman was held to be a surgeon because of his skill and speed with the knife and a rumour flew that he came from Argyll Street. That could only mean Dr Thomas Wakley and, as night fell, a sinister mob gathered outside his house, smashed his windows and set the place on fire. The police and the army were ordered to restore order and helped the bleeding and disoriented Wakley (who had been kicked by the mob and left for dead) to safety. They did the world a favour – not only was the surgeon unconnected with the executions, he would go on in later years to found that most eminent of medical journals, *The Lancet*.

The real culprit was probably a 'resurrectionist' named Tom Parker, hired for £20 by the Under-Sheriff. Before the law was changed in 1831, there was a vigorous trade in body-snatching, removing corpses from graves to provide 'subjects' for the London medical schools. Parker specialized in teeth – a spin-off outlet into the denture business, as he was 'in the habit of cutting off nobs for the purposes of getting the gnashers'.[1]

The widows and families who were left – Susan Thistlewood, Mary Tidd, Mary Brunt, Celia Ings and Sarah Davidson – petitioned Lord Sidmouth for the return of their husbands' bodies. This was, of course, refused, as it was contrary to custom. A channel had been dug alongside an underground passage at Newgate and at 7 that night, the five coffins were filled with quick lime and covered with earth and stones so that 'no trace of their end remains for any future public observation'.

Susan Thistlewood continued alone, presenting a petition to the Privy Council that was subsequently passed to the king. The official reply was laconic to the point 'that Thistlewood was buried'.

The next day, Tuesday 2 May, the remaining conspirators who had been sentenced to transportation were escorted in three post-chaises to Portsmouth and placed on a convict ship bound for New South Wales. It is not known whether any of them returned. Gilchrist alone remained in Newgate to serve an unspecified gaol sentence. The following Saturday, six men who had been arrested on suspicion appeared in the dock – Thomas Preston, William Simmons, Abel Hall, Robert George, William Firth and William Hazard. There was no case against them and they were discharged. Preston alone, as loquacious as ever, tried to make a speech and was immediately silenced by the court.

General histories of the period sweep swiftly from Cato Street to the Queen Caroline affair of the following year. At first sight, this is typically British – the public of all classes far more interested in the tittle-tattle of a salacious royal divorce than a people's revolution. In fact, serious rioting occurred in London between those who backed George IV and those who backed his wife and this was to be repeated on the occasion of her funeral in August 1821. This turned into an anti-police riot in which stones and brickbats were thrown. In the end order was only restored by the Life Guards firing their carbines into the air to disperse the mob. Ironically, most of the violence occurred near to Tyburn turnpike, within a stone's throw of both the Cato Street stable and Lord Harrowby's house. Two men died and many more were injured. One modern historian makes the interesting comment that Thistlewood's timing was poor; had he held off until the Caroline riots he might have succeeded in mounting his revolution.

In fact, there were three risings in 1820 which may or may not have been linked to Cato Street, and these in turn seem to have been part of a wider conspiracy in the weaving heartlands of Scotland, Yorkshire, Lancashire and Carlisle. Two weeks before Thistlewood's trial, trouble was brewing near Huddersfield. Secret cards labelled 'democracy' were distributed among potential revolutionaries whose aim was to establish a free government. Beacons, scythes, pitchforks, guns and the inevitable pikes were all part of the paraphernalia carried at Grange Moor near Barnsley on the night of 11 April. Led by two Waterloo veterans, Comstive and Addy, a 300-strong force marched twelve miles to rendezvous with a Scottish contingent that failed to materialize. There were transportations and a bitter sense of disappointment – 'I hope', ran a letter found among the effects of a weaver-conspirator, 'that we may all meet in one body and one voice yet.'[2]

More serious was the violence near Glasgow on 5/6 April when weavers clashed with the authorities in what became known as the 'battle of Bonnymuir'. As with Brandreth's Pentrich rising, the disaffected marched on local ironworks (at Carron) to grab weapons. For months, there had been strikes in the area (all of them illegal under the Acts of 1799 and 1800) and three armed units converged on the factory to be met by two squadrons of Hussars. Three ring-leaders were hanged.

In the days before he died, Arthur Thistlewood received a visitor in the condemned cell at Newgate. The result of that visit appeared in the *Leeds Intelligencer* two months later:

> Exhibition, Music Hall, Leeds, by Particular Desire, New Addition .
> . . a likeness of the celebrated notorious Arthur Thistlewood taken
> from life.

If Thistlewood hoped that his wax image in Madame Tussaud's 'special room' would make him a part of history, he was mistaken. Two years later, neither he nor Colonel Despard was part of the waxworks' catalogue and the world had moved on.

We have some tantalizing insights into the mindsets of the Cato Street hanged from their writings in Newgate. Thistlewood's poem is typically anti-government – 'Oh what a twine of mischief is a Statesman'. There is no introspection here and certainly no remorse. The government is corrupt – that is the only reason for Thistlewood's death. Richard Tidd, who had difficulty expressing himself on paper, wrote nothing, but James Ings wrote separate letters to his wife, his daughters, his son and the king.

To Celia, at 4 o'clock on Sunday afternoon, 30 April, he lamented the fact that he had to leave his family

> in a land full of corruption, where justice and liberty has taken their
> flight from, to other distant shores . . . I conclude a constant lover to
> you and your children and all friends. I die the same, but an enemy
> to all tyrants.

He asked her to give his love to his parents and siblings 'for I am gone out of a very troublesome world and I hope you will let it pass like a summer cloud over the earth'.

174 Enemies of the State

To his (unnamed) daughters, Ings wrote urging them to be kind to their mother and to put all their trust in God. To his son, William, he wrote – 'My dear boy, I hope you will make a bright man in society.' The lad should be honest, sober, industrious and upright and should treat all men as he would want to be treated. At the same time he cautioned him to trust no one – 'for the deception, the corruption and the ingenuity in man I am at a loss to comprehend'.

This was the last thing he wrote, because his petition to the king was almost certainly written first. It forms a mini-autobiography and we have already noted its details. He railed against Edwards the spy and assured his Majesty that should he spare his life, for the sake of his family, he would in future be a 'true and faithful subject'.

Davidson wrote to his wife and to Lord Harrowby. 'Death's countance is familiar to me,' he told Sarah. 'I have had him in view fifteen times and surely he cannot now be terrible. Keep up that noble spirit for the sake of your children . . .'

The Harrowby letter is extraordinary, a mixture of hopeless optimism and downright lies in which Davidson hoped to curry favour by mentioning the fact that he had once been employed by his Lordship and that Edwards knew perfectly well that he was not 'that man of colour' in the revolutionary group.

John Brunt was the most poetic of all, even when he was complaining to Sidmouth about the lack of cutlery in Newgate –

> Let them eat and drink and sleep,
> But knives and forks pray from them keep,
> As they'll commit assassination –
> The rogues would overthrow the nation.

As a sort of PS he wrote:

> Life's but a jest and all things show it,
> I thought so once, but now I know it!

He placed his poetry in an envelope to his wife, together with a shilling, the last money he had, urging her to keep the coin for as long as she lived.

On 30 April, facing the drop the next day, he finally wrote –

> Let Sidmouth and his base colleagues

Cajole and plot their dark intrigues;
Still each Briton's last words shall be
Oh! Give me death or liberty!

Along with the four others, Sidmouth and his colleagues gave Brunt death.

Of the men who were to dine with Lord Harrowby that bitterly cold night in February 1820, Lord Liverpool, the Prime Minister, suffered a massive stroke almost exactly seven years later and lingered on, a vegetable, until December 1828. The nebulous Vansittart, Chancellor of the Exchequer, resigned from the Cabinet in 1822 and took a vague interest in education and factory reform thereafter. The Duke of Wellington, who had advised his Cabinet colleagues to let Thistlewood and his company arrive and then shoot it out with them, spent his last days in 1852 surrounded by an adoring family. He was the hero of Waterloo still, the Iron Duke and a legend as large as that could never be diminished by an appalling two years spent as Prime Minister as the Cato Street decade ended. Lord Eldon lived on, as reactionary as ever, until 1838, by which time there were new revolutionaries – the Chartists – baying for change. The hated Sidmouth, who had done so much to bring down the men of Cato Street, lived on until 1844 when Britain was a nation of cities and railways and steel. At a stroke however, the 'old guard' of Eldon, Vansittart and Sidmouth were removed from the Cabinet two years after Cato Street. It would be nice to believe that this fall from grace was linked with the conspiracy but that is simply not true. They resigned because of age or for personal reasons and probably never thought consciously of Cato Street again.

The oddest fortunes befell Lord Castlereagh. As the only senior Cabinet member in the Commons, he became the government's mouthpiece on all sorts of problems, not merely his own Foreign Office, and the strain, shortly after Cato Street, was beginning to tell. Friends and colleagues became increasingly worried about him and an unsavoury scandal may have been at the bottom of it. At the trial of the Cato Street men we saw how low-life like Dwyer made a precarious living by blackmailing gentlemen over homosexual allegations. According to H Montgomery Hyde,[3] Castlereagh was in the habit of frequenting prostitutes as he crossed St James's Park from his home. One of these turned out to be a man in drag and Castlereagh was caught 'in flagrante' by the man's accomplice. Unlikely as all this sounds, the Foreign Secretary made various veiled references to it to Wellington, among others and it is possibly true.

With all this and the cares of the political world on his shoulders, Castlereagh cut his throat in the presence of his own doctor at his country house of Cray's Farm, Kent, in August 1822. The men of Cato Street would have been delighted.

Of all the shadowy figures stalking the radical night in the Cato Street story, the name that stands out is George Edwards. Documents in the Home Office files prove that Edwards was a spy, that he often used the alias Windsor and that he reported, not only to Magistrate Stafford and his Bow Street Runners, but directly to Sidmouth too. Childish code letters have survived for use by political revolutionaries, signed 'G.E.' on the back. A number of sworn statements still exist (not, of course, made available to the court in 1820) which paint Edwards in a damning light. One of the potential 'Committee of Two Hundred', Pickard, writes of a plan by Edwards to enter the Houses of Parliament carrying hollowed out books which carried bombs – 'What bloody destruction it would make,' Edwards had said.

Alderman Wood who had desperately tried to talk to Thistlewood on the eve and then the morning of his execution, was determined to nail Edwards and raised the issue in the Commons. Denied the right to do this, he approached Sidmouth direct, to stop Edwards from fleeing the country. Sidmouth, of course, refused to help. It was not until 22 May, over three weeks after the execution that a warrant for high treason was eventually raised against Edwards. Harmer, the conspirators' solicitor, put up a vast reward of 1,000 guineas. By that time, the ever-reliable Home Office stooge, Cam Hobhouse, had spirited Edwards away to Guernsey. Using the alias G E Parker, Edwards complained that he was running out of money, that his model-making tools were still locked away at his lodgings in Fleet Street and that his wife was living separately as Mrs Holmes. He was concerned that his new whereabouts were already known. His last letter, written at the end of July, asks for money to buy a house where he can feel safer. There, the trail stops.

One of the many anonymous threatening letters written to the Home Office in the spring of 1820 is this one:

> To Ministers, Privy Councillors, Bloody-minded wretches – Ye are now brooding with hellish delight on the sacrifice ye intend to make of those poor creatures ye took out of Cato Street on pretence of punishing them for what your own horrid spies and agents instigated

. . . But know this, ye demons, on an approaching day and in an hour when you least expect it ye yourselves shall fall a sacrifice to the just vengeance of an oppressed and suffering people who shall behold your bloody corpses dragged in Triumph through their streets.

It never happened. Today, astonishingly, the hay-loft of Cato Street has survived. It is the last building on the left along a quiet cul-de-sac which still bears the name. With an irony which would have appalled Arthur Thistlewood, a nearby street is named after Lord Harrowby and a block of flats only feet from the hay-loft is called Sidmouth Court. In Grosvenor Square, in front of the incongruous statues of American generals from the Second World War, Lord Harrowby's house is now the imposing 5-star Millennium Hotel. Across radical London, Baldwin's Gardens, where Richard Tidd lived in Hole-in-the-Wall Passage, has a church built in 1863 and new flats and a school. Fox Court, the home of John Brunt, is no longer an alleyway, but a huge office block, symbol of the wealth that Brunt despised. Newgate gaol and its Sessions House have long gone, and the grey of the Old Bailey with its gilded figure of justice, stands over the last resting place of the men of Cato Street, its granite determined still not to turn them into martyrs. By contrast, the conspirators' would-be targets have found honourable graves. Eldon lies beside his wife in the Old Churchyard in Kingston, Devon. Wellington rests in the crypt of St Paul's. Castlereagh, despite being a suicide, was laid to rest in Westminster Abbey.

Was there ever a chance of the Cato Street conspiracy working? That all depends on the existence of the Committee of Two Hundred and their links with the provinces. When the malcontents of Yorkshire and Scotland marched in the spring of 1820 they did so in the belief that a general rising of the people would occur. Arthur Thistlewood seems to have believed this too. All that was needed was the wholesale slaughter in Grosvenor Square and instinctively London would rise. If London rose, so would the rest of the country. One of those on the edge of the conspiracy had assured Thistlewood that he could bring twenty-six disaffected Irishmen out of Gee's Court. If all twenty-five men in the hayloft brought the same number, that would make a little over 600 – possibly enough to equal the scattered police forces in the capital but not the soldiery.

Two things are completely missing from the conspirators' plans; first, the exact mechanics of how London could be taken from the forces that held it; and second, if this could be achieved, what was to follow? Most historians have dismissed the men of Cato Street as lunatics, misguided madmen who had no clue as to how to proceed. But the same could be said – and was said – of the *sans-culottes* who stormed the Bastille; today, France is a republic run by its people. The same could be said – and was said – of the Irishmen who occupied the British-held Dublin in 1916; today, Dublin is the capital of an independent Eire. The same could be said – and was said – of the men who took power in Russia in the October of 1917; these were the communists who controlled one of the world's greatest superpowers for nearly three-quarters of a century. It is easy to dismiss plots that fail and British history is full of them.

No doubt Arthur Thistlewood, and the men who stood with him that bright May day in 1820 as they faced the mob and ultimately their God in the yard outside Newgate, felt a sense of failure and of being let down. But what they proved, perhaps once and for all, was that conspiracy, assassination and revolution were no longer the British way. The future, of democracy and justice lay instead with Henry Hunt and William Cobbett, with the men of peace who dealt in moral, not physical force. What 1820 proved at last was that the British way was by the ballot, not the bullet, even if it was to take another hundred years for the ballot to arrive.

In that sense, and in that sense alone, the men of Cato Street deserve their place in history.

NOTES

Chapter 2

1. Literally, 'shit!'. Cambronne had been called on to surrender by the pursuing British and this was his reply. The more polite version is 'La Garde meurt, elle ne se rend pas' (the Guard dies, but does not surrender). Perhaps he said both.

2. The first news in England of the victory had actually been received at Harrowby's house in Grosvenor Square.

3. See below.

4. George Wilkinson, *An Authentic History of the Cato Street Conspiracy* (London, Thomas Kelly, 1820), p. 192.

5. It is noticeable that even in an historic edition of *The Times*, such as that which featured Wellington's Waterloo dispatch, the first page was always given over to advertisements – For Sale and Wanted.

6. *The Wealth of Nations* (1776).

7. In fact, it was well into the twentieth century that such systems became a de rigueur part of domestic arrangements.

8. The Health and Morals of Apprentices Act which affected pauper children only and was widely ignored by industrialists.

9. The conversion of money is complicated. Some economic historians assume a multiplying factor of 40. On that basis, however, we run into difficulties. A better yardstick is in comparison with the poorest working wage – that of a farm labourer at 7 or 8 shillings a week.

10. See Ch. 8.

11. This finally came to an end in 2006.

12. Hector Morrison's testimony from the *Trial of James Ings* – Wilkinson, *Cato Street*, p. 264.

13. Wilkinson, *Cato Street*, p. 183.

14. See Ch. 8.

15. Thomas Malthus, an Anglican vicar, wrote *An Essay on Population* in 1798. Nauseatingly moral, he was over-pessimistic for his time, predicting that population would soon completely outstrip food supply and the result would be disaster of biblical proportions.

16.   For the importance of radical literature, see below.

17.   See Ch. 8

Chapter 3

1.   Almost certainly the metabolic illness porphyria.

2.   Edmund Burke, *Reflections on the Revolution in France* (1790).

3.   Quoted in Lord John Russell, *The Life and Times of Charles James Fox* (1859), vol. 2, p. 361.

4.   Wordsworth, *The Prelude*, bk 2.

5.   Customs officer.

6.   Paine, *The Rights of Man* (1791), p. 260.

7.   Ibid.

8.   Paine is a more visionary version of Cobbett in some ways. In the end he managed to alienate almost everybody, falling out with the French and the Americans.

9.   Ironically, the Revolution's ideology did not take this up. De Gouges herself was guillotined in Nov. 1793 and French women did not get the vote for another 143 years!

10.   Astonishingly, he was rescued on the way by a French ship and went to live in France.

11.   The *Chronique de Paris* for 26 April said 'Yesterday, at half past three, there was . . . used for the first time a machine destined to cut off the heads of criminals condemned to death. This machine was rightfully preferred to other forms of execution. It in no way soils the hands of the man who murders his fellow man and the promptness with which it strikes . . . is more in the print of the law, which may often be stern, but must never be cruel.'

12.   Jacques-Pierre Brissot de Warville wrote 'Each soldier will say to his enemy: brother, I am not going to cut your throat, I am going to free you from the yoke which burdens you; I am going to show you the road to happiness. Like you, I was once a slave; I took up arms and the tyrant vanished.'

13.   Although Fox famously lost his, twice, on the turn of a card!

14.   *The Trial of Joseph Gerrald* (Edinburgh, 1794), pp. 197–9.

15.   Edmund Burke, *Two Letters addressed to a Member of the Present Parliament* (1796).

16.   The importance of informers, spies and *agents provocateurs* will be dealt with elsewhere.

17. We do not have Ings's age. He had four children by 1820 and I have made the assumption he was born about 1780.

18. Quoted in Graham Wallas, *Francis Place* (1895).

19. No relation to the shoemaker Jacobin.

20. 'The Wearing of the Green' was a folk ballad from the time. The Green referred to the shamrock, the visible symbol of the rebels.

21. Quoted in G Manning and B Dobré, *The Floating Republic* (London), p. 200.

22. At one point, Bonaparte actually referred to the long-dead Louis XVI as 'my poor uncle'.

Chapter 4

1. The McNaghten Rules, named after Daniel McNaghten who tried to assassinate the Prime Minister, Robert Peel, in 1843.

2. Southey and Coleridge, *The Devil's Thoughts*, 1829.

3. Quoted in Christopher Hibbert, *Nelson: A Personal History* (London, Viking, 1994), p. 316.

4. All quotations from the Despard trial from *The Newgate Calendar*, vol. 3.

5. As part of the Act of Union with Ireland in 1801, Pitt proposed that Irish Catholics be given equality with Protestants. As head of the Church of England, George III could not accept that and the Prime Minister was forced to resign.

6. *Observer* (Feb. 1803).

7. Charles Dickens watched Mr and Mrs Manning hanged here in 1849, for their part in the Bermondsey Horror.

8. The Bow Street Horse Patrol, which might otherwise have carried out this duty, was not formed for another two years.

9. The actual whereabouts of Despard's grave are shrouded in mystery. One account says that he was buried in the medieval church of St Faith's, long demolished, which stood within the precincts of St Paul's.

10. Condemned to death by his own system, Robespierre tried to commit suicide the night before his execution but he was interrupted by guards and only succeeded in shooting himself in the jaw.

11. Ironically of course, the Revolutionary exhibits are among the most popular in the Chamber of Horrors today. It would be fascinating to see Despard and even more Arthur Thistlewood in wax.

12. *The Newgate Calendar* (1802), vol. 3.

13.   The Foot Guards, like their mounted counterpart the Life Guards and Royals, were raised in 1660 as a personal bodyguard for the king.

Chapter 5

1.   Waiting in the wings was James Catnatch, the doyen of the dying speech. Operating his own printing press in London, Catnatch made a fortune in the 1820s with blood and guts confessions (totally spurious). He sold 500,000 copies of the trial of William Thurtell in 1823 and 1,166,000 of the confession and execution of William Corder in the Red Barn Murder of 1828.

2.   Quoted in E P Thompson, *The Making of the English Working Class* (London, Penguin, 1991), p. 792.

3.   *Works of John Keats*, vol. 5 (1901), p. 108.

4.   Quoted in Thompson, *English Working Class*, p. 803.

5.   *Shorter Oxford Dictionary* (1993), p. 2522.

6.   G M Thomson, *The Prime Ministers* (London, Secker & Warburg, 1980), p. 77. As Thomson points out, he was beaten on all three counts and in that order by Lord John Russell, the Duke of Grafton and Robert Peel!

7.   Quoted ibid., p. 76.

8.   Quoted in Carl Sifakis, *The Encyclopedia of Assassinations* (London, Headline, 1993), p. 337.

9.   Quoted in Thompson, *English Working Class*, p. 623.

10.   Quoted in Brian Bailey, *Hangmen of England* (London, W H Allen, 1989), p. 44.

11.   So-called because safe seats like Cashel were under the total control (in the pocket) of certain families.

12.   Quoted in Thomson, *Prime Ministers*, p. 71.

13.   Not everyone believed that. Some over-eager tourists, believing the war was permanently over, went over to France and found themselves in prison there when it was renewed. Some of them were not released until 1814!

14.   Quoted in Geoffrey Treasure, *Who's Who in Late Hanoverian Britain* (London, Shepheard-Walyn, 1997), p. 289.

15.   A quirk in the constitution meant that Irish peers could sit in the Commons.

16.   Thomson, *Prime Ministers*, p. 92.

17.   Ibid.

18.   Henry Legge, MP.

Chapter 6

1. Quoted in Geoffrey Treasure, *Who's Who in Late Hanoverian Britain* (London, Shepheard-Walyn, 1997), p. 351.
2. No one at that early stage in education considered the possible indoctrination of children; that Thomas Spence was busily turning Newcastle into a Communist state!
3. He even wrote an account of his 1801 trial in this form.
4. He spoke French tolerably well.
5. Grinning matches were usually played by toothless old men contorting their mouths. The most hideous was the winner.
6. Quoted in Clive Bloom, *Violent London* (London, Sidgwick & Jackson, 2003), p. 189.
7. For a brilliant discussion of the complexity (and ineptitude) of pre-Peelite policemen see T A Critchley and P D James, *The Maul and the Pear Tree* (London, Sphere, 1971).
8. Paraphrased from *The Examiner* (16 Nov. 1816).

Chapter 7

1. Richard Belfield, *Assassination: The Killers and their Paymasters Revealed* (London, Magpie (Constable), 2005).
2. The parallels with Cato Street can only go so far. The king's power was still paramount in the reign of James I whereas by 1820, George IV was almost an irrelevance. Half-baked though the Gunpowder Plot may have been, the idea was almost certainly to replace James with a Catholic alternative. In both assassination attempts, the conspirators expected the country to rise to back them.
3. Quoted in E P Thompson *The Making of the English Working Class* (London, Penguin, 1991), p. 530.
4. Treasury Solicitor's Papers, 6 March 1817, 11.351
5. Moscow had been burnt almost to the ground by the Russians in 1812 in an attempt to drive the invading French army under Napoleon out.
6. *The Trial of Jeremiah Brandreth*, Oct. 1817.

Chapter 8

1. Quoted in Joyce Marlow, *The Peterloo Massacre* (London, Readers' Union, 1970), p. 50.

2.   This is a very odd reference and presumably refers to the Pendle witch trials of 1612. Were the witches seen as earlier examples of poor, oppressed people suffering under the tyranny of arbitrary law?

3.   Pikes are referred to consistently in this period. They were homemade and the authorities seem to regard them as almost the weapon of choice, the symbol of insurrection.

4.   In fact the wording contained the equivalent of a double negative. It said that the Magistrates 'do hereby caution all Persons to abstain at their peril from attending . . .'

5.   Henry Hunt, *An Address to the Reformers of Manchester and its Neighbourhood*, 11 Aug. 1819.

6.   No relation to the lady on the hustings with Hunt.

7.   One of those swords, supposedly from Peterloo, was the inspiration for Howard Spring's *Fame is the Spur*.

8.   Samuel Bamford, *Passages in the Life of a Radical* (1967 edn; originally published London, T F Unwin, 1893).

9.   Ibid.

Chapter 9

1.   *Works of John Keats*, p. 108.

2.   Wilkinson, *An Authentic History of the Cato Street Conspiracy* (London, Thomas Kelly, 1820), pp. 56–7.

3.   Ibid., p. 398.

4.   The pre-1832 voting system was highly complicated. A tiny handful of the working class *could* actually vote depending on the property in which they lived.

5.   'Trial of Richard Tidd', p 326.

6.   Bradburn (also spelt Blackburn), Gilchrist, Cooper and Monument are not listed on the original document.

Chapter 10

1.   Percy Bysshe Shelley, *England in 1819*, 1839.

2.   'The Trial of James Brunt'.

3.   'The Trial of James Ings'.

4.   In fact, the likeness of Thistlewood, judging from the drawing made at the trial, is quite accurate.

5. Technically, a carbine is a short musket used by the cavalry and capable of being fired in one hand. A blunderbuss is an early shotgun, scattering pellets in a wide arc. This would have been more useful at Grosvenor Square.

6. There is some confusion over the man's rank. He was presumably promoted by the time of the Cato Street trials, but there 'Lieutenant' and 'Captain' are used interchangeably.

7. So either Thistlewood fired three guns or somebody else was shooting too.

8. The engraver of the Cato Street building, A Wivell, actually shows this in his work.

9. Robert Burns, *March to Bannockburn*.

Chapter 11

1. This is still the law today and for the worst modern example of its cruelty and injustice, see M J Trow, *Let Him Have It, Chris* (London, Constable, 1990).

2. Perhaps another spelling of Surman or Sarmon.

3. A commission empowering a judge in Great Britain to hear and rule on a criminal case at the assizes.

4. One of hundreds of examples where the law used archaic or downright wrong words in its official capacity.

5. Technically, James Wilson's case was delayed pending the misnomer plea. He was in fact 'trying it on' because the only difference was that his middle name, William, had been added in the indictment. The decision to over-rule the plea however lay with the Attorney-General, hardly a disinterested party.

Chapter 12

1. This may have been to save time and ultimately money.

2. Shackled with chains at the wrists and ankles, making escape impossible. Ings was only cuffed because he had been ill in gaol.

3. Marcus Tullius Cicero, one of the best known advocates and orators in the ancient world.

4. Technically the word implies belief in a remote Creator who does not interfere in the present world. I suspect that several of the conspirators had probably abandoned God altogether.

5. Interestingly, an account of this case – Holloway and Haggerty were accused of murdering Mr Steele on Hounslow Heath – was written by James Harmer, the Cato Street conspirators' solicitor.

6.   £2 2s or £2 10p. In today's currency about £200.

7.   By 1820, this was a generic term for the hangman. The original Ketch, John Catch, took up the job in September 1663 and officiated at the execution of the Duke of Monmouth and the pillorying of Titus Oates.

Chapter 13

1.   Quoted in Brian Bailey, *The Hangmen of England* (London, W H Allen, 1989), p. 50.

2.   Letter to Joseph Tyas, quoted in E P Thompson, *The Making of the English Working Class* (London, Penguin, 1991), p. 777.

3.   H Montgomery Hyde, *The Strange Death of Lord Castlereagh* (London, Heinemann, 1959).

BIBLIOGRAPHY

BAILEY, BRIAN. *Hangmen of England* (London, W H Allen, 1989)

BLOOM, CLIVE. *Violent London* (London, Sidgwick & Jackson, 2003)

BOSTON, RAY. *The Essential Fleet Street: Its History and Influence* (London, Blandford, 1990)

BYRNE, RICHARD. *Prisons and Punishments of London* (London, Grafton, 1992)

CHAPMAN, PAULINE. *Madame Tussaud's Chamber of Horrors* (London, Grafton, 1985)

CLOUT, HUGH, ed. *The Times London History Atlas* (London, BCA, 1991)

COBBETT, WILLIAM. *Rural Rides* (London, Thomas Nelson & Sons, 1830)

COLE, HUBERT. *Things for the Surgeon: A History of the Resurrection Men* (London, Heinemann, 1964)

EVANS, ERIC J. *Britain before the Reform Act: Politics and Society 1815–32* (London, Longman, 1989)

FIDO, MARTIN. *Murder Guide to London* (London, Grafton, 1987)

HIBBERT, CHRISTOPHER. *George IV* (London, Penguin, 1972)

HIBBERT, CHRISTOPHER. *Nelson: A Personal History* (London, Viking, 1994)

LINNANE, FERGUS. *London's Underworld: Three Centuries of Vice and Crime* (London, Robson, 2004)

LONGFORD, ELIZABETH. *Wellington: Pillar of State* (London, Weidenfeld & Nicolson, 1972)

MARLOW, JOYCE. *The Peterloo Massacre* (London, Readers' Union, 1969)

MONTGOMERY HYDE, H. *The Strange Death of Lord Castlereagh* (London, Icon, 1967)

SIFAKIS, CARL. *Encyclopaedia of Assassinations* (London, Headline, 1993)

STANHOPE, JOHN. *The Cato Street Conspiracy* (London, Jonathan Cape, 1962)

THOMPSON, E P. *The Making of the English Working Class* (London, Penguin, 1991)

TREASURE, GEOFFREY. *Who's Who in Late Hanoverian Britain* (London, Shepheard-Walwyn, 1997)

WILKINSON, GEORGE THEODORE. *An Authentic History of the Cato Street Conspiracy* (London, Thomas Kelly, 1820)

WILSON, BEN. *Decency and Disorder 1789–1837* (London, Faber & Faber, 2007)

INDEX

Abbott, Mr Justice 58, 91, 95, 146, 150, 155, 162
Act of Union (Ireland) 39, 53, 67, 71
Adams, Robert 121, 125, 129-130, 134, 143, 147-148, 150-151, 153, 155, 157-160, 162
Addington, Henry – see Sidmouth
Adkins, Governor 145
Adolphus, Barrister 148, 150-151, 158-159
Artillery Ground 8, 128
Ashton, John 109
Ashworth, Joseph 109
Ashworth, Thomas 109
Baker, John 109
Baldwin's Gardens 119, 124, 177
Bamford, Samuel 23, 32, 60, 83, 100, 101-103, 107-109, 110–111, 114
Barnes, Thomas 65, 115
Bartholomew Fair 114-115
Basey, Pte James 136-137
Bastille, The 25-27, 29, 43-46, 52, 65, 85- 86, 102, 178
Bathurst, Henry 73, 139
Bayley, Mr Justice 91
Bellingham, John 62-64, 164
Best (Barrister) 47
Binns, John 33-34, 36
Birley, Capt. Hugh 106-107
Birmingham 29, 35
Birnie, Richard 134, 136-138, 140, 143, 148
Bishop, Daniel 138, 143
Bissex, Charles 4-5, 151
Blanketeers 92
Bolland, Barrister 139, 151, 159
Bonaparte, Napoleon 11, 13, 17, 18, 20-22, 27, 37, 39, 53, 57, 63, 67, 69, 81
Botting, James 165-169
Bow Street Runners 15, 46, 50, 133-134, 136-137, 142-143, 148-149, 176
Bow Street 46, 84, 137, 138
Bradburn, Amelia 148
Bradburn, Richard 5, 15, 124, 137, 141, 146-147, 160, 162
Bradshaw, William 1 09
Brandreth, Ann 97
Brandreth, Jeremiah 94–8, 126, 149, 150, 163, 173
Broderick, Barrister 148, 160

Brookes, William 136, 142
Broughton, Thomas 46, 50
Brunskill, William 50-52, 64
Brunt, John 2-3, 7, 11-12, 120–1, 125, 128-130, 134, 145-147, 149, 151, 153-154, 158–9, 162-163, 166-169, 174-175, 177
Brunt, Mary 120–1, 148, 171
Buckley, Thomas 109
Burdett, Sir Francis 23, 32, 44–5, 60, 65, 84-85, 89, 93, 114, 118
Burke, Edmund 25, 27- 29, 31, 33, 69, 76
Butterworth, William 109
Byng, Major General John 94, 102, 105, 115, 117
Canning, George 66-68–70, 89, 139
Carlile, Richard 58-59, 105, 114-115, 120, 159
Carlton House 4, 31, 85, 127
Caroline of Brunswick 127–8, 172
Cartwright, Major John 59, 60, 102, 103, 114
Castle, John 86, 89–93, 96-97, 125-126
Castlereagh, Lord 1, 2, 7, 8, 17–18, 65–66, 69, 70–2, 89, 96, 127, 130, 139, 142, 144, 152, 154, 160, 161-162, 175-177
Catholic Emancipation 49, 62, 67, 69, 71
Cato Street 3, 7-8, 12, 50, 124, 129-130, 134, 137, 139, 142-143, 145, 151-153, 157, 160, 162, 172, 177
Chambers, Thomas 158
Cheapside 85-86, 89
Christian Polity, the Salvation of the Empire 78
Cobbett, William 12, 21-23, 30, 32, 57, 59-60, 74, 83-84, 93, 98, 100, 102, 117–18, 144, 178
Coleman, Catherine 109
Coleridge, Samuel 44, 51, 64
Committee of Two Hundred 116, 176-177
Commonsense 28
Conant, Sir Nathaniel 84, 85
Cook (conspirator) 128, 134, 158
Cooper, Charles 5, 15, 124, 137-138, 142, 146-147, 160, 162
Corn Laws 22-23, 72, 87, 100, 102
Cotton, Reverend 163, 166-167
Crompton, James 109
Cross, Barrister 96-97

Cruikshank, George 87, 89, 97, 133
Curtis, Pte William 137
Curtius, Dr Phillipe 52
Curwood, Barrister 125, 148, 150, 152-155, 157-158
Dallas, Mr Justice Robert 95, 150, 157
Davidson, Sarah 124, 148, 171, 174
Davidson, William 2-3, 5-7, 15, 25, 41-42, 57, 72, 75, 121-4, 132, 134-138, 143, 145-147, 149, 151-152, 159 163, 166-169, 174
Dawson, William 109
de Launay, Bernard 26,46
Denman, Barrister 96, 97
Dennison, Henry 109
Despard, Catherine 42, 44, 45, 49, 52, 67
Despard, Edward 41-55, 57, 59-60, 64, 77, 82-83, 86, 88, 93, 119, 122, 129, 159, 163
Despard, James 42
Dwyer, Thomas 153-155, 161, 175
Edgware Road 12, 129, 136
Edwards, George 2, 4-6, 8, 24, 119-120, 125-126, 134, 138, 150, 152-156, 158-161, 165, 168, 174, 176
Eldon, Lord 4, 45, 65, 70, 139, 175, 177
Ellenborough, Lord 48, 53, 58, 91, 116
Ellis, James 134-137, 142
Elrington, Capt. J H 145
Equiano, Olaudah 42-3
Erskine, Thomas 40-41
Ethelston, Reverend Charles 100, 102
Evans, Thomas Jnr 78, 82, 90
Evans, Thomas Snr 78, 82, 90
Fildes, Ann 106
Fildes, Mrs 105-106
Fildes, William 106, 109
Firth, William 132, 145-146, 172
Fitzclarence, Capt. 135-137, 141, 148
Fox Court 125, 129-130, 151, 177
Fox, Charles James 27, 28, 30, 32, 58, 62, 93
Foxen, James 165, 168-169
Francis, John 46-7, 50-51, 53
Friends of the People 40
Furnival's Inn 36, 43, 151
Gee's Court 43, 152, 177
George III 27, 31, 34, 40, 66-67, 70-71, 92, 127, 133
George IV (Prince Regent) 31, 70, 84-85, 89, 92, 102, 110, 114, 127, 147, 157, 167, 172
George, Robert 146-147, 172
Gerald, Joseph 32-33
Gilchrist, James 5, 15, 124, 137, 142, 146-147, 160, 162, 172
Gill (Bow Street Runner) 147
Gilray, James 35, 87

Goldworthy, George 160, 161
Goodwin, Margaret 109
Gordon Riots 43, 46, 54, 55
Graham, Arthur 46, 50
Gray's Inn Lane 152
Grosvenor Square 8, 72, 116, 125, 127, 129, 132, 139, 151-152, 159, 160, 177
Gurney (Barrister) 47
Hadfield, James 39, 40-41, 133
Hall, Abel 124-125, 134, 143, 146-147, 172
Hampden Clubs 59, 60, 95, 100
Hanson, Sgt Edward 19
Hardy, Capt. Thomas 35
Hardy, Thomas 31-33, 40
Harmer, James 109, 148, 176
Harrison, Caroline 148
Harrison, William 7, 127-130, 132, 134, 145-147, 160, 165
Harrowby, Lord 1-9, 22, 63, 65, 68-70, 72, 125, 127, 129, 132, 138-139, 152, 154, 157, 163, 172, 174-175, 177
Hay, Reverend William 100
Hayle, Joseph 121, 125, 151
Hazard, William 172
Healey, Dr Joseph 60, 101, 104, 109
Heys, Mary 109
Hobhouse, John Cam 116, 144, 153, 176
Holborn 36, 43, 54, 76, 124, 128, 149
Hole-in-the-Wall Passage 3, 19, 119, 125, 129, 177
Holroyd, Mr Justice 91, 95
Hone, William 58-59, 97
Hooper, John 79, 85, 91
Hucklestone, Edward 13, 154
Hulton, William 107
Hunt, Henry 3, 83-86, 89, 90, 93, 98, 101-105, 107, 109-110, 113-115, 117, 119, 158, 178
Huskisson, William 66, 73, 144
Hyden, Thomas 13, 150, 152-153, 155, 157-158, 161
Ings, Celia 171, 173
Ings, James 3, 5-8, 12, 15, 19, 24, 34, 72, 119-20, 124- 125, 129-130, 132, 134-137-8, 142, 145-147, 149-150, 157-158, 161-163, 166-169, 173-4
Ings, William 174
Jenkinson, Robert – see Liverpool
Jervis, Mary 109
John Street 130, 132, 135, 160
Johnson, Joseph 60, 101, 107
Jolliffe, Lt Hylton 108
Jones, Dr John 78, 116-117
Jones, Sarah 109

Kaylock, George   130
Keats, John   58, 113
Keynes, John   79
King's Bench, Court of   91, 114
Knight, John   60, 100, 105
L'Estrange, Lt Col Guy   106-107
Lander, Despard conspirator   49
Lavender, John   138
Lees, John   109
Legge, Sergeant   136, 142
Litchfield, Treasury Solicitor   90
Littledale, Barrister   151
Liverpool, Lord   5-7, 14, 22, 24, 65–6, 68-69, 73-74, 92, 127, 138, 175
London Corresponding Society (LCS)   33-34, 43-44, 75, 82
Londonderry, Marquess of – see Castlereagh
Louis XVI   25-26, 30, 34, 52, 66
Luddites   18-19, 21, 58, 62-64, 89
Ludlam, Isaac   94-96
Mansion House   8, 128, 158
Marie Antoinette   30, 52
Marx, Karl   15, 17
McNamara, John   46, 50-51
Meagher, Trumpeter Edward   107, 114
Ministry of All the Talents   62, 68, 71
Mitchell, Andrew   154
Mitchell, Joseph   92, 93
Monday, Richard   132
Monument, John   5, 15, 124, 132, 137, 142, 145-147, 153, 155, 159
Monument, Thomas   157
Morris, John   151
Moy, Giles   136, 142
Muddock, Pte John   137
Muir, Thomas   30, 32
Nadin, Joseph   100–1, 103, 105, 107, 109
National Assembly   26
National Convention   28, 32
Nelson, Horatio   35, 47–8, 49, 58
Newgate Calendar   47, 53
Newman Despard conspirator   49
Newspapers/journals
  Anti-Jacobin   68
  Black Dwarf   58, 94, 103, 115, 158
  Cap of Liberty   117
  Gorgon   97
  Independent Whig   91
  Lancet   171
  Leeds Intelligencer   173
  Leeds Mercury   96, 101
  London Gazette   139
  Manchester Mercury   104

Manchester Observer   101, 104, 106, 110, 114-115
Medusa   117, 158
Morning Chronicle   77
New Annual Register   77
New Times   1, 129, 154
Observer   49, 58
Political Register   100
Republican   117
The Times   11, 58, 65, 105, 115
Twopenny Trash or *Weekly Political Register*   22-23, 57- 58, 115, 144
Nodder, Governor   145
Norris, James   100, 103, 113
Norwich   31, 34
O'Neill, Arthur   109
Old Bailey, Sessions House   33, 125, 148-149, 156, 160, 164, 177
Oliver the Spy – see Richards, W J
Oxford Street   43, 76, 120, 124, 152
Paine, Thomas   26, 28-30, 40, 43, 48, 59, 60, 76-77, 102, 118, 159-160
Palin, John   8, 124, 128, 134, 138, 143, 151, 158, 164
Parker, Tom   171
Parkins, Sheriff   165
Partington, Martha   109
Peace of Amiens   52, 82
Peel, Robert   23, 33, 66, 144
Perceval, Spencer   57, 62-66, 68-69, 71
Peterloo   19, 21, 23, 72, 99–111, 113, 117, 150, 161, 165
Pig's Meat   76
Pitt, William   18, 20, 22-23, 25, 27, 30, 32-36, 39, 45, 49, 62, 65-69, 71, 73, 80, 88
Place, Francis   32, 34, 60, 76, 78
Portland, Duke of   66, 69, 71, 78
Portman Street   8, 134, 142, 151
Potter (conspirator)   134
Preston, Ann   144
Preston, Charlotte   148
Preston, Thomas   79, 84, 91, 113-114, 117, 144-146, 148, 166, 172
Prisons
  Coldbath Fields   44, 101, 139, 145-148
  Fleet   93
  Gatehouse   46
  Horsemonger Lane (Surrey County Gaol)   50
  King's Bench   43, 116
  Marshalsea   157
  New (Clerkenwell)   46

New Gaol (Borough) 49
Newgate 21, 46, 64, 76, 86, 148-150, 163-164, 171-173, 177-178
Tothill Fields 46, 144-146
Public Houses
  Bell 31
  Black Horse 59
  Bleeding Heart 59
  Brown Bear 59
  Coach and Horses 59
  Cock 85, 92
  Flying Horse 47, 59
  Ham and Windmill 59
  Horse and Groom 2, 3, 132, 136-137, 141, 152, 160
  Merlin's Cave 84
  Mulberry Tree 85
  Oakley Arms 46
  Tiger 47
  Two Bells 59
  White Hart 120, 125
  White Lion 2-3, 117
Ranelagh Place 125
Real Rights of Man 76
Reeves, James 31, 33
Reflections on the Revolution in France 27
Regiments (in order of seniority)
  Life Guards 50, 97, 114, 127-128, 148, 151, 164-165, 167, 172
  Blues (Royal Horse Guards) 11, 12, 114, 121, 143
  7th Hussars 102
  15th Hussars 94, 106-108
  23rd Light Dragoons 22
  Royal Artillery 19
  Royal Horse Artillery 106, 164
  Coldstream Guards 36, 134-135, 140, 143, 164
  Grenadier Guards 54
  31st Foot 106
  88th Foot 106
  Cheshire Yeomanry 106
  Manchester and Salford Yeomanry 106-107, 109-110, 114, 130
  London Light Horse Volunteers 128, 164
Restorer of Society to its Natural State 75, 77
Revealed Knowledge of the Prophecies and Times 32
Revel, Pte John 137
Richards, Lord Chief Baron 95, 150, 159
Richards, W J 89, 93-8, 126
Richardson, Mr Justice 150

Rights of Man 28-29, 77
Robespierre, Maximilien 27, 31, 39, 52, 80-81
Robinson, Frederick 66, 73-4
Rothwell, Sheriff 164-165
Royal Exchange 86, 128
Ruthven, George 132, 134-135, 138, 141-142, 144, 146, 148
Salmon (Bow Street Runner) 138, 146
Sampson, Henry 94
Sarnon, William (John Sermon?) 142
Saxton, John 101, 105, 114
Scott, John – see Eldon
Shaw, Alderman 86
Shaw, John 5, 15, 124, 134, 137, 141, 146-147, 160, 162
Shaw, Mary 148
Sheffield 29, 31, 34
Shelley, Percy 70-72, 98, 127
Shelmerdine, Pte Thomas 108
Sidmouth, Lord 3, 8, 35, 49, 62, 64-67, 70, 73, 84, 89-90, 93, 96, 101-102, 110, 113, 116, 130, 139-140, 142, 144, 150, 153-154, 158, 160, 162, 164, 171, 174-176
Simmons, William 172
Simpson, Cpl Major Edward 151
Six Acts, The 3, 72, 115-117
Smart, Thomas 1, 4, 151
Smithers, Richard 133-135, 137-144, 147
Smithfield 103, 114, 156, 158, 166
Snow Hill 86, 166
Southey, Robert 44, 51
Spa Fields 21, 78, 83-6, 90-92, 101, 113, 117, 125, 129, 139, 144, 149-150, 153, 156
Spence, Thomas 75-8
Spenceans 32
Spitalfields 34, 114, 149
St Peter's Fields, Manchester – see Peterloo
St Vincent, Earl of, Admiral 58
Stafford, John 86, 138, 176
Stanhope Street 138
Stewart, Robert – see Castlereagh
Take Your Choice 59
Tatton, Thomas 105
Thelwall, John 32-33, 114
Thistlewood, Arthur 1-2, 4, 5-8, 13-14, 16, 19, 50, 60, 62, 67, 79-82, 84-86, 90- 93, 95, 101-102, 104, 111, 113 114, 116-118, 125, 127-130, 132-135, 138-145, 147-151, 153-158, 160-169, 172, 173, 175, 177-178
Thistlewood, James 82
Thistlewood, Susan 116, 146, 148, 163, 171
Tidd, Ann 119, 148

Tidd, Mary (Barker)   3, 119, 125, 171
Tidd, Richard   3-5, 15, 19, 57, 118–19, 124-
    125, 129, 132, 134-137, 141-142, 145-147,
    149, 159–60, 162-163, 166-167, 168-169,
    173, 177
Tone, Theobald Wolfe   35-36, 39, 43-44, 71
Tooke, John Horne   33, 40, 93
Tower of London   45-46, 85, 86, 93, 95, 102,
    128, 145-148
Townshend, Viscount Charles   14
Trafford, Major   106
Truelock, Bannister   41
Turner, William   94-96
Tussaud, Marie   52–3, 173
Tyndall   (Despard conspirator) 49
United Englishmen   36, 43-45
United Irishmen   36, 44
Vansittart, Nicholas   72–3, 139, 175
Vindication of the Rights of Women   29
Waddington, Samuel   117, 144
Wakley, Dr Thomas   171
Walford, Barrister   148, 160
Walker, Eleanor   151
Waterloo, Battle of   3, 11, 17, 21, 98, 108,
    109, 172, 175
Watson, Dr James   78, 85, 90-93, 95, 96, 101-
    102, 113-117, 125-126, 153
Watson, Jem   78, 85-86, 90-91
Weightman, George   94, 95, 96
Wellington, Duke of   2-3, 7, 11–12, 21, 65-
    66, 69, 121, 127, 138, 175-177
Westall, Elizabeth   132
Westcott, William   135, 142
Westmoreland, Lord   4, 139, 145
Wetherell, Barrister   91-92
Whitbread, Samuel   65, 89
White Street   138
Wilberforce, William   23, 29, 67
Wilson, James   5, 15, 124, 132, 134, 141, 145-
    147, 150, 152, 160, 162, 165
Windsor, Thomas   47
Winkworth, William   51
Wood, Alderman   163-165, 176
Wood, John   46-47, 50, 54
Wooler, Thomas   58, 97, 103
Wordsworth, William   28
Wratten, James   46, 50
Wyville, Christopher   29, 32